CHICKENS IN THE GARDEN,

WELLIES BY THE DOOR

An American in Rural Ireland

V. J. Fadely

Published by IREUSA Press, Long Beach, California, USA
ireusapress@gmail.com

First Printing: February 2016
Second Printing: April 2016

ISBN-13: 978-0692543429

ISBN-10: 0692543422

Dedicated with love and gratitude to my parents and my sister, always my biggest and best fans (whatever would I have done without you all these years?), and to the good people of Kenmare, Co. Kerry, Ireland.

'Would you tell me, please, which way I ought to go from here?'

'That depends a good deal on where you want to get to,' said the Cat.

'I don't much care where – ' said Alice.

'Then it doesn't matter which way you go,' said the Cat.

' – so long as I get SOMEWHERE,' Alice added as an explanation.

'Oh, you're sure to do that,' said the Cat, 'if you only walk long enough.'

— Lewis Carroll, *Alice's Adventures in Wonderland*

CONTENTS

AUTHOR'S NOTE

The people, places, and events on these pages are real, but in the interest of privacy most of the names are fictitious and some of the events have been combined or moved in time. You'll note an absence of people in most photos; again, this is to protect privacy. The book was initially printed with the fictitious town name of Ballyglen which has now been replaced by the real name for a very real, very special town, Kenmare.

I hope readers, especially my Irish friends, will overlook any errors in pronunciation or interpretation of Irish words and expressions, and any confused, missing, or incorrect details. I did my best to report on my Irish world, as seen through my American eyes and heard with my American ears. Nothing in this book is meant to be anything but positive about Ireland and its people – excluding those responsible for Ireland's nonsensical immigration policies regarding retired non-EU citizens.

A big city editor once told me to cut back on reflective passages, 'make it read more like a novel!' For a time I struggled to find a different way to convey the color of an Irish summer afternoon and the sound of birds singing in my back garden. To explain the cozy camaraderie of the local pub on a rainy winter evening and the way a warm fire, chat and laughter ward off the damp and gloom. It didn't work for me and it changed the book, moved it away from what I originally intended. Because it *isn't* a novel, it's a sort of journal. So I ignored that editor and did what felt natural, and reverted back to my mostly narrative style to describe my reactions to the rich wonders around me.

I hope I've chosen the right words to help bring others some of the same amusement, joy, wonder, and magic Ireland has brought to me.

Sláinte!

Prologue

I dreamed I was an old woman, but not too old, living in Ireland. I went for morning walks, sipped tea with the locals in the afternoons, and sat before a cheerful fire on cool evenings...

I walked in all seasons, along high sea cliffs where waves crashed and sprayed diamonds across the azure sky, through damp and muddy fields past stone walls, grazing sheep, and trees blooming with birdsong, and down country lanes where bees drank from red fuchsia blossoms, wild blackberry bushes entwined with ferns and ivy, and willow trees bent gracefully over the roadway to form leafy green tunnels of secret, sun-dappled spaces.

I went to vibrant cities and colorful villages, enjoyed properly poured pints of Guinness while I laughed with friends and strangers alike, and tapped my feet to lively tunes. I learned the lingo, began to understand the accents, and always delighted in the sound of Irish voices.

I explored ancient ruins and never stopped being amazed by the history all around me. I marveled at the sight of mist hovering over green fields, rainbows arching across the sky, and miniature purple flowers miraculously growing from stone walls, sprouting from tiny pockets of soil carried on the wind and deposited in the nooks and crannies of the old, rough, stone.

I spent time in quiet places where silence sings, like old churchyards where Celtic crosses, their elaborately carved designs muted with time and weather, stand guard among the headstones leaning with age like stooped old men, bent but still strong, some towering above those so worn they are little more than suggestions of stones, mere whispers of another time hiding in the tall grass.

I was far from Southern California, far from the blare of traffic and flash of neon signs where one can go nearly unnoticed among the many who scurry around absorbed in their own busy lives; far from the routine boredom I called my life. I was in rural Ireland where people greeting passersby on the street is customary, and a chat with a complete stranger is not at all out of the ordinary. Where people know life is short and don't let time get away without enjoying it.

It was like coming in from the cold, tired and shivering, and sinking into a soft bed under the warmth and comfort of a finely stitched patchwork quilt made of forty-shades-of-green. I was an American in Ireland – but I felt like I was home.

1

CÉAD MÍLE FÁILTE!

September 2, 2013: After a tearful goodbye and 16 hours of airports and airplanes, I made it!

I stood in line at the Dublin airport, waiting my turn to go through Customs, tired after the long trip, but buoyed by my excitement and not impatient as I would have been in the past. I had time; I wasn't going anywhere. It felt strange. The familiar CÉAD MÍLE FÁILTE![1] signs I'd so often seen on previous visits now held a different significance for me. They welcomed me to Ireland, not for a two week holiday, but to live. After many months of planning and preparation, I had finally made the move from California to Ireland.

My emotions were a little out of whack those first days. I went from bliss to apprehension mixed with bewildered disbelief, and all levels in between. Questions niggled away at the back of my mind like pesky mosquitoes and I swatted them away with annoyance. Had I made the right decision? *Z-z-z-z.* Would I like living in Ireland? *Z-z-z-z.* What would it be like not having a car? *Z-z-z-z.* Would this really be the change I hoped for? *Z-z-z-splat!* But overall, I felt happy anticipation. Life in Ireland would be what I made it.

I was on the edge of something big; I felt certain of that. A little like being in a cool, air-conditioned theater on a hot, sweaty

---

[1] A hundred thousand welcomes (*kayd-meeluh-fall-chuh*)

day, right before the blockbuster film is to start, the one you've been wanting to see. Filled with happy anticipation, you know even if the movie doesn't live up to the hype, so what? It's still great to be sitting in the cool darkness of the theater eating buttered popcorn and a theater-size box of candy. It felt something like that, but bigger – way bigger.

That first day I stood on Dublin's broad and bustling O'Connell Street with its statutes of Irish heroes like Daniel O'Connell, and the Dublin Spire, said to be the tallest sculpture in the world, jutting up into the blue sky. People walked briskly past me in both directions on the wide sidewalk and cars and buses zoomed by, seeming to move *en masse* on the busy roadway. A small city by world standards, Dublin is still impressive and very much has the feel of a big city. I felt like I should show my exuberation by spinning around, smiling face turned toward the sky, and joyously tossing my hat in the air like Mary Tyler Moore did in the opening scene of every episode of her 1970's television sit-com. If only I'd been wearing a hat.

The day after arriving in Dublin I walked to a large department store to buy some odds and ends I needed to set up house, things I knew would either be more expensive or unavailable in Kenmare. After shopping more than an hour, I stood in line to pay, my arms heavy with the last few things I'd chosen, eyeing the stack of duvets, throw rugs and other goods the clerk had agreed to stow behind the counter as a courtesy while I shopped. A substantial pile had collected. My original list of bed sheets and a few towels had somehow multiplied into far more. I liked to shop and moving to Ireland hadn't changed that.

It wasn't until I stood in line that the first inkling of a problem hit me. How would I get everything back to my hotel? It wasn't far, but I realized walking wasn't a good plan unless I wanted to do it Sherpa-style. That wouldn't work unless the cashier had the time, interest, and know-how to strap it all onto my back. I had not thought this through well.

As the items were rung up and the evidence of my over-buying grew larger before my eyes, I knew for certain walking back to my hotel was not an option. What should I do? I waited for a solution to come to mind. When nothing did, I wondered aloud to the cashier.

The young man said I could catch a cab on Parnell Street. Of course! How obvious. I should have thought of it myself. But the idea wasn't as simple as it sounded. The store was large with three levels and numerous exits leading outdoors as well as into a mall. I had no idea which direction to go to reach Parnell Street. I inquired of the cashier.

'Oh, it's just downstairs – it's not far.'

This was not particularly helpful – of course I knew Parnell Street would be downstairs. We were not on the ground floor. Well, I would just have to ask directions once I arrived at street level. As my mind hit the next stumbling block, I again wondered aloud. How would I transport everything from where I stood, down the escalator, and out the store to the pickup point?

'I guess you'll need to make two trips,' the clever young man said. I wondered if he was a stand-up comedian in real life, moonlighting as a cashier.

I had hoped he might offer himself or another employee to assist. This was, after all, Ireland. That's the sort of thing that happens.

He continued bagging my purchases while I pondered my dilemma. I'd have to take whatever I could carry down two flights to the ground floor, determine the correct exit for Parnell Street, go out the door and abandon the bags on the sidewalk, while the rest of my goods sat in the store, also abandoned, then go back upstairs and do it again. And this was the best case scenario, assuming I could do it in two trips.

I suppose as I considered this I looked stressed as my purchases piled up around me, penning me in. I didn't know what to do. As the cashier handed me the last bag, I looked at the rest gathered around my feet, then looked blankly at the couple behind me in line, knowing I was holding them up.

Before I could offer an apology, the man spoke.

'You're needing a lift? I can take you – I have a cab outside.'

Did I hear correctly? He was a cab driver?? Before relief dissolved me into hysterical, helpless laughter, I snapped myself out of it.

'Oh! Are you sure?'

'No problem, if you don't mind waiting a moment while we pay.'

He looked normal, ordinary, as did his wife. He sounded friendly and sincere. There didn't seem to be any catch or any danger. It wasn't like I would be accepting a ride from a random stranger; the man was a cab driver. Hardly believing my good luck, I thanked him.

While he paid for their purchases, his wife chatted with me, telling me how he'd finished his shift and met up with her to do some shopping before she had to go to work at one of the stores in the mall.

Together, we trooped out of the store, the wife carrying their shopping bag while the cab driver carried everything I couldn't, and we were on our merry way into the mall, chatting like old friends. When we arrived at the wife's place of work, we bid her farewell and walked on, out the exit to Parnell Street, a fair distance from where I'd paid for my purchases and an exit I'd never have found on my own. He loaded everything in his cab parked nearby and drove me to my hotel. He unloaded my bags and took them into the lobby, then hopped back into his cab with a wave and a smile. I swear his eyes twinkled. What a relief to find out I really was in Ireland, after all.

2

IRELAND OF MY DREAMS

August 1, 2009: One more month and I'm off – my first trip to Ireland! I just finished a 'test pack' to see what will fit in my suitcase. There definitely won't be room for the kitchen sink!

Like so many who dream of visiting far-away places, my far-away place was Ireland. From the time I was a young girl I was as fond of wishful thinking as my mother was of the expression, 'If wishes were horses, beggars would ride.' Well, Mom, after many years of wishing to go to Ireland, in 2009 beggars *did* ride and I took off on my first trip to the Emerald Isle.

In the months leading up to the trip I was so filled with anticipation I could barely think of anything else. It reminded me of that feeling of being a teenager in love, that all-consuming excitement making you nearly sick with an overload of adrenalin. I had every detail planned – over-planned – well in advance, and I was counting the days until departure, my excitement building daily.

There was little doubt the vision I had of Ireland, based on movies and books and further embellished by my big imagination, had little to do with reality. In my mind Ireland was a place of green and mossy forests where shamrocks grew, trees were filled with birdsong, and waterfalls cascaded in the sunshine. There were quaint cottages and cozy pubs, and sheep placidly grazing in fields crisscrossed with stone walls. I could hear the Irish voices, see the rainbows and the smiles, taste the perfect Guinness while I talked with a friendly Irishman... I couldn't help myself; I was a dreamer. Maybe I could blame part of that on my O'Rourke ancestry?

In the months before I left I worked on toning down those great expectations. I didn't want to be disappointed, as I surely would be, when the vision I'd crafted with such care collided with the real world.

No such collision took place. There was no disappointment, none at all. I was immediately and deeply enchanted. The real Ireland surpassed the land of my dreams and the entire trip passed by like a magical mystery tour; a swirling, colorful, delightful feast for the senses and the soul. Time was seamless, days and nights flowing together. I was surrounded by smiling faces, ancient places, laughter, green, music, and fresh air. I felt like I was exactly where I was supposed to be in this world, and it was heavenly.

Alas, after fifteen glorious days it ended and I was unprepared for how wrenching it would be to leave, and how difficult the re-entry back into my real life would be. Those details had never been a part of my dream.

In Ireland my soul danced and my heart beat stronger, and I smiled and laughed in a way I hadn't for a long while. I felt incredibly alive and as though I was young again. I didn't want that feeling to end.

I'd fallen head-over-heels in love with the Emerald Isle.

◙

Over the next three years I made annual pilgrimages to Ireland, spending two beautiful, refreshing weeks in the land that I became more passionate about with every visit. The green vistas, rugged coastline, and stone ruins, the friendly people and the music in the pubs all became familiar to me, but never less intriguing.

The other fifty weeks of the year I spent my days inside the bland, confining walls of a law office working as a legal secretary, never a career goal, simply a job to pay the bills. The stress of unrealistic deadlines (so much a part of the job) and the monotony and teeth-gritting boredom of endless paper-pushing were sandwiched on either end by the aggravation of fighting the snarl of Southern California traffic.

After work and on weekends I immersed myself in all things Irish, from music to books to photos. I watched Irish films, newscasts and sporting events. I even studied the Irish language, a tricky one, and taught myself a few words and phrases. Anything to feel connected to Ireland. Initially, it was the way I eased myself through the culture shock of returning to California after that first trip, but it soon became a way of life.

◙

Maybe discovering Ireland brought it on or maybe it was a delayed mid-life crisis, but I was becoming acutely aware of the steady forward march of time. Life was going by and not in the manner I'd planned. I wasn't satisfied to think this is it. I felt restless; I wanted something more.

I'd devoted twenty years to being my son's mother, but he had married young, quickly grown away from me, and was living his own life in a world quite separate from mine, leaving a giant chasm, a void that would take years to learn how to live with, without constantly falling into it – another story for another time.

Divorced twice, once from a highly intelligent, loving, but disloyal man, and once from a fun-loving but troubled alcoholic, I was single. I'd grown accustomed to that status and wasn't unhappy with it, but something was missing other than my son and a husband. I felt there must be something else out there waiting for me.

For years I'd fantasized about living by the ocean or in a cabin in the woods, somewhere different, somewhere wilder, earthier than suburban California. But that persistent old dog we call life has a long-standing habit of getting in the way and I never did anything toward turning such fantasies into possibilities. I wondered if it was too late.

The combination of my restlessness, passion for Ireland, and big imagination resulted in rainbow-colored daydreams of how it might be to *live* in Ireland, to feel year-round the way I felt on two week holidays. Not that moving there was a practical idea. I wasn't a rich woman or even close to it. I hadn't done the best job of managing my finances, and those failed marriages and raising a child on my own had done nothing to contribute to a more secure financial future.

No, moving somewhere like Ireland simply wasn't practical. Making such a move would mean early retirement, lowering my Social Security income, and I wouldn't be allowed to work in Ireland. I couldn't see how it would be financially feasible, never mind all the complicated logistics of such a move.

The impracticality of it didn't keep me from wishing and the daydreams continued to grow, becoming more elaborate and vivid as I effortlessly embroidered fanciful details, woven in and out and around that wondrous corner of my mind, the place I could go when Ireland was too far away. I spent many hours there.

Before each trip to the real Emerald Isle there was something unsettling hovering just beneath my excitement, tiny flickerings of apprehension, erratic gusts of wind giving the butterflies a bumpy ride. I alternated between feeling dizzy with joy and tensing with worry: would the magic still be there? I hoped it would be, I needed it to be, but the practical side of me said I ought to be trying to cure myself of such an intense and expensive addiction, an addiction requiring me to spend nearly all my savings every year just for two weeks in Ireland. Yet it seemed logical if I spent enough time there my passion would naturally begin to diminish, so why worry about it? It would play out in due time.

Ireland had other ideas and I was a highly cooperative follower. Each time I set foot on Irish soil I cradled and protected the passion in one hand, holding it gently against my chest like a fragile robin's egg, and in the other, my arm outstretched, I held the apprehension loosely, like an offering to the gods. The breeze dutifully played across my palm, sweeping it clean, catching the apprehension and carrying it far out over the sea, where it dissolved in the Irish mist. It always made me smile, and my soul danced and my heart beat stronger as I set out on another adventure in Ireland.

3

YOU'RE NOT GETTING ANY YOUNGER

August 12, 2012: Only 3 weeks and 2 days before my next trip to Ireland! I suppose some (many?) might say I've been spending too much time planning the trip and writing poetry about sheep and green fields...

Three years had passed since my first visit to Ireland and my next trip was just a few weeks away. I was still bringing home a paycheck for typing, reading, filing, and general shuffling of legal documents. The high point of my day was my lunch hour when I could sit in my car and listen to Irish traditional music or a podcast from or about Ireland. I tried not to notice as days flew by like autumn leaves in a high wind because if I thought about it, and the sameness of my days, and my inability to make my life more exciting and meaningful, alarm gripped me. My Ireland trips and my Ireland daydreams were little therapeutic pockets of time holding my life together.

One balmy California evening in mid-August I was living real life at a backyard party at my sister and brother-in-law's Southern California home, instead of dwelling in the mist and magic of my by then perfectly honed Irish daydreams. Surrounded by family and friends and buoyed by the excitement of knowing I'd be back in Ireland soon, my fourth sojourn, I was feeling good.

Fairy lights twinkled and reflected in the swimming pool, and the party guests chatted and laughed around me. I drank a Guinness, a taste I'd acquired in Ireland though it never tasted quite the same in the USA, and watched as the light breeze taunted a flickering candle.

I was visiting with my brother, monopolizing the conversation, talking too long on my favorite subject, as was my habit whenever I had a good listener. Yes, this was real life, but it didn't mean I couldn't *talk* about Ireland. And believe me, I *could* talk about it and did so at length, with great enthusiasm. I knew there was every chance I was boring my brother silly, but it was his fault. He brought it up.

'I hear you're going to Ireland again pretty soon?'

'I am!'

'Cool.'

I began rattling on about the scenery, the traditional Irish music I so loved, and the friendly people; about the way it felt to wander through ruins and touch an ancient standing stone thousands of years old, or lean against a crumbling castle wall. Just talking about it put me on a high.

My brother smiled. I wasn't sure I was doing a good job of expressing the magic and mystery of it. How many times had I tried to explain it in talking with someone? The emotional connection, the delight I found in Ireland wasn't an easy thing to put into words. As much as I loved talking on the subject, I wasn't very eloquent; I knew that. It had always been easier for me to write than to tell.

I kept at it. 'There's just something about it, the way it affects me. I don't know, exactly... It probably sounds dumb, but it's like a feast for my soul. I just love how I feel when I'm there...'

He seemed to be listening, or maybe I just hoped he was, so I continued. 'There's a beach on the Antrim Coast, up north, a place I went to on my first trip. I was the only one there. It was a gorgeous, sunny day...' Just thinking about it took me back. I could smell the salty air, hear the cries of the gulls, and feel the warm sun and the cool breeze against my skin.

'The ocean looked like blue glass that day, blue glass covered in glittering diamonds... Reflections of the sky and moss-covered rocks made the tide pools shimmer with iridescence. It was *so* beautiful... mesmerizing...but there was another feeling, too. Comfort? I don't know exactly...'

'What do you mean?'

'I don't know… something happened. It's hard to explain. I was sitting on this big flat rock writing, a little poem about being on the beach. The waves sounded like… like a lullaby?… I'm not sure, but it was so extraordinarily peaceful. I felt such a sense of calm and belonging…' I paused. The memory was causing the same strong emotion even after three years.

'I felt like I was in a place I'd been before, a place I'd missed. Like coming home after being away for a long time. I was moved to tears…' I didn't really know how to explain it to myself; explaining it to someone else was impossible. I was losing my audience, anyway.

My good listener was looking across the yard to where my nephew was playing with his dog. I'd gone on too long about Ireland; it was time to wrap it up. No matter how excited I was about it, how profound my experiences, other people could only be expected to take so much.

'Anyway, there's just something about it that I love. I wish I could figure out a way to *live* there!'

It was the usual way I ended my monologues on Ireland. People usually just smiled blankly, or looked at me with sympathetic indulgence as if to say 'There, there, dear; you'll be okay when you pull your head out of the clouds.' I didn't figure my brother had even heard me at that point. But he did. He definitely did. He looked at me in a different way, without speaking, studying me for a moment. And then he spoke.

'So…Why don't you do that?'

I stared at him. *What?* No one had ever said that before. He made it sound so simple. Like it could happen. *Like it wasn't such a big deal.*

Why didn't I, indeed? I smiled at the very thought of it.

'Well… maybe I will!'

It seemed the right response, but as soon as I said it the statement became more than just a casual remark. His question planted a seed and the speed with which it took root surprised me, although I suppose, knowing myself and my tendency to become obsessed with ideas that intrigue me, it shouldn't have. Maybe it didn't have to be only a dream. I wasn't living the life I wanted; maybe I could build a new one?

The next day I went out to lunch with my parents and my sister. We'd just started eating when my mother said, 'So, your brother tells us you're thinking about moving to Ireland!'

Oh, for heaven's sake! My brother had shared our conversation! Dang. I hadn't thought he'd do that and I was annoyed. I had no illusions about what my parents' opinion of such a wild idea would be and it wasn't something I'd intended to tell them at that point. Given my less than secure financial picture it wasn't a plan they'd like; and anyway, it wasn't even a plan! They wouldn't be impressed.

I certainly couldn't see how it would be a good topic to discuss over lunch. Before presenting such a grandiose idea to my conservative, financially responsible, sensible parents I at least needed to have the outline of a plan, have my ducks in a row or at least all heading in the same general direction. It surprised me to realize I still needed my parents' approval.

My mother's statement hung in the air. The noise of the restaurant seemed to recede into the background and the silence was deafening. Befuddled, stomach in a knot, I froze and stared wide-eyed at my sister across the table. I was a startled deer on a dark country road, paralyzed by the headlights of an oncoming car. She was the wise owl perched in a nearby tree, calm, unruffled. I had to say something; it was starting to feel awkward. *Breathe.*

Doing my best to downplay the whole crazy idea I said, 'Uh, well, I guess. I mean, yeah, I've *thought* about it, but...' I wasn't in my sixties, I was twelve years old again.

I finished the sentence with raised eyebrows, shrugging my shoulders as if to say, 'who knows?' and hoped that would close the subject. I made a show of eating my lunch, but I was tense and swallowing was difficult, knowing the disapproval and words of caution soon coming my way.

My mother looked at me. Here it comes. I braced. *Breathe.*

'Well, we think it's a great idea. You should. You're not getting any younger, you know!'

My father, deep into enjoying his burger, smiled in obvious agreement with my mother, raising and lowering his eyebrows in the funny way he sometimes does to show he's pleased.

I was thunderstruck; I may have dropped my fork. Time stopped. It was one of those rare moments when 'you could have knocked me over with a feather' wouldn't have been just a figure of speech, but a literal description. I could not believe what my mother said. Did she *really* say it? I sat there unmoving, returning to my deer-like state, the sounds around me reduced to indecipherable noises, like the adult voices in a Peanuts cartoon.

My sister continued to placidly eat her salad (no wonder she's the skinny one) with a Mona Lisa smile, as if to say, 'What's the big deal? I always thought you should do it!' She is always so calm, matter of fact, and unfailingly encouraging.

I eventually snapped out of it, relaxed, changed the subject, and we finished lunch without further incident.

Later that day when I'd more fully recovered from the surprise of my parents' reaction and registered the fact that it hadn't been a false illusion, I knew their support of the idea was the encouragement I needed. It nurtured that seed my brother had planted and over the next few weeks, it began to sprout. With the approval and enthusiasm of my family I would pursue my dream and find out if it could become reality. I knew they were as hopeful as I was that I could create a new life in a place which promised so much happiness.

◙

My fourth jaunt to Ireland was no less magical than the others and fired my enthusiasm to begin a quest to find out if living there was a possibility for me. I fought to keep my hopes in check knowing the chances weren't good, but I was energized, buzzing with the very thought of it.

I felt so sure it would be the adventure and the life change I needed. Perhaps that certainty is why, up until my brother's query, I had never made any effort toward serious consideration of the possibility. It sounded too perfect, it meant too much. I was afraid of finding out it couldn't happen. That would kill the dream – and then what would I do? If not the reality, I needed the dream.

Actually living there wouldn't be perfect, I knew that. It would not be the same as being there on a holiday. I'd miss family and friends. There'd be inconveniences and annoyances. And I'd still be me. But even trying to look at it with some of the shine off, it was difficult to imagine not feeling as I always did whenever I was there: comfortable in my skin, happy in my heart, and at peace in my soul.

For two months my evenings and weekends were spent on my computer researching, planning, calculating. I did little else. Studying maps, bus and train schedules, immigration policies, housing availability, rental prices and other costs of living became my second job. I prepared a budget and made endless lists, among them my most often edited and referred to list, *Pros & Cons*. I wanted to go, but my mind had to agree with my heart. It all had to add up logically on paper.

One day, there it was in front of me in black and white, almost as if someone had handed me a free pass. *Wait – what??* Yes, the pros outweighed the cons, the logistics could be worked out, and with the exception of a few hurdles I would have to overcome to make it happen, everything was pointing in the direction of Ireland.

So great was my disbelief that something I'd dreamed of, something I'd thought for so long *couldn't* happen actually *could*, it took time for it to sink in. When it did, it wasn't easy to contain my over-enthusiastic self. Where before I'd felt excited at the prospect, discovering I could make the dream a reality turned excitement into elation and I dove head first into the real planning stages of my quest. I think I was fearful if I took my eye off the prize it wasn't going to happen. Surely my enthusiasm and drive couldn't have had anything to do with my obsessive nature…

I chose picturesque Kenmare, a small town in County Kerry, as the place I wanted to settle. I'd been there twice and it was where I'd first thought, 'Wow! I'd love to live here!' I considered many places, but always came back to Kenmare. It was small, but not too small to have the amenities I was looking for, and the access to public transit I would need without a car. I wondered if I was crazy to think I could switch from being a Southern California freeway dweller where my car was like a spare room, to living in rural Ireland and relying on trains, buses, and my own two feet. But it was part of the plan to keep expenses down so crazy or not, that's how it would be.

On an Irish lodging website I found a cottage in Kenmare available by the week. The owner, an Irish woman named Noreen, responded to my e-mail inquiry. When she learned I was an American planning to move there, her interest was piqued and further communication ensued. Within weeks she'd found me a monthly rental I could afford in what seemed a perfect location, steps from town. The photos she sent me showed a furnished two bedroom, one-and-a half bath place. It looked great, I didn't see how I could go wrong. The dwelling in my dream world had been a thatched-roof stone cottage with a red half-door and a furry kitten on the doorstep in an idyllic country setting, but that was out of my price range, and impractical without a car. Some bits of the dream would have to be altered.

Between e-mails, Noreen telephoned me twice. Her thick Kerry accent prevented me from understanding everything she said, but I delighted in hearing her Irish voice. She was as you might imagine a friendly Irish woman would be. She talked fast, she was funny, and she was very kind.

I expressed my interest in her friend's place. How great to have a place upon arrival!

'What shall I send to secure it? How much of a deposit?' My departure date was still several months away.

'Oh, you needn't send anything!' she said.

'Well, what about references? How many references would you like?'

She laughed. 'Oh, no, you needn't send anything! I can tell you're a nice woman. You know how sometimes you just know that about people?' I supposed I did, having thought the same about her.

She then offered references for herself and the rental cottage...

I told that story many times afterwards. Her kindness and instant trust tickled me then and would later become traits I appreciated in a valued friend.

The pieces were falling into place nicely and a picture was emerging of life in Ireland, but two issues remained which I'd been ignoring up until then. It was time to confront them.

I had amassed a fair amount of credit card debt, thanks in part to all those trips to Ireland. I couldn't retire if I had any debt outside of normal living expenses. Period. It had to be paid off.

I owned my condominium. Paying rent in Ireland in addition to the condo mortgage was outside my budget, and I didn't want the hassle and responsibility of owning a rental. If I could sell it – and that was a big 'if' – I might make the extra money I needed. The real estate market had been in a down-turn for years and it didn't look promising. But selling it was the key to my plan so I had to try, and hope for the best.

With the help of a confident realtor friend, I decided to put the condo up for sale four months before my planned departure to Ireland. I was terrified, despite her encouragement and cheerful, smiling support.

My state of terror, while intense, was short-lived. In the first of many times to come, the luck of the Irish was with me. My home went on the market at just the right time, on the edge of a sudden rapid and dramatic come-back for California real estate, the first in several years. By day three we'd received multiple offers at or above asking price, a price set by my optimistic realtor at much higher than I thought reasonable. Within a week I'd accepted a cash offer for thousands more than I'd ever imagined would be possible. I could hardly believe my good fortune. It wasn't an *actual* fortune, it didn't make me rich, but it meant I could go forward with my grand plan and that's all I cared about.

The day escrow closed I sat on my front deck with my savvy realtor friend, looking out across the distant mountains and drinking champagne to celebrate.

She raised her glass. 'So, here's to you! You did it! Now you can move to Ireland!' We clinked our glasses together and the grin on my face didn't leave for the rest of the day.

I knew it was meant to be. The future looked bright and debt-free, and the green hills of Ireland looked close, very close.

4

OBSTACLES OF THE HEART

July 5, 2013: Fireworks last night, but while others are enjoying the long 4th of July weekend today, my nose is to the grindstone, fighting my way through too many possessions. How is it possible that I have this many things?

I wished I was the cram-some-basics-into-a-backpack-and-go type, but I never had been. To make the nearly 5,200 mile move to Ireland the majority of my possessions had to go. Shipping costs were too expensive so I'd be taking only a few cartons of things with me. My intent was to get rid of anything I couldn't take, but I soon realized I was asking the impossible of myself so rented a small storage room for safe-keeping of those things I couldn't bear to part with.

A repeated cycle of sifting, deciding, and sorting began. At times it seemed an insurmountable task. My living space, rather than becoming emptier and less cluttered, went the other way. The unsorted and the sorted seemed to multiply like rabbits. It was a distasteful task and the constant chaos of living among the piles and boxes was irritating and unsettling.

The memorabilia was the hardest to deal with, my natural instinct being to keep all of it. The albums, cartons and storage tubs of photographs, from childhood to recent times, more than sixty years of snapshots, thousands of them, each one telling its own story. Old letters, greeting cards, half-finished stories and poems, childhood drawings and craft projects by my son and my nieces and nephews. I couldn't keep everything; it was too much.

My heart ached and my mind balked at getting rid of any of the memories, but I did. Not all of it; I couldn't. But much of it. For too many days I shed tears and gritted my teeth while I tossed out letters, artwork and other things I never would have parted with under other circumstances. But it had to be done.

Things, they were just things, but the power they had to stop me was tremendous. Unearthing yellowed envelopes with postmarks dating back decades, I couldn't help but begin reading letters, many of which I'd written myself to my sister, who had saved and returned them to me years later. Tales of living in a work camp and working on the Trans-Alaska Pipeline... The heartbreak of a disintegrating marriage and later, the naïve hopes and dreams stemming from my latest romance. I carefully selected some of the letters and tied them up with a blue ribbon.

From the bottom of a box I picked up a curled rectangle of construction paper and traced with one finger the outline of a boat made by my six year old son with red-painted elbow macaroni. It drifted on fuzzy blue yarn sea waves, white cotton ball clouds dotting the sky. *I love you mommy* was written across the bottom in a child's unsure hand. I could still see his big grin and the sparkle in his blue eyes the day he'd proudly given it to me for my birthday twenty-two years before. So long ago, but like yesterday.

The hardest were the photographs, hundreds of them, many duplicates, or photos already scanned for safe-keeping. For days on end I was lost in pictures, memories filling the room like the heady scent of lilacs, needing only to look at a photo to find myself there, in that place, in that time, among those people.

I don't know how often such things caught me, how much time I spent lost in memories. On days when I felt I couldn't bear to let go of anything else, I wondered, is it worth it? Maybe moving to Ireland was crazy? Would it be easier to discard the dream instead of my possessions? Once I stepped away from the photos, the mementos, the over-full boxes, and the emptied drawers and closets, the cloud of emotions cleared along with the dust, and common sense returned. My quest to transform a dream into reality and create a new life took its rightful place, far above inanimate objects. My enthusiasm for the end goal restored, I felt certain I was going in the right direction, no matter how tough the journey.

Between sorting sessions, I searched for the documents I knew might be needed once I got to Ireland. As an American I had to apply for permission to stay in the country if I wished to remain longer than ninety days, but this couldn't be done until I was actually there. The available information on that process was vague and often conflicting, but based on what I learned, my chances for approval were good as long as I provided documentation of finances and identity. Taking periodic breaks from memorabilia sorting, I turned to the boring and thankfully emotionless task of finding and scanning every document I thought might be needed, and storing them all on a flash drive. When finished, I felt insignificant knowing a paper trail summary of my existence had been condensed and captured inside a two inch piece of smart plastic.

◉

It had taken months, but I reached the end of it. Everything was packed, sold, donated, discarded, gifted or stored. The day arrived to turn the keys over to the new owners and I walked out my door for the last time, my footsteps echoing in the empty exterior. Pausing on the front deck I looked out across the treetops to the mountains, the view I'd seen daily for thirteen years. I was leaving my home. A wave of loss and sadness washed over me, the undertow dragging at me. A pesky little voice asked me why I was leaving such an impressive vista and the snug little home attached to it. *Why?* At that moment, although 'Ireland' was on my tongue, I could give no answer.

I swallowed, steeled myself, and gripped the stair railing. I hadn't lost sight of the reason for leaving, but it was harder than I'd expected. I descended the stairs from the familiar, leaving my home and a life that all of a sudden didn't seem so bad. I didn't want to leave – but I *had* to leave if I wanted to pursue my dream. Walking away was painful, and Ireland was offering no comfort just then.

I'd taken the morning off and wasn't scheduled to be back in the office until after lunch. I had a few more hours so decided to make it a proper farewell. I began driving around town past old familiar places. They were common places, but rose up before me every bit as impressive and meaningful on that day as famous landmarks or historic monuments. There were no guided tours, no commemorative plaques, but each was special to me. The lake where I'd so often walked, but not as often as I should have. The Taco Bell where I'd treated myself for dinner, more often than I should have. My parents' old neighborhood. The tennis courts where I'd watched my Dad teach his grandsons to play tennis. The Starbucks where I'd met friends for coffee and conversation on Saturday mornings, and the Italian restaurant where we'd gathered for dinners, drinks and laughs. The hockey rink where I'd spent so many hours proudly watching my son. *Goodbye. Goodbye.*

I had been unprepared for the sadness that hit me that day, but saying goodbye to places and things would be nothing compared to the farewells to family and friends. During the last few weeks before my departure I said many goodbyes, some more difficult than others, all of them necessary, and none of them something I wanted to do. I knew I had to look ahead to when the hard bits were behind me. I reminded myself that change brings both gains and losses; that's just the way it is.

An adventure awaited.

◙

In the final days before leaving California I thought of the reactions expressed to my plan. I hadn't encountered anyone who did not seem, in varying degrees, admiring, excited over what I was doing and interested in hearing the details. I was complimented on finding a way to do it, on being brave enough to do it. I'm not sure how many of them realized I had a great motivator. I needed an adventure. Moving to a place I loved with the hope of creating a happier more satisfying life didn't seem to have much to do with bravery, but with a deep need for change.

It wasn't just close friends and family who seemed interested and impressed with the adventure I was about to begin, my fan base included acquaintances, co-workers, and virtual strangers. The first few times I concluded the reaction was just kind politeness. When it happened repeatedly I suspected it was more than that. An adventure of the kind others wished for, but either could not or would not do, based on personality or life circumstances. The next best thing was knowing someone who could – and did.

Perhaps the reactions were similar to the way I enjoy reading true stories featuring people exploring deep dark jungles, working in Antarctica, or climbing mountains. Things I wish I had the nerve to do because I'm fascinated by it, yet knowing it isn't my cup of tea. I'm satisfied to read about others doing it. I wouldn't equate living in Ireland with risking my life on a mountainside, using a machete to whack my way through a jungle, or living under a dome in Antarctica, but you get my gist. The folks who admired and encouraged me helped sustain my momentum during times of doubt. It seemed as though I was making the move not just for myself, but on some level, for others, too.

That little seed planted by my brother turned out to need more attention and nurturing to come to full bloom than I'd expected. Much more. The reality of it was nowhere near as simple as the concept. It was harder, took longer, and cost more than I'd anticipated, both financially and emotionally, but I'd made it. I was moving to Ireland. *I was moving to Ireland!* I couldn't wait for the adventure to begin, and already my heart felt lighter and my soul stretched and flexed, warming up to dance.

HOMECOMING

Oh, Ireland, how she greets me
All dressed up in smiles and greens
She cares not about my wrinkled shirt
Or my looking slept-in jeans
She doesn't notice I've put on weight
Or that my hair's more gray
She greets me with wide open arms
On this, my coming home day.

Like a loving mother
She so missed me while I was gone
And the red carpet she's rolled out
Is a broad and lush green lawn
And endless rolling hills
Dressed up in gorse and heather
And for me she's ordered sunshine and mist
A grand mix of Irish weather.

She sees not who I once was,
Nor wishes for what I might be
All she cares about is comfort
And an Irish welcome for me.
My failures are not noticed
My shortcomings waved away
She holds me and she rocks me
And we laugh and sing and pray.

She's pulled for me a pint
With a perfect foamy head
And a steaming bowl of chowder
Served with tasty fresh brown bread.
The fiddler's at the ready
The bodhrán's begun to beat
She's cleared a place for me to sit
To relax and tap my feet.

If anyone's more pleased than she is
It would, of course, be me
Back home in dear old Ireland
Where I've so longed to be.

5

HOME AWAY FROM HOME

September 7, 2013: I keep telling myself I'm here, I'm really here, but myself isn't listening! I suppose one of these days it will register.

After five days in Dublin I was on the road to Kenmare. Thanks to Ciara, a friend in Dublin who kindly offered to drive me, I had transportation across the country without having to struggle with all my excess luggage and shopping bags overflowing with goods on trains and buses. There was that Irish luck again!

We stuffed Ciara's little Audi full and hit the road. Four and a half hours later we arrived in the southwest corner of Ireland, in Kenmare, nestled between the mountains on the shore of a beautiful bay. It felt unreal to be driving into town past the colorful pub and shop fronts I remembered from my first trip to Ireland, a place that would now be my new home.

We found my rental cottage on a narrow side road steps away from the center of town. From photos I'd received I recognized it, called a *cottage* by the locals, but actually one part of a long building housing eight two-story dwellings. Looking at the exterior no one would have trouble believing it was old, but the fact that it was built in the early nineteenth century took the concept of old to another level.

My landlord Michael's significant other, Ella, was there to open the door and let us inside. The cottage, once only one room and a loft, has been refurbished and expanded into its present state of a two bedroom, one-and-a-half bath home. Upon entering I was pleased to see it looked just as it did in the pictures. It seemed almost familiar. I was touched by the tall vase of fresh flowers in the front room, a note of welcome from my landlord and his family tucked among the blossoms. Ireland is known as 'the land of a hundred thousand welcomes,' and that would be the first of many I would have the privilege to receive.

Ciara stepped back outside to make a phone call while I inspected the old stone fireplace, running my hand across the rough cut gray stones shot through with streaks of brown and white. A brass log holder on the hearth held a few logs and chunks of turf, also known as peat. I loved the smell of a turf fire and couldn't wait to have one burning in my own fireplace.

I peeked through the single deep-set front window at the old, red, corrugated aluminum shed across the road, its color partly from paint and partly from rust, before continuing on my tour.

The kitchen was off the living room, with a sliding glass door to a small back patio. A concrete wall about four feet high separated the patio area from my neighbors and held back the hillside behind it. This was an area I'd come to know was my 'garden.' 'Garden,' – no matter what, if anything, was growing there – was the proper term in Ireland. It wasn't a yard or a patio, it was a garden. One of the first of many new things I'd learn.

The hillside was covered with vegetation stretching as far as I could see, giving the feeling of living in the country, despite the close proximity to town. Large willowy plumes of pampas grass waved their feathery fingers against the blue sky, and enormous tree-like rosemary bushes grew from the dirt and rocks at the bottom of the hill just behind the wall.

On the right, behind the adjoining cottage, was a pretty rock garden, shrubs and flowers blooming in various colors and heights between the rocks on the terraced hillside. I'd later learn the garden and cottage belonged to one of Michael's sisters. I would come to enjoy my view of that changing garden year-round.

On the left side was a wild overgrown open space, the back garden of an unrestored vacant cottage, partially obscured by a large green oil tank. Oil would supply the energy to operate the hot water boiler.

Back inside I looked around the kitchen. All the major appliances appeared to be accounted for, including a small combination washer/dryer, something I'd heard of, but had never used. The refrigerator was a 'mini-fridge,' the kind one might see in a hotel or college dorm room. I peered inside at the diminutive interior and wondered how it would work out for me. I could foresee frequent trips to the market.

The place was clean, more than spacious enough for one, and completely furnished. Over-furnished. I was perplexed by the bounty of duplicate and triplicate kitchen supplies filling the cupboards and drawers but assumed it had all just accumulated over time. The same was true upstairs where sheets, blankets and towels in multiple sets crowded the two small closets. With Michael's permission, I later packed up much of it and he kindly hauled it away.

After thanking Ciara for carting me across the country and bidding her farewell, I continued wandering around my new home in a daze, feeling as though I'd been abruptly awakened after a deep sleep. After four years of fervent wishing and a year of extensive research and careful planning, it wasn't easy to grasp that I was finally living the dream. While it was exciting, it was a bit bewildering. I felt a little like Alice-through-the-looking-glass.

When I climbed into bed that night between the new sheets I'd bought in Dublin, I was physically and emotionally tired, but looking forward to beginning my new life. Laying there beneath the skylight I looked up at the stars glittering in the night sky. Before I could marvel at the beauty of such a sight I was hit with an odd, empty feeling, something like sadness. It caught me off guard and I began to feel anxious, apprehensive… but I didn't understand why. Wasn't this where I wanted to be?

My mind spun in crazy circles and my heart was beating too fast. It was more than apprehension; it was fear. But fear of what? I was happy to finally be in Ireland, but maybe my subconscious wasn't as adventurous as the rest of me? It *was* a major life change. I tossed and turned and tried to be logical, knowing it was purely a mind game, but even repeating my usually helpful mantra during times of stress, *mind over matter*, wasn't helping at all.

And then it occurred to me that what I was actually feeling was a terrible, deep homesickness. I felt further away from home than I could even comprehend. Like I always imagined it would feel to be in space – not somewhere I'd ever had any desire to go. I felt like I was up there with those stars I could see through the skylight, alone, way out there, somewhere so far away, a distance so impossible to cover... My mind buckled and folded over on itself, refusing to comprehend. I was saved by exhaustion and cradled by sleep.

I awoke the next morning feeling well-rested, made coffee, and built a small fire in the fireplace. I opened the back door and stepped out into the cool quiet of the morning, the only sound the birds singing in the trees. I gazed out across the hillside, looked up at the blue sky and took deep breaths of the sweet Irish air before returning indoors. I drank my coffee, my first cup on my first morning, by my first fire, in my new Irish home, and imagined my elation was surely glowing like an aura around me. It had been a long road from dream to reality, but I'd made it. I smiled and laughed at myself remembering my anxiety the night before. Strong as it had been, it had disappeared along with the starry night sky. My mind had caught up with my heart. I was fine; I was more than fine. I was in Ireland!

◙

In those first weeks I felt as I always had on all my travels to Ireland. Life was peaceful, yet full of entertainment and stimulation, and a sense of freedom. The world around me was intriguing, solid, and filled with ancient places and timeless traditions, delightful people and experiences. An old world, but to me it was new. And new was just what I needed. I'd seen and experienced much of it on those annual treks, but it was different now. I began seeing things through different eyes, no longer a tourist, and that seemed to further enhance the beauty and wonders around me.

The modern suburban landscape of my old neighborhood in Southern California was replaced with roads lined with old stone walls, quaint buildings, and an early nineteenth century dwelling where, I'd discovered on my first day, chickens scratched and clucked their way through my back garden. I walked in the rain in my wellington boots – better known as *wellies* – with no thought toward whether I looked fashionable, and met friends with lovely Irish accents for window shopping or a cup of tea. The neighbors brought me fresh eggs and garden produce. Random remarks to strangers could develop into full-blown chats and a few minutes could melt into half an hour. An evening outing was a few pints of perfectly-poured Guinness in a pub a short walk up the road, where the warmth of a fire, friendly folks, and jigs and reels provided the Irish ambiance I'd only experienced in movies. In those first days I often felt I was *in* a movie, so hard was it to fully comprehend that I was actually living what had once been just a dream.

◙

It was a simple life and an interesting one, but that dream world I'd lived in before, no matter how detailed and elaborate, hadn't prepared me for all the things I needed to learn to live comfortably in Ireland. Many of the mechanics of my new life were mysteries, but figuring them out was all a part of the fun – most of the time, anyway.

My fire-building skills needed work, but I was getting daily practice. Reorganizing the wood pile to keep it protected from the rain, restocking the indoor wood basket, and cleaning out the fireplace ashes became a standard part of my routine.

Visitors dropped by unannounced on a regular basis, not something to which I was accustomed. It was considered neighborly, and being at the ready with tea and a biscuit was customary and expected. I learned early on that Noreen, the lady who found the rental cottage for me, would pop in often. She proved to be every bit the kind and funny lady I'd imagined after speaking with her on the phone. Her habit of knocking on my door with one hand as she jiggled the handle with the other startled me at first, but soon became an amusing part of my new life. Living in the country, Noreen's not accustomed to locked doors.

Likewise, seeing my landlord Michael or his sister Liz appear in my back garden after hopping over the garden wall was something it took time to get used to, but eventually just became the way of things. I discovered it would be their usual approach, so knew better than to walk around in my underwear. Not that it was my habit to do so, but just in case I ever had the urge.

In between chores, visitors, and pub outings, I cooked and baked. I was never much of a baker; that title belongs to my mother and sister. Never really much of a cook, either. But in Ireland I began to enjoy both, and every few days found me in the kitchen making soups and stews, and baking biscuits, cookies, or banana bread. It occurred to me if I continued in that vein I'd need to add longer, faster, and more frequent walks in the rain to my daily list of activities.

The stove, known as a 'cooker,' wasn't familiar and I wasn't quite sure how to use it, even beyond the fact that the dials showed Celsius instead of Fahrenheit. I didn't know how to operate the combo washer/dryer machine. I wasn't sure if the heat was broken, ineffective, or if I was turning it on incorrectly. There was a nice fireplace, but I wasn't an experienced fire builder and where did one buy firewood in Kenmare, anyway?

I spent time daily translating Celsius to Fahrenheit, centimeters to inches, grams to ounces and Irish-English to American-English. I sorted compost-eligible items from other garbage, all of which used to be one category – trash – and reminded myself repeatedly that it wasn't called trash or garbage anymore, but rubbish, and the garbage cans weren't cans, they were bins!

Using an oil-fired boiler which required one to switch it off and on to heat water or suffer the expensive consequences of using too much oil was completely foreign to me. I struggled to remember to turn it on in advance, and turn it off when I finished showering or washing dishes. It would take time before that became less of an afterthought and more of a habit.

The mini-fridge was a puzzle. It took days to figure out where to position items to maximize the space, and crouching on the floor to find things was one of the new experiences I could have lived without.

And who knew 'Emergency' was 999? Or that the emergency room of a hospital wasn't called 'Emergency' or 'ER,' but A&E (Accident and Emergency)? Or that the reason for the tiny openings in the litter bins on the streets, barely large enough to toss away a paper cup, was to prevent people from dumping their home garbage free of charge? And when the bus driver asked you if you wanted a 'return' ticket that meant round-trip, and if you wanted only a one-way ticket you needed to ask for a single?

At the supermarket for the first time, I was clueless about the shopping cart system. The carts were chained together. I didn't know the trick was to insert a one-euro coin into the little slot in the handle to release the key on the end of the chain. An excellent way to help eliminate the abandonment or theft of carts, but some sort of instructional signage for newbies would have been nice.

Shopping itself was an adventure. I knew after my first shopping trip it would be awhile before I could find things because I first needed to learn the correct terms for them. I was mildly distressed to discover I couldn't buy some favorites like beef jerky and dill pickles. I went without the jerky except when I received it in care packages from my sister.

Pickles were another matter. After trying various brands of what were billed as 'sour gherkins' and finding nothing tasting remotely like the dill pickles I loved, I ordered them online from amazon.co.uk at a staggering price, quadruple what I would have paid in the USA. 'Just this once,' I told myself, closing my eyes, and clicking 'Place Order.' I love dill pickles. A lot. I rationed them out carefully, but it wasn't a bottomless jar. Repeating the ordering process was far too easy and it became a regular habit.

Without a car, I needed something to increase my carrying capacity. As would become the solution for many things, I again turned to amazon.co.uk. I was looking for a small rolling shopping cart-thing to help me truck groceries home (before I discovered the miraculous invention of the grocery delivery service). It wasn't easy to find what I was seeking because it was yet another item known by a different name. I couldn't have guessed a shopping cart is called a trolley. I thought a trolley was like a cable car. Somehow, after much searching, I managed to find the right product and in doing so, ran across a humorous description:

'A range of simply stylish shopping trolleys, designed by British designers, … are a simple and contemporary way to surpass the plastic carrier bags to transport your shopping whilst allowing you to wave hello to the neighbours in a stunning way.'

Well, of course, I had to order one. I was no spring chicken; I could use some help with looking stunning.

I had devoted ridiculous amounts of time to serious research and planning during the year before I moved. But there was no course available, no book to study, offering the 'how to's' of the practical, day-to-day functions of living in Ireland. I hadn't learned as much as I thought during all that research and my four two-week trips traveling around the country. I knew how to count to ten and make a few toasts in the Irish language; I was aware ordering a glass of Guinness would get you a half-pint; that a sign advertising *CRAIC AGUS CEOL* meant 'fun and music,' and traditional Irish music was called 'trad music.' I was nearly a pro at finding the tourist spots in Dublin. I'd been to many of Ireland's historical sites, from Glendalough to the Skellig Islands. I'd walked on white sand beaches, through mossy forests and boggy fields, along quiet country lanes, and on steep mountain roads. So what? Very little of it had any particular relevance to the practicalities of daily living. I had much to learn. Trial and error would be the order of the day for a while.

◻

One of my first bits of settling in business was to buy an international calling card so I could call my family in the USA. This turned out to be an interesting experience, second in complexity and perplexity only to Ireland's immigration procedures, but much more amusing – in retrospect. At the time, it made me wonder about the friendliness of the locals.

I was told I could purchase a calling card at the convenience market near my cottage. I headed there my second day in town, full of enthusiasm and extreme cheerfulness, so excited was I to be in Kenmare. Inside, I inquired brightly of the clerk who stood in front of a five foot square sign posted to the wall advertising in bold black lettering, INTERNATIONAL CALLING CARDS!, accompanied by an illustration of two yellow smiley-faces, one waving an American flag and the other an Irish flag, talked on telephones, presumably to each other.

'Hello!' I said. 'I'd like to buy an international calling card, please.'

She shook her head. 'We don't have any.'

I looked at her, then at the advertisement on the wall, then back at her, but she didn't seem to get it. I pointed to the sign. She shook her head again and directed me 'up the way' to another market. I would later learn that directions never involved distances in blocks; this was not a known unit of measurement in Ireland, at least not in County Kerry. It was always something like 'up the way,' 'at the top of the town,' or 'down below,' or something far more complicated and detailed but somehow, ultimately vague and confusing.

I wasn't one for being confrontational and I didn't want to seem rude, so I said nothing about the giant advertisement on the wall, and continued on my way.

I found the second market by walking until I ran into it. A sour-faced older gentleman I thought must be the proprietor stood behind the counter. I didn't see evidence of any advertisements for calling cards, but given the situation at the last market, maybe that was as good thing. I smiled at the man and made my cheery inquiry.

'Hello! I'm told you have international calling cards for sale here?'

He looked at me like I was asking for a ticket on the space shuttle and said nothing. I was perplexed by his decidedly un-Irish response. The young woman standing next to him pointed outside and said, 'Three doors up.'

I had to assume they didn't have any calling cards, but like the first market, I didn't know if they were out of them or no longer carried them, or maybe never had any. This information was beginning to seem like a mysterious, closely guarded secret.

The woman failed to mention the place she was sending me was on the other side of the street, but I did deduce from the 'up' part of the directions that she intended for me to head uphill, so I did. I didn't see any shops that looked like possible purveyors of calling cards, but spied a small market on the other side of the street, so crossed over.

Smiling was feeling a little forced at this point, but I managed a small one.

'Hello! I hope you can help me!' Maybe being less cheerful and playing up the pity angle would produce better results. Practically wringing my hands I said, 'I'm having a terrible time trying to find international calling cards! I was told you might have them - ?'

This time, I did at least get some sympathy. 'Sorry,' the clerk said, shaking her head in the negative. She had no idea where I might find such an item.

After three strikes, I took the hint and gave up.

I went home and turned to the Wonders of the Internet. Within minutes I found an excellent deal online. So much for my effort to support local businesses. Accustomed as I was to speaking with my sister at least a couple of times a week I was happy to know though I was far away, it would not be cost-prohibitive to call her and others in America. It was my little security blanket and added to my enjoyment of my time in Ireland. I would never again feel as far away as I had that first night.

I should mention that I would also never again be met with such an odd and unfriendly reception from shopkeepers in Kenmare as happened on the strange day I went on the hunt for the illusive international calling card.

◙

Finding a calling card had required some patience, but awaiting the arrival of my possessions required many more days of patience, and patience was never my strong point. The brand-spanking newness of being in Ireland was beginning to wear off a little as I sat and waited for my things, the specially selected possessions I spent far too much money to ship overseas from California. Like every other task I'd completed in my journey toward Ireland, I had spent time and effort choosing and packing those things and calculating the right shipping date so their arrival would occur shortly after mine. That last part hadn't panned out.

I was in a lull, days that weren't going according to plan. Time and quiet were allowing a few doubts and concerns to begin creeping in again and I was still feeling somewhat like Alice after falling down the rabbit hole. Could I *really* become accustomed to turning on the boiler every time I wanted hot water and waiting up to thirty minutes before I could take a shower? Would I be warm enough in winter? Would the novelty of hanging clothes outdoors to dry wear off and become just an annoyance? Would my budget work out? Would I become too lonely for family and friends in the U.S.? Could I live with the tiny old-fashioned television set? (The answer was a resounding 'No!' to the TV question. A couple of months later Amazon.co.uk came to the rescue again, and for a few hundred euros sorted that one out for me. And while I was there I put a jar of pickles in my cart.)

I wrestled for a brief time with all those questions and doubts then shook them off, becoming more irritated with myself and my worrying than with the delay in receiving my things. I thought about the good times I'd already had, settled in or not. All that was really missing to make me feel at home were those boxes from California. I knew when I had some of my familiar things around me I would feel more settled. It was just a minor glitch.

Sixteen days after I arrived, those long awaited boxes which had departed the USA two weeks before I did, finally arrived, too, looking as though they might have circled the globe more than once. One was crushed nearly beyond recognition, but fortunately it contained only non-breakable items. I'd covered all of the boxes with what I told myself at the time was a ridiculous amount of packing tape, but I patted myself on the back for the overkill as it had prevented all chances of any of the contents spilling out, despite the severe crushing.

Feeling like a child at a birthday party, I opened those cartons, pulling out and examining and admiring various items as if they were new, as if I'd never seen them before. But the reason I was enamored was not because they were new, but because they were comfortingly familiar. I told myself I'd been a little silly in bringing so much, yet couldn't stop the feeling of excitement each time I unwrapped something.

I spent several days arranging and finding storage for everything, the chosen few selected to accompany me on my journey into a new chapter of my life. Afterwards I sat and gazed around, my eyes stopping and focusing on each treasured item. The value was not monetary, it was in the warm feelings attached to them. The sun, moon and star trio of blue glass candle holders, a much-loved, long-ago gift from my sister. A small black and white snapshot of my mother in a big floppy hat, my chubby one-year old self safe in her arms, frozen in time, and a dog-eared copy of *Benedictus*, a book of blessings by Irish philosopher and poet John O'Donohue.

With my possessions around me, the cottage was being transformed into a place that was beginning to feel like my own. I wanted a new life but that didn't mean giving up all of the past. I'd always been a 'nester' and I guess living in a rental cottage in a land far across the sea didn't change that.

When I went to bed that night relishing the feel of my fluffy comforter and my own pillow cradling my head, I felt different, more at ease. Was it only weeks before when I'd convinced myself 'things' weren't important? Yes, but things can have such meaning and comfort attached to them, and they become so much more than that. I was in Ireland, where I'd so longed to be, but something had been missing: some of the flotsam and jetsam of my life. Reunited with a few familiar bits and pieces completed the process. I was at home.

In those first days as the autumn evenings unfolded, night's shadows descending and the temperature cooling, I'd light the fire. I'd sit and eat dinner by the flickering flames, feeling safe and sheltered by the roof and walls of my new Irish home. In the quiet warmth I thought about the simple things that formed such an easy framework for my life in County Kerry. I felt proud of myself for all I was learning how to do and loved the tickling feeling of looking forward to what the coming days might bring, what new pleasure or discovery.

A small step at a time, I was relaxing into my Irish life. Like a chameleon dropped into a different landscape, my color was changing. While I would always show the Stars & Stripes and be *That American Woman* living in Kenmare, I was settling in. I thought often of the lovely dream I'd once spent so much time in and gave thanks for the blessing of being able to live it.

6

MEET THE LOCALS

Sept. 20, 2013: Noreen just stopped by with firewood from their farm. I've long known Irish folks are generally nice people, but I'm amazed daily by just how kind and helpful they truly are.

A great number of people in Kenmare are in some way related. Everyone seems to know everyone or at least someone who knows someone else. Combine that with the propensity for chat, a high level of interest in what's going on, and you have a human communication network rivaling Eircom, the largest telecommunications operator in Ireland. Gossip and news spread like butter dropped into a hot fry pan. The first time a friend of mine asked me if I'd enjoyed myself at the pub the evening before, I wondered how she knew. I hadn't yet realized the intricacy and effectiveness of the Kenmare grapevine. I suppose being a newcomer – *That American Woman* – made me more noticeable and for a time, an interesting topic, no matter what I did.

I often thought how strange, but wonderful, to meet so many people in a place so small compared to the large metropolis I'd lived in before, where I rarely met anyone. The people I met and came to know, with their kind ways, and the sweet and funny things they do, are such a big part of what living in Ireland is all about. Of course I didn't click with every person I encountered, but most turned out to be good, down-to-earth folks who enjoy life and love to laugh.

Noreen and my neighbors were the most constant people in my new world. On my first day in town I met Noreen. I was walking to the nearby market and she came careening down the narrow roadway in her little car, saw me, whipped around the corner onto a side street, screeched to a stop, hopped out of the car and introduced herself. Knowing everyone on the street, I guess she assumed the stranger was the new American woman.

Noreen doesn't just know everyone on the street, she knows everyone in town. She loves to chat and I suppose that helps in getting to know people. Her rental cottage is just down the street a short ways and she's often there taking care of business. She frequently combines that with a stop to see me, or my landlord Michael and his family.

Noreen's funny knock-and-turn-the-door-handle approach, entering the room in her lightning-quick way with a cheery 'Hello!' the instant the door opens, is in keeping with the way she does everything – with quickness and intensity, no messing about. She often leaves in the same fashion, like a whirlwind changing direction, on to the next event or duty because she is a very busy lady. She switches activities as fast as she switches conversation topics. With all she has to handle, it's a must.

Noreen and her husband Paudie are sheep farmers and do it all on their own, from lambing to shearing to taking the sheep to market. They live on the land where Noreen has lived her entire life. On top of that and her holiday cottage, she takes care of her sister's holiday home and often Liz's cottage, the one next door to me. And then there are her two part-time jobs, one in a shop in town and another housekeeping in the holiday home of some English folks. It is a mystery to everyone how Noreen keeps everything straight with all that she does.

I'm not the only one impressed with her energy and juggling ability. With her gift of the gab, dry sense of humor, strong Kerry accent, and high energy no-nonsense ways, she is a genuine Irish character with enough warmth and complexity to be the lovable central figure in a wildly entertaining film I wish I had the talent and funds to make. I can picture someone like the actress Julie Walters perfectly portraying the role of Noreen similar to the character she played in the film, *Mama Mia*.

Noreen would always be a fun, helpful and trustworthy friend, a friendship that began while I was still sitting in my kitchen in California talking to her by phone, and she was judging me to be a good person, sight unseen.

Michael is my neighbor. He lives next door to his father Daniel's home, one building down from mine. At first he seemed a shy, quiet man, but I soon learned he loves to talk (he is Irish, after all!). He is interesting and witty with a knack for telling stories, usually funny ones, and is very kind. He turned sixty during my first summer in Ireland.

I thought of Michael's sisters, Liz and Mary, who both live in England, as my 'alternating neighbors' as they took turns staying with their dad so he could remain living in the place he loved, in his home of seventy years, the house where they'd all been raised. Daniel's mobility and stability were issues, and as a very independent, proud man he didn't like asking for help. They feared he might fall and injure himself if someone wasn't there to assist when needed.

I didn't get to know Daniel well, his failing health preventing him from socializing beyond cups of tea in the kitchen of his home. He'd sit in his chair and watch his beloved sports on television and his equally beloved birds through the back window as they flittered around and pecked at the multiple feeders hanging in the trees and from the eaves of the house. I never heard him say too much, but he always had a pleasant look on his face, and a ready smile. I could tell just by knowing his children and the way they spoke of him that he was an exceptional, and loved, man. He made me think of my own father and grandfather, both remarkable and well-loved men.

I met Liz within days of arriving in Kenmare. She was here in Kenmare caring for Daniel. She's a small woman and looks young, certainly younger than her sixty-something years, but her bountiful energy and frequent smiles are probably as much responsible for that as her genetics. We became instant friends and I can't imagine that will ever change. The garden behind her holiday home, the one I so admired on arrival, made it clear she has a very green thumb.

Liz is a doer, a helper, a giver. She is constantly thinking of and caring for others. From the day I met her she made me smile and even more often, laugh. Since she lives in England I don't see her regularly, but from the day we met she always felt very much a part of my life in Ireland. We never seem to run out of things to talk about. When she's not here, I think of her whenever I'm admiring her beautiful garden.

Liz's husband, Frank, is a good-humored and helpful Englishman, nearly twice as tall as Liz. He loves to tease and joke. Individually or together, Liz and Frank are fun to be around.

When Michael and Liz's sister Mary, a nun, arrived to stay with their dad, she knocked on my door one day and introduced herself. Like Liz she is an attractive lady. As I did with everyone in the family, I took an immediate liking to her. A sweet and soft-spoken woman with kind, intelligent eyes, being in her company is peaceful and pleasant, in keeping with her chosen profession. I'm told she was a firecracker in her youth and after getting to know her better, I caught glimpses of her wit and high spiritedness beneath the calm facade. Although we are close in age, her genteel and wise ways, and quick sense of humor are reminiscent of my grandmother. It is always a pleasure to see her.

Before long I'd also met another sibling, Colin, and his long-time significant other, Clare, who regularly come from Dublin to visit and spend time in their holiday home in Kenmare. They are also warm, caring folks with a great sense of humor, just like the rest of the clan. Colin is soft-spoken like Mary, but when he gets to talking he can tell stories to rival his brother. Clare is another one with whom I immediately felt comfortable. She's funny and fun, and easy to talk with. I am always delighted to see both her and Colin.

It was only a matter of days before I realized my good fortune in meeting this exceptional family, people who were my neighbors and became my friends, and oftentimes seemed like my second family.

I met many other people, too, like Kieran, born and raised in England with Irish parents. Kieran was one of the first people I became friends with in Kenmare. It's Kieran's habit to go out for a pint or two after his work as a painter a few times a week. His favorite pubs are my favorites, too, and we met within days of my arrival. His English instead of Irish accent made understanding him easier, such a relief in those early days when I so often struggled during conversations with the locals. As I got to know him better it wasn't just the way he talked that I appreciated, it was his kind Irish nature and obvious sincerity. He's a good guy.

In his late forties, Kieran isn't too young to be able to talk about the 'old days' and we can discuss the current state of the modern world and be on the same page, or at least relate to what the other is talking about. We've covered a variety of subjects, from Irish immigration policies to the Rolling Stones, and past loves to the Viet Nam War. We share local gossip, trade favorite books, and just listen when that's what one of us needs.

There were many others I met early on, too, like Dierdre, a hardworking young woman from Dublin, always ready with a kind word and a smile regardless of how busy she might be with customers in the Kenmare pub where she works. She's a nice young lady.

Liam, a young man who grew up in Kenmare, is similarly hardworking and friendly. He mans the bar at what has turned out to be my usual pub because of the regular twice-weekly traditional music sessions. Only in his twenties, there is something in Liam's dark eyes which hints of an older soul. At times he's quiet and serious, but he enjoys joking around, too. He's the kind of guy you can have a serious conversation with or lots of laughs, depending on his mood – and yours.

A number of transplants add an international component to the mostly Irish population of Kenmare, people like Bob and Rose, ex pats from America who share my passion for Ireland, several ex pats from England, and countless pub and restaurant workers like high-energy Mandy from Scotland whose serious working demeanor is frequently punctuated by her infectious smile and laugh.

I met and became friends with Molly and Eric, ex-pats from Germany, through Noreen. Like me, they moved to Ireland after spending many holidays here and falling in love with the place. They're congenial folks, always up for a road trip or an evening of socializing. Avid motorbike riders, they cruise around whenever weather permits and have traveled much of Ireland in that fashion. They're a fun and interesting couple and in no time I counted them among my good friends in Ireland.

Volunteering with the local theater group also led to the opportunity to meet more interesting and fun folks and an ever-widening circle of acquaintances and friends.

Ireland's climate, culture, and landscape were but the backdrop for my new life; it was definitely the people who provided the punctuation, the commas and the exclamation points to string all the discoveries and adventures together, making me feel valued and creating clarity of experience, enhancing the excitement, and deepening the enjoyment. Whether our paths briefly crossed or they walked with me for a ways, I feel lucky to have met them and I know there will be several with whom I'll want to always keep in touch, no matter where we all end up in this life.

7

Days of Yore

September 21, 2013: I can't seem to get over living in the middle of all this history. It's amazing. Plan to walk up to the stone circle this evening. It is a magical place in the twilight.

Born and raised on the west coast of America, living among the visible history of Ireland was mind-boggling. The antiquities seemingly around every corner never became commonplace to me.

The area now known as Kenmare, where cattle once grazed on open fields, was granted to an Englishman in the mid-seventeenth century by the infamous Oliver Cromwell, as was the cruel habit in those days of taking Ireland from the Irish. In the late eighteenth century the town's development began.

The same three main streets in their triangular layout, Henry, Main and Shelbourne, and many of the original buildings still exist. The street I live on is one of the older roadways. If you could have walked upon it before the town was developed, you'd have likely found a worn path through the fields, and could easily have encountered a cattle drover taking his cattle to market.

The cottages at the end of the street nearest to town were built in the 1860's. On one side of the street stone walls and pretty front gardens separate the cottages from the road; on the other side the homes are built in the more traditional Irish style with doorsteps right on the narrow sidewalk.

Further down the street is my building, a limestone structure built to house tradesmen employed by the English landlord's estate. Although no records exist to document the exact year it was built, it is thought to be one of the oldest still occupied buildings in Kenmare, estimated to date back to the first or second decade of the nineteenth century. Almost two hundred years before I called it home, a tradesman such as a blacksmith or a wheelwright and his family lived here. I repeated that fact to myself many times, but it never sounded less fantastical.

Most of the cottages have been refurbished in the last twenty-five years, doubling in size, with additions built onto the rear, behind what once was only a single room and a loft, but the exteriors of most are unchanged.

A few cottages are vacant and haven't been restored. Their faces show their status, with cracked wooden doors, peeling paint, and dusty lace curtains still hanging in some of the windows. Peering through those windows clouded with cobwebs and time one can just make out the dim interiors with their huge open fireplaces, buckled or non-existent floors, rusted tools and equipment, barrels, and fallen timbers. For several weeks during my first winter a tattered lace curtain yellowed with age flapped in the wind through the upstairs half-broken window of the cottage next to me, like a flag beckoning from the past. One day it was gone, probably torn loose by the persistent and ferocious storms that pounded Ireland that winter.

I had the opportunity to step inside one of the vacant cottages. The high, jumbled stacks of scrap wood and other miscellaneous items crowding the space and the dim light from the open door and small lace-curtained window didn't invite a tour of the place. But I could see enough to get a sense of how it once must have been.

As my eyes adjusted to the darkness and the sun peeked out from behind the clouds, a ray of dust-flecked sunlight filtered in through the front window illuminating the deep set frame and a rusty tin cup resting on the sill. A stone fireplace overwhelmed the space, taking up most of the wall on one side of the room. Thick cobwebs nestled in the corners and hung from the rafters supporting the sleeping loft. It smelled of age and dust, of wood and metal, but I could imagine how it once smelled of a turf fire and soup simmering over it, or perhaps of soap and fresh linens from a recently finished morning's wash before it was hung on the clothesline in the dirt yard to flap in the breeze.

When I stepped back outside I saw an old, rusty horseshoe partially embedded in the earth near the back door. I picked it up and was given permission to keep it. It had probably been laying there for many years. I would guess the area has seen neither horses nor blacksmiths for a long while.

I was told when one of the old cottages was being restored and expanded, a discovery was made. Over the alarmed protestations of a neighbor ('Oh, don't tell her that!'), afraid that it might spook me, I learned that during the excavation for the new foundation, it is thought a stone circle was uncovered. This was no small discovery; stone circles date back to as early as 2,000 years B.C. The owners looked the other way and built over it. That's how the story goes, anyway. I'm not superstitious, so I was interested in hearing about it, but I must admit to having it lodge in my head and periodically surface, causing an occasional small shiver down my spine, especially when I heard unidentified noises in the night. But I preferred the idea of spirits of the ancients to the field mice seeking food and shelter, which was the more likely possibility.

A few months after I moved in my landlord was preparing to reline the chimney. In the process, an old, corroded piece of metal fell into the fireplace. It was what was left of a hook, the kind used in fireplaces long ago to hang pots for cooking and heating water. It was, for me, as one who is not accustomed to such encounters with history, an eerie and exciting find. Like that unearthed stone circle, and the curtain blowing in the wind, it was something else reaching out from the past.

Michael and his siblings remember some of the people who once lived in my cottage when it was still just one room and a loft, including the man who lived here alone. The stairway leading to the loft had deteriorated with age and part of the steps near the top had gaping holes I them. The man never fixed them. To get up to or down from the loft, he had to jump over those few steps. Michael remembers seeing the man cook his meals over the open fire, in the fireplace I was using to refine my fire-building skills.

After cooking his dinner, he'd eat from the pan, then set it and the remains of the food on a table under the front window. The next day he'd return the pan to the fire and warm up the leftover food for another meal.

'Ah, he was crazy!' Michael said, but I didn't know him so could think of him in a more romantic light. The story made a strong impression on me and when I ate sitting by the fire or looked out the front window, I sometimes thought of that man. It was easy to picture him setting his cast iron skillet on a heavy rough-hewn wooden table, peering out through the window, searching the sky for any hint that the sun might soon break through the clouds. I liked to think he wasn't lonely; he enjoyed his simple life and was grateful for what he had.

My street ends just past the old cottages, turning into a now private road where a pathway leads to a large stone circle, this one having escaped being buried. The wealthy landowners charge an entry fee to visit the circle, much to the dismay of most of the locals. During my first days in Ireland, it was a favorite destination, so fascinated was I to live near it. I made visits at different times of the day, but twilight on a clear evening always seemed the most magical. I blithely ignored the honor system bucket with its '2 euros' sign. I wasn't really a local, but I wasn't a tourist, either.

In another move which I suppose did even less to endear them to their neighbors, those same people blocked the road which continues on past the stone circle. It is no longer open to the public. They surely knew they were closing a once favorite pathway used by many to walk through the countryside down to the edge of the sea. Looking through the tall, imposing black iron gates slicing across the roadway, one can imagine how it might have been… An open dirt lane flanked by fields with tall grass swaying in the breeze of the summer afternoon, bees busy among the blossoms of overgrown thickets of blackberries and fuchsia. Look – a couple strolls arm-in-arm on their way to have a picnic by the sea. If you're quiet, you might hear the voices and laughter of two small children, and it's then you'll notice them skipping along ahead of their parents, scuffing at the ground with their feet, kicking stones into the field, and playing a rhyming game...

Perhaps one day the landowners will stop by the gate, too, and pause long enough to see and hear those folks, and be moved to reopen the road to the water's edge. You never know. The spirits of the ancients move in mysterious ways.

In a hushed voice with deep conviction a friend told me about walking along the Finnihy River, which winds its way through town and runs close behind my cottage, and seeing a man standing there on the river bank, perfectly still – a man who had passed away many years before. She didn't feel afraid, just awed.

A curved stone bridge, Cromwell's Bridge, believed to have been built in the eleventh century, arches across that same river. The stones are partially obscured by overgrown weeds and grass, and in spring and summer wild flowers sprout from it. No matter how many times I pass that old bridge, it never fails to catch my attention and imagination. It's another place where it's easy to envision days gone by.

My imagination was set free by living in that historic building, by the stories, the unearthed artifacts, and the nearby ancient places. It gave me a stronger connection to the past and made me think more about the people whose footsteps came before mine. And that horseshoe I found? I later put it atop my wood stove, open end up to receive good luck, a tiny altar to the past, a nod to those who once passed by or took shelter inside these old walls and warmed themselves before the fire.

8

TEA FOR THREE

September 23, 2013: Guests for tea this afternoon! As I write this, two fat chickens are walking around in my back garden. I wonder if the sight will ever become routine?

It was time to host my first real event in my new abode. Just days after I received the long-awaited boxes from California, new friends Noreen and Liz were coming for tea. I was looking forward to having guests. It seemed almost like a rite of passage, another step toward settling in.

I was ready ahead of time, wanting to make sure everything looked nice for them. As two of the three times I'd been out for tea had also included lunch, I wasn't certain if that's what 'tea' at two-thirty in the afternoon means in Ireland. To be safe, I put out a spread of mini-sandwiches, deviled eggs, cherry tomatoes, strawberries and cookies ('biscuits') and, of course, tea. I remembered that most folks in Ireland drink their tea with milk so included a small pitcher of it on the table.

At the appointed hour there was a knock on the door. I opened the door and was greeted by a large potted mum plant. I could see Noreen's laughing eyes just above it and a small elbow jutting out on one side.

The plant moved in my direction and I could then see it was being held by both Noreen and Liz, the owner of the small elbow, at first nearly completely obscured by the large mum.

'For you, my dear!' said Noreen.

I thanked her. 'Oh, 'tis from Liz, too!' she exclaimed.

Another round of thanks and smiles, and 'Oh, not a'tall, not a'tall!' from both of them, followed by laughter, which would prove to be a dominant sound during every gathering in the months to follow.

Liz was a talker, as so many Irish folks are, but with her habit of using her hands when talking, one might wonder if she's Italian. Probably because of her years married to an Englishman and living in England, her accent was easier for me to understand than many of the other Irish folks I met. I appreciated that fact on many occasions. One can only say 'Excuse me?' so many times before it becomes embarrassing and wearing, and surely annoying to the person who is not being understood.

Calling Liz a talker was accurate; it would be a complete understatement to use that term to describe Noreen. She is the champion of talkers. She can talk to anyone, anywhere, anytime, on any subject. She speaks rapidly and switches topics faster than the speed of light. Understanding her Kerry accent would be something I'd struggle with for some time, and following her quick-change, shifting gears would be something I'd never keep up with.

The ladies appeared to be delighted with the food and between the two of them there was no shortage of witty chat. They either loved the deviled eggs or were good at pretending. 'What do you call these?' they wanted to know. I had not known I was providing a foreign dish.

As we ate and sipped our tea, we chatted about the weather, gardening, and food. We discussed the differences between egg mayonnaise and egg salad (none), Irish/English biscuits (what I know as cookies) and cookies (large biscuits), biscuits versus scones, and scones versus American buttermilk biscuits, another foreign food in Ireland.

In the course of our conversation I learned the chickens I'd been seeing in my back garden belonged to my landlord Michael.

'You should put out a nest and maybe they'll lay you some eggs!' Noreen said, with a straight face, her brown eyes sparkling.

Liz laughed and I followed suit, thankful for the help in determining whether it was said in jest or was a serious suggestion.

There would be many times to come when I'd be unsure, but more often than not, she would be joking.

They told me of the recent death of Michael and Liz's father's little black cat. No one knew what happened, the poor thing just died. They said his death hit Daniel hard. I had not known he had a cat, but felt sad for his loss. I would later learn he loved all animals.

After we finished eating and I refused their clean-up help, I collected the dishes as they wandered around looking at and admiring my things. It was almost as if they were in a gift shop or museum. They raved about all the changes I'd made to the place.

'Oh, a woman's touch! That's what it needed!'

The new curtain on the front window was a hit, as was the lace runner I'd hung as a valance above the window in the front door. From time to time they reached out and gently touched or stroked something that caught their eye, showing the genuineness of their fascination. I was pleased they liked everything and flattered they were so taken with the humble home I was creating.

Just before they left, Noreen's husband Paudie stopped in, on his way back from having sold some of their sheep at the mart outside of town. He'd brought me a bag of firewood, or *timber* as he called it, from their farm. (Noreen and Paudie would kindly and generously provide me with a steady supply of that timber, chunks of logs and branches cleared from their land, some with bits of sheep's wool clinging to them.)

I'd heard Paudie was good looking and been told there was a resemblance to Paul Newman. Seeing him in person, I understood the comparison. He is a nice looking man and his twinkling blue eyes which crinkle at the corners when he laughs are indeed reminiscent of Mr. Newman. With his thick Kerry accent I found him even harder to understand than Noreen – and heaven help you when they spoke to each other! But it wasn't necessary to understand all that he was saying to learn early on that he loves to joke around.

We all stood near the door visiting for a few minutes that afternoon after he arrived, then Noreen's eyes widened.

'Oh! I must run!' She'd suddenly realized she had to meet some folks at her cottage.

Before she stepped outside she grabbed Paudie by the shoulder and spun him around while he was in mid-sentence, declaring, 'I'd better not leave you here, Jane might want to keep you!'

'Oh, I don't really think she's that interested,' he said as he meekly followed her out the door with a wink and a sly smile in my direction. And of course, everyone laughed.

9

Jigs & Reels & Immigration Blues

September 27, 2013: I'm up early today to catch the bus to Dingle for a music festival. Can't wait to hear the music and be back in Dingle town, one of my favorite places!

Dingle isn't too far from Kenmare and I could travel there by bus. It involves two bus changes, but I didn't mind, so excited was I to attend the Dingle Tradfest, a three-day Irish traditional music festival. After the Killarney-Tralee leg of the journey I had two hours before the connecting bus to Dingle.

The bus station was clean, as is everywhere I've been in Ireland, but there was nothing there aside from four long rows of plastic chairs, a rack holding bus schedules, a ticket counter and public toilets. No coffee shop or snack bar, not even a vending machine, and I saw nothing in the immediate surrounding area.

The station was packed with people. They sat in the plastic chairs or sprawled on the floor. Others stood looking out the window with wishful eyes, yearning to see their bus arriving. A long row of people stood outside smoking, leaning against the front of the station building.

I looked around the station and spied one empty chair. After inquiring of the people who sat on either side of it to make sure it was not already taken, I sat. On my left an elderly, thin man in a brown suit jacket and a red knit hat, a folded up newspaper under his arm, appeared to be falling asleep. Quite a trick in those hard, uncomfortable chairs. On my right a girl wearing a hippie-style woven leather headband across her forehead and a tie-dyed T-shirt chewed gum with her mouth open. She smelled of strong perfume. It was harsh and unpleasant, like a floral-scented bathroom deodorizer in a public restroom. Glued to her mobile phone, she tapped out text messages with multi-colored painted nails and read frequent incoming messages announced by a series of rapid beeps. Maybe her bus would arrive soon.

Except for the murmur of Irish voices, I could have been in a bus station anywhere, but I hoped looking back I might see something good in it, something special. I was becoming accustomed to having nearly every day be an adventure; I was getting spoiled.

As I dug into my backpack for a book to read to pass the time, a young woman I guessed to be the mother of the two crying children trailing after her, came through the door. She looked rushed and stressed as she stopped, pulled two lollipops out of her bag and hastily unwrapped them for the kids, then got in the ticket counter queue. I watched as smiles and quiet replaced the children's wails. The miraculous power of sugar. The woman's shoulders relaxed and I breathed a sigh of relief for her.

I read my book as buses arrived, engines idling while passengers boarded. A Bus Eireann worker announced each one both inside and out, like a town crier of old. I felt for him as he swam his way through the heavy cloud of cigarette smoke outside the glass doors to make his announcements. When his loud cries of 'Cork! Bus to Cork!' pierced the smoke, the smokers ground out their cigarettes, those lolling on the vinyl station floor arose and exited, and the plastic seats emptied. Every one of them, except mine.

The town crier approached and inquired with a nice smile, 'Are ya' alright?' I thought how Irish it was that he was even asking.

'I'm fine,' I assured him. 'Just waiting for my bus to Dingle.'

He checked his watch and nodded, seeing it wouldn't be arriving for another hour. Continuing on with his Irish helpfulness, he said 'Now it isn't a far walk into town if you fancy something to eat or just want to walk. You'll go straight down the road here and make a right at the market.'

I was impressed with the very un-Irish clarity and simplicity of the directions he gave me.

'I wonder have ya' been to the Rose Garden?' he asked.

'No, I haven't.'

He gave me further easy to follow directions. 'Oh, 'tis a beautiful place; you'll enjoy it, you will!' he said with an enthusiastic smile. 'And 'tis a lovely day, so!'

I thanked him and he shared his hope that the roses would still be in full bloom for me.

That plastic chair was taking its toll and I was glad to heed the man's suggestion. I found the rose garden which was indeed still in bloom, admired the pretty roses and snapped some photos before heading back to the bus station.

I reached the station with only minutes to spare before I heard, 'Dingle! Bus to Dingle!' I thanked the good Irishman for his directions, watched his eyes light up when I told him the roses were still in bloom, and boarded the bus.

It could have been just a boring, uncomfortable wait at a nondescript bus station smelling cheap perfume and cigarette smoke, but it wasn't. There'd been Irish kindness, a pleasant walk, and roses to boot. This whole Irish thing was panning out wonderfully.

◙

Along with hearing as much music as I could that weekend, I also hoped to get an appointment to see an immigration officer so I could register and begin the application process for permission to stay in Ireland. That was the one step everyone seemed to agree was the first one. One doesn't speak with immigration headquarters in Dublin; any phone or in-person contact is at the local level. My local officer was in Killarney.

After checking into my Dingle hotel on Friday, I telephoned the Killarney gardaí (police, usually called *garda* or *the guards*) station where the immigration office was located. I hoped to register on my way back through Killarney that Monday. It would save me another bus trip. I'd tried to call a few times before, but hadn't reached the immigration officer who was either busy or not in.

The garda officer I spoke with that day was polite and friendly, but I was having trouble with his pronounced Irish accent. I don't think he was having the same difficulty with my American accent, but there *was* a communication problem. He knew nothing about what I was asking him. Although the garda and immigration shared offices, it didn't appear they shared even the most basic information. The officer didn't even seem to know what 'registering' meant. He asked me to call again and speak with the immigration officer who wasn't there on Fridays.

It was frustrating, but I wasn't surprised. Even during the research phase of the permission to stay procedure I'd learned things were vague; there didn't seem to be any cut and dried rules. Those I'd talked to who'd gone through the application process all had different experiences, depending on the office and officer dealing with their case. Multiple inquiries were generally required to determine exactly what was needed, and guesswork was sometimes more dependable than the information obtained. It was complicated.

I hung up the phone and made a mental note to try again Monday on my way back through Killarney, and set out in pursuit of my other, far more fun and interesting, objective for being in Dingle.

Always a fun place to visit, the festival atmosphere that weekend made it even more so. After a bowl of steaming hot (the only way hot food is served in Ireland – *hot*, as in be-careful-not-to-burn-your-tongue hot!) chowder and a cold pint of Guinness, I strolled along Dingle's picturesque waterfront, thoughts of immigration far from mind. It was a sunny afternoon with a few high, snowy white clouds. The late September air was warm and still and the water in the bay was as smooth as a protected pond deep in a forest, its glassy surface reflecting the boats, the sky, and the far hills. It was like a Photoshop-enhanced picture, except for the fact that it was the real thing.

I listened as the cries of gulls and other sea birds mixed with the tunes played on fiddles and guitars and accordions by people of all ages standing on street corners or sitting on low stone walls.

I walked up and down Dingle's hilly streets with other festival goers, enjoying the music and the sea air. Passing pretty shop fronts I window-shopped, ducking into those that looked inviting and sometimes chatting with shopkeepers, and wherever I heard music, I stopped to listen.

As the evening sun sank low in the sky I returned to the waterfront to take advantage of the new light for more photographs. In the cooling, damp air the mist descended like a slow motion video, draping a delicate bridal veil across the green hills. It was magical. I knew pictures wouldn't do it justice, without the feel of the air and the scents and the sounds. I wished for a way to capture all of it. There I was again, me and my wishfulness.

I sat down on a bench facing the water to call my sister and my wishful self persisted. I wanted so much to be able to transmit the scene to her, to do more than talk about it and take photos, to somehow pour a dollop of it into the phone where it would instantly bounce from cell tower to cell tower, then emerge on her end, an iridescent, fragrant and harmonious bubble of sight, scent and sound, a little piece of Ireland in California.

For the rest of the evening I wandered in and out of pubs, never able to get my fill of the music. It didn't matter if it was a jig or a reel, or a slow mournful tune; I loved it all. I wormed my way into the Courthouse Pub when I heard uilleann pipes. Uilleann (*IL-len*) is the Irish word for elbow. Uilleann pipes are smaller than Scottish bagpipes and are played differently. The air is not blown in, it is produced by pumping a bellows held under the arm. A softer, sweeter sound is produced. Chances to hear them are infrequent, so I never pass up the opportunity.

The low-ceilinged pub was crowded with patrons of varying ages, most there for the music. If you were looking for good trad music in Dingle, it was a sure destination. I created a small pocket of space for myself, sandwiched between a support post and a tall woman wearing large hoop earrings and a thick sweater. She nodded at me, her masses of white hair threatening to escape the loose topknot on her head. Her tanned skin crinkled when she smiled.

During a break between songs we chatted and drank our pints of Guinness. After responding to her inquiry as to where I was from, I asked her the same question.

'England, originally, but my husband and I are traveling around on our boat. We're docked in Dingle Bay.' That explained the tanned skin.

'Wow! Really? That sounds great!'

'We love it! We've been doing it for a few years now and we stop in Dingle regularly.'

She said her husband had stayed behind on the boat. From her description, I deduced that the boat was actually a yacht. She mentioned they were hoping to find a cook, someone who wanted to sign on with them and join them in their travels. I knew I had neither the skills nor the youth to do such a thing, but that didn't keep me from entertaining the idea for a fleeting moment. It sounded like a grand adventure.

The first notes of the uilleann pipes began again and I stayed, transfixed by the music, as did the boat lady, until it ended.

After the tuneful weekend on Dingle Bay I was back in Killarney on Monday. I phoned the immigration office. Sorry; said the garda officer who answered the phone, try again on a Tuesday or a Wednesday. Those, then, were the office hours for Killarney immigration. The original officer hadn't mentioned that fact, he'd only said no one was there on Fridays. But the fault was mine. I had jumped to conclusions, assuming 'not in on Fridays' meant the rest of the week was fair game. I should have stayed an extra day in Dingle. Perhaps I would have had another opportunity to hear those uilleann pipes, or been persuaded to sign on as a cook on the English lady's yacht.

I was eager to get my status sorted and frustrated with trying to see the Killarney immigration officer. When I got home, I made an executive decision. I went against the recommended protocol and mailed my application for permission to stay and the associated documents directly to the big boys in Dublin – the Irish Naturalization and Immigration Service, better known as INIS.

Within three days I received an acknowledgment letter from Dublin. I telephoned Killarney once again and wonder of wonders, reached the immigration officer. I explained I was having trouble getting an appointment to register and had gone ahead and mailed my application to Dublin. He said it didn't matter. It didn't matter? No, he said, I needn't go in until I received, if I received, permission to remain. Apparently none of my earlier attempts to follow what I was told was the correct procedure had been necessary. Sometimes it's just better to think for yourself.

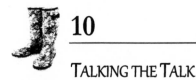

10

TALKING THE TALK

October 1, 2013: I don't seem to be doing much better at understanding folks, especially those with strong Kerry accents. Tried to talk to a man last night at the pub but it got so embarrassing repeating 'What? What did you say? Excuse me?' I eventually had to give up on the conversation altogether.

After returning from Dingle, I got back to the business of settling in, familiarizing myself with new customs and developing new skills. Learning the language was something I hadn't anticipated would be on my *to do* list. While Ireland is an English-speaking country, it wasn't the American English I knew. There were many unfamiliar words, expressions, and accents, with a bit of Irish Gaelic, known more commonly as 'Irish,' thrown into the mix.

I began detecting the different Irish accents, but more time was needed to better understand them. Likewise, I quickly learned there are different terms and expressions for certain things, but learning them and incorporating them into my own speech took longer. It took longer still before I developed a hint of an accent (so say some).

I wasn't completely clueless; I did have *some* knowledge. Why, I'd known since my first visit to Ireland a restroom or ladies' room is known by neither of those terms, it is called simply *the toilet*. Using the term felt funny and seemed impolite, but after a while I adapted to using it. I also knew to look for 'Mna' (*mean-uh*), the Irish word on the signage for most ladies' toilets. And I was a pro at pronouncing and using *sláinte* (slaw-n-chuh), a toast meaning 'to your health,' similar to saying 'cheers!' I'd long known a bodhrán (*bo-rawn*) is an Irish drum. I was familiar with the term *craic*, with its basic definition of fun, and knew it could be used a couple of different ways. 'What's the craic?' means 'What's up?' and if asking about the atmosphere in a pub, 'How's the craic?' works. If the place is hopping, you might say 'The craic is mighty!' or 'mad craic!' None of those phrases ever felt completely comfortable on my tongue, but I did begin using the word from time to time.

Two more phrases I'd learned during my holidays pertained to sports and expressing support for your team. Rather than 'Go [team name]!' it was 'Up [team name]!' – or the Irish language version, '[Team name] abú!' Knowing County Kerry is called 'The Kingdom' by the proud locals, 'Up The Kingdom!' or 'Kerry Abú!' became my cheers of choice.

The belief that swearing is commonplace in Ireland, particularly use of the 'F-word' and related forms thereof, is true in my experience. It is a standard part of the vocabulary of many people, particularly males. Sure, I've known people in the USA with an affinity for using those words. The primary difference is I rarely hear anyone apologize for saying them in Ireland, regardless of the company they're in. The words don't seem to carry the same intensity, maybe because they're so often heard. Even my own ears were not as offended after a while.

Some folks use alternatives to such words. While they are easily identifiable, the alternative versions don't have any particularly negative connotation. *Feck, feckin'* and *fecker* are common. So is *shite*, the polite form of the same word, minus the 'e.' *Jayzus* or *Jayzus Christ*, and sometimes *Jayzus, Mary and Joseph*, are all in regular use and again, wouldn't raise any eyebrows.

I made a concentrated effort to avoid adopting the majority of the swearing, including most of the alternatives, but I picked up a few other terms. Before too long I could effectively communicate with my hair stylist because I learned *fringe* is the correct term for bangs. I knew to stand in a *queue* instead of a line and after two or three times dining out I'd learned *starters* are appetizers, *mains* the main course, *afters* dessert, and *serviettes* are napkins.

I picked up the correct words for potato chips (*crisps*) and French fries (*chips*). I knew if someone described a dish as *gorgeous*, it had nothing to do with appearance, but with taste. And if the food is described as *nice* it doesn't mean friendly, it means it tastes good, although not as good as gorgeous.

The first few times a bartender or server asked me, 'Ye' okay, then?' my reaction was to wonder if I looked ill or had a sour expression on my face. I later learned it was synonymous with 'May I help you?/What would you like?'

'Are you happy with that?' is like asking if you're okay with the situation, but it isn't at all the same as 'Ye' okay then?' The two are not interchangeable. For example, you're perched on a barstool in a crowded pub, squished between two others, but it's the only seat in the house. Your companion might say 'Are you happy with that?' trying to find out if you're alright with the seating arrangement.

When someone gives me a ride I learned 'thanks for collecting me' or 'thanks for the lift' is appropriate, not 'thanks for the ride,' which has an entirely different meaning. I also caught on that cars don't run on gasoline, but petrol, the trunk is not a trunk but a boot and if you're looking to park it will be at the aptly named *car park*, not the parking lot.

I don't take 'You're grand!' as a compliment, or an insult meaning I'm huge because I know it's a phrase like 'no problem' - you're not in the way, or haven't been a bother or made a mistake. Let's say I accidentally bump into someone and apologize for doing so. A common response would be 'Oh, you're grand!'

You can be brilliant as well as grand, but the term has nothing to do with intelligence or illumination, it means 'excellent.' It can be used to describe a great many things, from a book to a party to an entertaining individual. It could be compared to the overly used 'awesome' in the USA, but somehow sounds better. Maybe that's partially due to the Irish accent.

'Done and dusted' is a phrase meaning handled, completed. 'Sorted' has a similar meaning – and I heard that one so often I began using it as though I'd said it all my life.

There are zillions of items with names different than those I've always known. The first time I heard someone say 'brelly' I hadn't the slightest clue she was referring to an umbrella. A sweater isn't a sweater but a jumper, and sneakers are trainers. A valance is not the curtain that goes across the top of a window, it's a bed ruffle. Guinness is known as 'the black stuff,' a roast is a joint, and if you'd like to order the salmon fillet, ask for the salmon 'fill-it.' A cooker is a stove, but to further complicate matters, the top part, the surface where the burners are located, is called a hob.

I've become accustomed to hearing 'Mind yourself' (take care of yourself) and 'How are you keeping?' (how are you?), but haven't developed the habit of using either.

I hear cray-ter ('creature' with an Irish accent) often, but have never been sure I have a grasp on the true meaning. Even if I eventually figure it out, I'd never use it with my American accent. I do know it isn't derogatory, but more of a sympathetic or humorous term for someone, usually spoken gently with a sing-song lilt. 'Oh, the poor crayter.'

'Your man' is an expression that initially confused me even more than crayter and though I have the general idea now, I've never felt I understand it well enough to use it correctly. When someone says, 'Here comes your man,' they don't mean he belongs to me. It could be a reference to someone I know, but not necessarily, or someone I've recently mentioned. Let's say I'm standing at the checkout counter in a small shop, but there's no one at the register. My friend spots the owner, a stranger to me, making his way to the counter. She says, 'Ah, here's your man!' Or another customer walks in the door, someone I know, and my friend says, 'Isn't that your man?' There is no similar expression to refer to a female.

Various places have been referred to as 'God's country,' but I'd venture to say God's country just might be the Emerald Isle, so frequently is God made a part of everyday conversation. 'Thanks be to God' and 'Please God' are uttered frequently.

There is a perplexing penchant for uttering multiple goodbyes when ending telephone conversations. If you were to hear someone saying, "Bye. Buh-bye. 'Bye-bye-bye,' it's guaranteed you've just heard the end of a phone conversation. If you can't tell from their accent they're Irish, the multiple 'byes' are a dead giveaway. I've never heard a phone conversation ended with any fewer than three of them; once or twice is never enough. Strangely, this only applies to phone conversations, not in-person farewells.

An interesting habit is the use of 'so' at the end of sentences, as in 'She is in love with him, so.' Maybe an abbreviated way of saying, 'She is in love with him, so she is'? I think there's more to it than that, or maybe less, but when I asked someone to explain it I became more confused, so [I did].

'Like,' a favorite in County Cork, is similarly used. 'She's in love with him like.' Like what? Like nothing; it's just an extra word tacked on for fun; I don't believe it has any meaning.

'Desperate' is a commonly used adjective not usually followed by any further descriptor to clarify how it's being used. It doesn't really mean distressed or frantic, it's more a way to emphasize any variety of generally negative conditions. Maybe someone is a heavy drinker, or a gossip, or clumsy. It could be anything. 'Sure he's desperate' applies regardless, and sums it up. Desperate is also used to describe the weather, politics, the economy – again, just about anything. ''Tis desperate!'

One of my favorite expressions will always be 'away with the fairies,' as in 'she's away with the fairies.' The equivalent to 'la-la land,' I find the Irish expression more descriptive and amusing.

And then there is the ever-popular, widely known and used Irish expression, 'Top o' the mornin'!' Only it isn't an Irish expression at all, and in Ireland it is used only in jest.

After several months it wasn't just different words and phrases I was picking up, it was also syntax and pronunciations. I was starting to say words in a different order than I would have once said them. 'So we're leaving about 7:30?' became 'Will we leave about half-seven, then?' ('We will!') Instead of 'Do you have any plain crisps, or just the cheese & onion?' it's 'Have you any plain crisps...?' (Note that it doesn't matter in what order you place the words in that last query, the answer will generally be 'No, we haven't any' or 'No, but we've salt and vinegar flavor.')

Even using some of the words, expressions and phrasing, I never had any doubt that I still sounded decidedly American and probably would, no matter how many years I spent in Ireland. I wonder how often I say something my Irish friends find odd, funny, or confusing? Probably more often than I know. 'Fall!' someone said to me one day, 'I love that American expression!' At first I was confused, but then realized I'd just used the word in speaking about autumn, unaware that it was an American expression. I like the idea that while I'm being entertained with colorful and often amusing terms and phrases, perhaps I'm providing some entertainment, too.

11

AROUND TOWN

October 3, 2013: I've been in Kenmare almost a month and still feel like I'm on holiday. Every day seems to bring something new!

Moving to Kenmare was a good decision and I soon felt quite pleased with myself. Setting aside the fact that handsome, rich, age-appropriate, unattached men looking my way seemed in short supply, I found all the amenities I wanted, a variety of quintessentially Irish scenes I'd hoped for but not expected to actually find, a growing group of friends, and the change in life-style I'd been seeking. I was having a grand time.

On a bright blue and gold late autumn morning, I headed out for the nearby market for a loaf of the delicious, rich, calorie-intense brown (wheat) bread I was eating too often, the scent of peat fires in the air. The church bells rang clear in the quiet morning, chiming the hour. I liked hearing those bells and seeing the church's tall steeple where the bell-tower was housed, jutting high into the brilliant blue of the sky, the tiny cross on top barely visible.

The last chiming faded away and a tuneful trilling of wrens, thrushes and blackbirds started up, rising above the occasional hoarse, insistent cries of the jackdaws, rooks and magpies lining the telephone wires and rooftops. I was surprised to discover the mockingbirds I'd heard were in all likelihood starlings, another bird with the ability to mimic songs and sounds. I promised myself one day I'd learn more about the birds of Ireland and be better able to identify them.

At the end of the street I reached the car park and turned the corner toward the market. I was met with a sight that made me stop and stare before I even realized what I was doing. A section of the street, one of the main streets of town, was partially fenced off with low metal barriers. Inside the enclosure sheep milled about. In the street. Sheep! This was the stuff of movies, not real life – not for an American from California, anyway.

Two sheep farmers, one in a flat cap and the other in a knit beanie, both wearing the old-school traditional uniform of wool sport coats, baggy trousers, and wellies, sat on a bench on the sidewalk watching over the sheep. So old and worn was their clothing it had no discernable color or style; it was like a part of them, a second skin. They chatted, heads close together, leaning forward with their hands resting on their sticks, eyes trained on the sheep. Next to them at a small table in front of the Atlantic Bar, an old man quietly drank his morning Guinness.

I'd never seen anything like it. Maybe it was a movie set? A photo shoot? No cameras were in sight; no one was directing the action. It was my first in-town sheep sighting and it took some wide-eyed staring before I could get my brain to make sense of it. I later learned farmers sometimes bring their sheep to town to sell, rather than taking them to the mart a few miles further up the road. Whatever the reason, I was delighted with the scene.

Several days later I was sitting in a small restaurant waiting for a friend to join me for afternoon tea, gazing around at the dark wood and old photos lining the walls. My mind had just wandered to the sheep encounter when another scene tested my belief in what I was seeing. An older gray-haired man sat at the bar, possibly a sheep farmer as he was dressed similarly to the farmers I'd seen on the street. Every time he picked up his pint glass of Guinness and raised it to his lips, his elbow protruded through the large gaping hole in the sleeve of his jacket, multiple long threads dangling from it. He had money for a pint, but not for a new jacket. Well, who was I to judge? We all have our priorities.

A week later I splashed up the street in the rain headed for the little market again and came upon more sheep in the street, but double the number I'd seen before. The sight was just as fascinating the second time, and not something I'd probably ever find normal. Several farmers stood on the sidewalk, dressed in the traditional garb, some chatting, others quiet, all with their eyes on the sheep. Neither the sheep nor the farmers seemed bothered by the rain which had been coming down at a good pace for several hours. Like the wooly sheep, the farmers were kept warm and dry by their wool caps and clothing.

A few tourists huddled under umbrellas and pointed, taking photos and giggling. I, on the other hand, played it cool. I nonchalantly walked by in my wellies with barely a glance, acting as if this was an everyday part of my world, hoping to seem like one of the locals. I'm not sure what compelled me to do that, and it probably didn't fool anyone but the tourists. I guess I was hoping for the anonymity of just once blending in with the locals and not being *That American Woman*. I wondered if I would ever be known as anything else.

Inside the busy market the strong, pungent odor of wet sheep drifted in each time the doors swung open. It couldn't be missed; it permeated every corner of the store. It was the kind of smell that makes you wrinkle your nose as though that might help keep it at bay. It was quite unpleasant.

That smell was the predominant topic of conversation and reason for raised eyebrows, wrinkled noses, wry smiles and shaking heads, but neither customers nor clerks were complaining – only commenting. It was not so unusual, but rare enough to make it something interesting to talk about that day. That fact elevated its value and made the smell more bearable. It was a reprieve from, or addition to, the usual discussion of the weather and thus, not an unwelcome event at all.

Those farmers I was seeing were from my generation and older. Noreen and Paudie are sheep farmers, too, as are many folks in the area, and none of them dress in the 'movie set' attire or offer their sheep for sale in town. I realized that it wouldn't be many more years before such sights were no longer a part of the

Kenmare scene and I felt privileged to be a witness. It was sad to think the day would soon come when such scenes would be things of the past.

◙

Kenmare's weekly outdoor market is held in the same area where the sheep and their farmers sometimes took up residence. The market is a changeable thing, depending on the time of year and the weather, but it is only in very desperate weather that it doesn't spring up every Wednesday. It is a far more fragrant event than the sheep gatherings.

On pleasant days and during the tourist season and bank holiday weekends, the vendors are out in full force, lining the street on both sides. Market day brings a festive atmosphere to Kenmare with its gaily striped awnings, colorful merchandise, and extra people on the streets and sidewalks.

Over the months I learned that rain or shine, tourists or not, you can count on seeing a few regular vendors; others come and go. Rarely a week passes without the honey guy, an American who moved to Ireland as a young man in the 1970's and is now a beekeeper. The artisan selling his ceramic creations. The purveyor of assorted olives and cheeses at one end of his long table, and on the other end, scented homemade soap and lovely bunches of lavender when in season. The bread man, the made-to-order crepe lady, the coffee guy. You can depend on the fish man in his white wellie boots and his table of ice-packed just-caught orange-pink salmon and other fish appearing twice a week, on both Wednesdays and Fridays. It is a nation of Catholics and fish is still a Friday staple in many homes in Kenmare.

From late spring to early fall the sidewalk is crowded with folks shopping and when the market is at its peak size, it extends around the corner into the car park. It is then the occasional busker appears playing guitar or fiddle, case open on the sidewalk hoping to collect the spare change of passersby. The music adds another layer to the market's soundtrack, a background rhythm for the voices and laughter of shoppers and vendors exchanging smiles and greetings.

In high season all number of things are sold at the market including shoes and boots, vintage clothing, balloons, organic produce, plants, toys, souvenirs and jewelry. The ice cream lady is probably there, standing in the sunshine with her little cart of homemade ice cream. And there's every chance Gypsy Breda's caravan will be parked on the corner, Gypsy Breda herself sitting in her lawn chair awaiting curious customers, those who want to be told what their future holds.

The market is a nice perk to living in Kenmare, no matter the season. While the colors and textures, scents and sounds are intensified when it is full scale, even in the off season when it's smaller, it provides liveliness to the winter quiet.

I don't often buy anything but always enjoy walking by and sometimes stopping to peruse the goods. The market is a treat for the senses and it came to be a pleasant weekly habit for me. Of course, one does have the option of just scurrying past and ignoring the sensory delights there free for the taking. I suppose there are some folks who do that, although I can't imagine why. I am definitely not one of them.

◫

Halfway up the main street of town, not far from where the market is held, is Morgan's, a hair salon. Before leaving California, I had a hair stylist I loved, Courtney, who became a fast friend. She warned me I'd never find a salon I liked in Ireland. Well, she said, maybe in Dublin. Certainly not in a small town in County Kerry. I figured that would be one of the things I'd have to live without.

Luck was with me and my first week in Kenmare I stumbled upon Morgan's. Seeing the same products in the window as those carried by my old salon, I went in, had my hair cut and colored and was pleased with the result. I've been going there ever since.

Morgan's is owned and operated by two sisters and their niece, all attractive, enthusiastic and nice ladies. The niece, in her twenties, is talkative and friendly, and we hit it off right away. No, she is not my beloved Courtney, but nevertheless, I like her, enjoy chatting with her, and she knows how to do my hair.

I was intrigued with the way the shop operates from my very first visit. No appointments, people drifting in and out, one sister washing a customer's hair, the other sister cutting it, and the niece coloring or blow-drying and styling. Customers simply walk in, sit down and wait their turn. It's an ever-changing assembly line yet each customer is treated as an individual with great care and personal attention. It is amazing how the three women work together with few or no words needed to communicate with each other and keep the process moving smoothly.

Customers continually flow from one chair to another and out the door. Except for me, the big boulder rising up from that smoothly running stream, bucking the system. I trust the niece with my hair, so will spend hours in that salon waiting my turn for her and only her, and do so without complaint. It isn't that I don't trust the other two ladies, but when you find someone who gets along well with your hair… well, it's a female thing, I suppose. Or maybe it's just a human thing and has nothing at all to do with gender.

The chat is constant, the atmosphere always friendly. Everyone knows everyone and there's always something to talk about. Recent holidays in Spain or Italy, the birth of a baby, someone's wedding, celebrity gossip, funny stories, and let us not forget the weather. Depending on the topic, the conversation can just as easily involve the entire shop as the stylist and customer only. One day when the town and indeed, all of Ireland it seemed, was buzzing with news of an upcoming Garth Brooks concert in Dublin, it was the headliner topic in the shop. The place hummed with salon-wide excitement and chat as the popular Mr. Brooks was discussed with great enthusiasm.

The talk and the laughter is almost constant in Morgan's, interspersed with offers of a cup of tea, queries such as 'Now then, how's that?' or 'Will we cut your fringe?' and greetings and farewells called out over the hum of blow dryers. Something like the feminine version of the old-fashioned American barber shop. The three stylists definitely have their fingers on the pulse of Kenmare and it's highly unlikely anything goes on in town or anywhere nearby that they don't know about.

As if all of that isn't enough to make Morgan's interesting and unique, at least to an American, there is this: one of the sisters makes hats. One can purchase or rent the hat of their choice. The other is a painter and she sells her artwork in the shop. One of the two front display windows is filled with beautiful hats; lovely oil paintings of landscapes and flowers adorn the shop walls. You can get your hair done and leave, if you wish, with a painting and a custom hat.

Finding a good stylist in a quirky and fun hair salon a three minute walk from my front door was an unexpected bonus to living in Ireland, and I became a regular customer.

◙

A few doors down from Morgan's is Hallisey's Hardware - not to be confused with Hallisey's Market, Hallisey's B&B, or Hallisey's Cash & Carry. Hallisey's Hardware is my favorite place to shop in town. It's the closest thing to an authentic old-fashioned general store I've ever seen, minus the pickle barrel and the old guys playing checkers. It has everything from milk to paint. I always enjoy the place and go there regularly, even when I don't need anything. It is hard to escape without buying something because I so often find a useful or interesting item.

Just browsing is an adventure. Every shelf, every corner, every possible nook and cranny is filled with merchandise. In fair weather more is stacked out front. If you can imagine it, you can probably find it at Hallisey's, from greeting cards to cookie cutters, welcome mats to potato peelers, chocolate bars to coffee pots. And then there's my favorite shelf, the one full of unique knick-knacks, the tiny hinged treasure chests, glass hearts, polished wishing stones, cream pitchers shaped like cows, and miniature ceramic sheep.

Up the old wooden staircase in the back of the store, near the paint and hardware section, there's more. The wide plank flooring, uneven and creaking, is worn smooth with long use. Not to be outdone by the ground level of the store, more merchandise fills the second level space, stacked on shelves or on the floor, hanging from racks and walls. Clothes pins and plastic tubs, hand mirrors and snail bait. If you walk around long enough, the proprietor will hear the creaking of the floor boards and come up to inquire if you need help.

If ever an item eludes discovery, one of the employees or the proprietor will find it hidden from among the layers of goods. It seems they always have what you're looking for, or something like it that will do.

You can even buy peat briquettes at Hallisey's, turf/peat processed and compressed into brick-sized blocks. They're kept out back and sold in bundles of twelve strapped together. The briquettes are as heavy as the bricks they resemble and a bundle of twelve is twelve times heavier. The first time I bought them I hadn't thought about the weight, but was immediately offered the assistance of a strong and helpful young man who carried them all the way to my front door. That's the way they do business at Hallisey's. If you like to shop it's difficult not to be a regular patron and a big fan.

◼

There are many other interesting and unique gift and specialty shops, gastropubs, fine dining spots, and cafes along the two main streets of town. And there's more than food and drink and shopping. Not far from Hallisey's is the town's library and Carnegie Arts Centre, a lovely old stone building adjacent to Kenmare's golf course. There is always something to see at the Carnegie, be it a local play, an art show, music, touring productions, or a film. The building is near me and if blocks were a known distance descriptor in Ireland, I could say I only have to walk a few of them to get there. But in local lingo, it's at the top of the town.

One evening I attended a live show with some friends. A terrible storm with high winds, heavy rain, and hail hit shortly after the doors opened, and Kenmare lost electricity. But the performance, a one-man show about the Irish explorer Tom Crean and Earnest Shackleton's 1914-1916 Antarctic expedition, went on as planned. This was not only show business, this was Ireland. A little storm wasn't going to stop the evening; the show must go on.

Without electricity the stage lights were lanterns, the same illumination Shackleton's crew would have used, and we found our way to our seats by the light of many more lanterns.

We listened to the stories of the dark cold days and nights when Shackleton's ship, the Endurance, became trapped in the ice and the crew spent months trying to survive in the bitter cold of the barren, wind-swept, frozen world of Antarctica. It was fascinating hearing the tales about the strength of the men's will to survive against all odds and the unbelievable hardships they endured. As the lanterns flickered, the winds howled, and the rain and hail pounded like a herd of wild horses charging across the rooftop, the audience seemed to huddle closer together, as if we were out on the ice in a frozen wasteland, instead of sitting comfortably in a theater.

At intermission we gathered in the lobby and drank complimentary wine by candlelight. Without electricity the kettles couldn't provide us with hot water for tea and I guess regardless of how we were all imagining ourselves roughing it in Antarctica, management drew the line at further enhancing the reality factor by having an open cooking fire in the lobby to boil water for tea.

The show was great and the actor who portrayed Tom Crean did an excellent job, but the weather and those candles and lanterns clinched the deal, making it an impressive experience and a night to remember.

12

TRASH TALKS

*October 6, 2013: Michael should be here any time to pick up the trash —
I mean 'rubbish'! I can't seem to get used to calling it that, but I'm
trying...*

Every week Michael hops over my back garden wall to pick up
the rubbish and recycling bins. He takes them back to his place
and adds them to his own rubbish for a later trip to the dump and
recycling center, then returns them to me, sometimes dropping
off a bag of kindling. I don't think anyone has a garbage disposal
and there is no residential garbage pickup in Kenmare. Michael
picks up my rubbish and recycling as a service included with my
rent.

When I learned he was sorting through it to separate it (food
for composting and chicken feed, recyclables, basic trash), I
cringed — and at once told him I would be happy to use separate
bins, which he supplied. When he gave me the bin for waste food
he brought me a brick.

'Keep it on top of the lid or the fox will get at it. Have you
seen him? If you're a Night Watcher, you'll see him out here.'

Night Watcher? I didn't know what a Night Watcher, or
possibly a Nightwatcher, was. My best guess was it was someone
who peers out the window into the dark to see what they can
see? The opposite of a Peeping Tom, maybe? Michael offered no
explanation. Not wanting to come off as the dumb American, I
acted as though I knew about night watchers, like I was on familiar
terms with them — and hoped that was a good thing.

Those weekly rubbish pickups turned out to be much more than that. They were nearly always times of visiting with Michael. I began to look forward to hearing the rattle of the bins, my signal to open the back door and greet him. If the weather is inclement or he needs to check something inside the house, he comes in, often wearing his wellies, sometimes removing them and sometimes not – depending on how much rain we've had and how deep the mud – and we chat in the kitchen.

We've talked of many things and I learned much from him in those early days. We compared the merits of different kinds of fire fuels with regard to cost, ease of fire-building and heat output. It was from Michael I learned turf and peat are interchangeable terms. I learned coal was best for heat, but dirty to handle, peat briquettes were good for getting the fire started and smelled just as nice as regular peat, and regular peat wouldn't burn well unless you added it after the fire was good and hot. I was relieved to hear that last bit as it explained why I was having trouble getting those chunks of turf to burn.

Conversations on subjects like fire fuels and night watchers were foreign to me and before coming to Ireland, I never imagined discussing such things and how interesting it would be.

One day Michael was working on the sluggish drain in my back garden, the main drain from the house. Three of his hens walked around on the hillside above the garden wall, scratching at the earth, beaks to the ground. They followed him like baby ducklings following their mother when he was outdoors.

'Do you only have hens, or do you have roosters, too?' I asked.

'Oh, hens, just now I've hens.' A tale unfolded about a rooster he once had, a rooster who was 'too much!' for his hens, the creatures he calls his 'girls.' Seems the hens couldn't keep up with the young rooster so he got rid of him.

As we talked, Michael's eyes followed the hens. 'It's relaxing to watch them,' he said. It wasn't something I'd ever thought of before, but as I watched their calm scratching and pecking, their intermittent soft clucking noises sounding like a cross between a purring cat and the coo of a dove, I could understand what he meant.

He pointed at one stretching her wings. 'Look! See how she's stretching? They've been doing this for hundreds of years and isn't it funny that no one had to teach them to stretch before exercising?' He had a point.

The weekly bin pickups continued, usually on Sundays. If ever he was a day or two later, I would wonder if everything was okay, accustomed as I was to the routine. I looked forward to the chat and the interesting and humorous tales Michael told.

On a late autumn morning he began one of his tales with 'When we were picking up the sheik…' The sheik? Who was the sheik? He said he was just one of many in Saudi Arabia. He had numerous stories about working as a flight engineer on the sheik's private plane.

Michael and Ella grow mass quantities of vegetables in a cavernous greenhouse, several garden plots behind their home, and another on top of the hill above my back garden. There are patches of flowers everywhere in spring and summer, endless pots of seedlings awaiting planting, and large apple and evergreen trees. One day as Michael started up the hillside to the plot where he cultivates potatoes, covered in summer by a field of bright red poppies, he stopped to chat when he saw me tending to my container garden. We talked about what would grow in Ireland's climate and what wouldn't. Surely he was the man to know.

'What about tomatoes?' I asked hopefully. I love tomatoes nearly as much as pickles, and thankfully don't have to turn to amazon.co.uk to buy them. But there's nothing like home-grown.

'Oh, sure,' he said.

'Really?' I was pleased to hear it, but surprised. It didn't seem there would be enough sun. 'What kind? What variety would be best?'

He assured me just about any kind I wanted to plant would grow.

'Oh! I didn't think it would be sunny enough!'

He gave me a long, perplexed look and exclaimed, 'Oh, we've been growing potatoes for a long time in Ireland, Janie!' He chuckled softly.

It was then I realized the confusion. In Ireland, people say 'toe-mah-toes,' not 'tuh-may-toes' (rhymes with potatoes). No wonder he looked perplexed. I could imagine what he'd been thinking for those few seconds, about the dumb American's surprise over learning one could grow any variety of potatoes in, of all places, Ireland.

One afternoon we chatted about the beautiful sunset the evening before and I remarked how the changing sky fascinates me. I told him about the morning I went to Killarney with Noreen and Paudie and was captivated by a pale blue sky streaked with wispy, pink-tinged clouds. 'Oh, look!' I'd exclaimed. 'Look at the sky!'

Noreen had craned her neck, looked out the window and searched the heavens. At a loss, she said, 'What?'

We both laughed, but I'm sure Michael realized as I did how often people don't notice amazing things around them if they've always been there. Noreen's home, in a beautiful valley, is likely often surrounded by such skies; they are a common and expected part of her life. Like Noreen, Michael is a native, too, but a well-traveled man. He has lived and worked all over the world, but always returned to Kenmare, his favorite place. I think that makes him see things through different, more appreciative eyes.

One morning I was in my back garden and saw Michael walking to his garage, a building behind his house. He wasn't limping exactly, but he wasn't walking in his normal easy stride. That afternoon Liz told me he'd just returned from a trip with the sheik, bringing him back from Las Vegas. During the flight he leaned over trying to reach some mechanical something and somehow injured himself. Liz suspected he'd probably cracked a rib. She said he was in pain, and that was evident in the way he was moving. Laughing and rolling her eyes, she told me how he'd blamed the injury on a wild night with a prostitute.

A few days later Michael came over to pick up more of the items I'd finally finished clearing from cupboards and closets. I'd packed everything in boxes and stacked them on the back garden wall as instructed, where he could pick them up. After learning he was injured I was concerned about how he'd carry the boxes. When I heard him out back, I went outside.

'Hi – how are you doing?' I wondered if he would tell me the same tall tale of how the injury had happened.

All he said was, 'Oh, I'm fine!' and offered nothing further.

'Good. But be careful because several of those boxes are super heavy. Do you want some help? I don't mind helping.'

He waved me off, picked up a carton so large he couldn't see over the top of it, and turned to set off toward his place.

'Oh, it's no problem, Janie,' he said, 'I'm a man…'

Indeed, he is – and an entertaining one at that. I was glad to have him as my landlord, neighbor, and friend.

13

BECOMING IRISH

October 11, 2013: In some ways it seems as though I've always lived here. I guess that means I'm feeling settled.

'Ah, yer' becomin' more Irish than the Irish themselves!' I heard this more than once during my time in Ireland. Although said to me in jest, I liked hearing the old phrase, used as early as the twelfth century to describe the assimilation of non-indigenous peoples into the Irish culture. And anyway, I *am* one-eighth Irish!

On an October Friday afternoon I sat in Daniel's kitchen having a cup of tea with him and Michael and Liz. They were waiting for the priest's Friday visit. In rural Ireland, even in this day and age, the priest comes to visit the elderly or ill. I remarked how late I was sleeping since coming to Ireland.

'How late?' Liz asked.

'Oh, like sometimes as late as eight or eight-thirty!' I replied, almost embarrassed to admit it. Michael and Liz laughed and I saw a slow smile come to Daniel's kind old face.

'Oh, that isn't late at all!' said Liz. Michael and Daniel nodded their heads in agreement.

Accustomed to waking up to the sound of my alarm clock between six and six-thirty in the morning even on most weekends when I lived in California, any time much beyond that seemed late to me. Perhaps it was in keeping with the loose concept of time in Ireland. Someone could easily greet you with 'good morning' at two in the afternoon. I wasn't sure why, but it happened. Time has softer edges, more fluid parameters; '- ish' is a popular add-on, 'I'll collect you at six-ish.'

A few weeks after my conversation with the neighbors I was out walking and, as is customary in rural Ireland, said 'Good morning' to a man I passed by. The man smiled, said 'h'lo' and continued on his way.

A split second later I realized… it wasn't morning at all, it was one o'clock in the afternoon! I had not arisen that day until nine o'clock. It just *felt* like it was still morning. I had a good laugh at myself.

The next day my rent was due. I always paid in cash. I'd planned to give it to Michael when he came to empty the rubbish and recycling bins. Thinking he might come while I was out walking, I decided to leave the money out for him. I put it in a zip-loc bag in case of rain and anchored it to the patio table with a two-liter bottle of water. I was careful to place the bag so it hung from the edge of the table, just inches above the rubbish bin where he was certain to see it when he picked up the bin. I went walking and didn't think about it again.

The next afternoon I heard the rattle of the bins out back. Michael had apparently not made the pickup the day before as I'd anticipated. I opened the door to chat with him. While we were talking I remembered the rent money. It was still there, dangling from the edge of the table where I'd left it the day before. I pointed to it. 'Did you see the rent money? I left it there yesterday in case you came when I was out.'

Michael looked in the direction I was pointing and stared at the money for a moment, as though he was uncertain what he was seeing. Then he shook his head and laughed.

'Ah, yer' Irish, Janie!'

He was quite amused; I wasn't sure why. Then it dawned on me and I realized it was probably a little strange I had nonchalantly hung four-hundred and twenty-five euros in cash outdoors in a see-through plastic bag for two days and a night…Something I'd have considered more than a little crazy in America.

I thought about the euros in the plastic bag, the neighbors' assurances I was not a late riser, and what Michael had said about being Irish. *Was* I picking up some Irish habits?

I had started saying *mobile* phone (although I refused to say 'moe-bile') instead of cell phone, *car park* instead of parking lot, *toilet* instead of restroom, and *trad* music instead of traditional music. Those terms had become a regular part of my vocabulary.

I could find my way around the supermarket because I'd learned to look for bin liners instead of trash bags, porridge instead of oatmeal, and biscuits instead of cookies.

I'd adopted the habit of greeting people on the street. My perception of time was different and like some others, I might think it was morning even when it wasn't. I trustingly put cash on display in my back garden without giving it a second thought. And I knew if I crawled out of bed at eight-thirty my Irish friends would call that 'half-eight' – and not think of me as a late riser.

Was Michael on to something?

🔲

'Coo-ey, Jane!' I heard Liz's voice calling. She had hopped over the wall and was standing in my back garden. I'd learned this would nearly always be the preferred approach for both her and Michael; the front door was rarely used. In turn, when I went to visit them, I'd always go to the back door. The front door seemed to be reserved for strangers or more formal occasions.

Seeing me through the glass of the back door, Liz smiled and waved with both hands, a gardening trowel in one and a fistful of pansies in the other. My initial assessment of her gardening abilities was correct; she has one of the greenest thumbs I've ever met. Beautiful plants and flowers bloom year-round in her back garden. I enjoyed the changing colors and configurations through all seasons, even in the dead of late winter when her cheery yellow Jonquils defied below-freezing temperatures, sleet, fierce winds, and snow.

I opened the door and greeted her. She asked if I'd like her to plant the pansies on the hillside along the top of the garden wall. I agreed with enthusiasm. She got busy putting in the flowers, digging out small spaces in the rocky soil. She also planted the potted ivy plant I had purchased and intended to put into the ground in the hope it might trail down over the wall. We chatted and she planted, and then Clare, in Kenmare with Colin for a visit, strolled up to the wall. She'd brought a cup of tea for Liz.

'Would you like one, Jane?' she kindly asked.

'Oh, no, thank you – I have one inside.'

'Now 'twould be no problem! Are you sure?'

'Yes, thanks. I'm fine!'

She stayed and visited for a few minutes. One wonders why I didn't think of offering to make a cup of tea for Liz but to be honest, I hadn't thought tea went with gardening. Silly me. She wasn't only a guest, she was planting flowers for me! Apparently I had a long way to go toward becoming Irish. Such things were not yet second nature. I wondered if they ever would be.

The three of us chatted a while longer and then Clare had to leave to resume her relief shift staying with Daniel so Liz could continue her break.

Liz apologized for not coming over more often to visit. The woman stays with her father around the clock and can only leave if someone is there to take her place, which isn't often – and she is apologizing for not calling on me more often? When she finished planting she left, only to return two minutes later with the once empty ivy plant pot, now filled with fresh eggs from Michael's hens. I accepted the gift with exclamations of surprise and gratitude. Flashing one of her cheerful smiles, Liz waved goodbye and left.

Before coming to Ireland, I had imagined many things, but having a neighbor who kept hens, and being given free, fresh from the nest eggs, and having someone stop by with pansies for my garden were kindnesses beyond my imagination. I don't think I ever grew accustomed to them and I certainly never took them for granted.

The impression I'd formed of Irish folks during those holidays spent in Ireland didn't change. Overall, they are exceptionally caring and helpful. I tried to keep up, but I didn't think I'd ever make it to their level. No amount of sleeping in late, bidding folks 'good morning' in the afternoon, remembering to offer tea to visitors, or hanging bags of money in my back garden was going to fool anyone into thinking I was Irish. Well, not more than one-eighth, anyway.

14

WASH DAY

October 12, 2013: Okay, okay, I have to finally admit it: I miss my washer and dryer!

I awoke to a soft day, a slight breeze swirling the misty rain. Although already into October, the stretch of warm weather had been holding. The rain combined with the warmer temperature brought high humidity. As was my habit since arriving in Ireland, I had chosen yet another less than ideal day to do laundry. But then, in my defense, there were many less than ideal days for doing laundry in Ireland. And anyway, it wasn't called laundry anymore, it was wash. Doing the wash. Whatever it was called, on such days it would take ages to dry anything outdoors, even with the roof overhang partially protecting the clothesline.

I'd finally figured out how to use the dryer mode of the small combo washer/dryer, so decided to give it a try. I set it for forty minutes of drying time hoping to eliminate or at least decrease the length of time the clothes would have to spend outdoors. I watched as the machine started up and was perplexed by the design engineering behind the dryer function. It didn't operate like a normal tumble dryer. It turned one way a few times, then stopped. Then it turned the other way a few times. And stopped. This cycle continued and forty minutes later I opened the door. The clothes were pretty much as wet as when I'd started the cycle. I could see in future there would be little point in using it. I hung what I could around the house and the rest I put outdoors on the clothesline and hoped for the best. I saw no other options.

Laundry. A fact of life. It had to be done and there had to be a better way. It was time to begin perfecting the art of clothes drying. Warned that running the dryer function of the machine used a good amount of expensive electricity, I ruled out trying that again on a longer cycle. I didn't see how it could be very effective, anyway. In the days that followed I continued to hang my wash outdoors. And wait for it to dry. And wait. And wait some more. Upon arising one morning and finding most of what I hung outdoors twenty-four hours before still not dry, I knew a new plan of attack was needed. Thus, *Plan B* was born.

PLAN B:
THE ART OF DRYING LAUNDRY IN IRELAND

1. *Preheat the oven to any temperature while allowing laundry to partially dry outdoors.*
2. *Run a heavy cord (string or twine will suffice) from cupboard door handle above stove, across top of stove and around the corner into the laundry closet.*
3. *Affix laundry closet end of cord to leg of ironing board inside closet to anchor it.*
4. *Remove items from clothesline, bring indoors, and open the oven door partway.*
5. *Hang laundry, one or two items at a time, on the indoor line for 10-20 minutes.*

<u>*Warning!*</u> *Do not forget to turn off the oven and remove the cord when you are finished. Do not attempt to cook on the stove top when drying is in progress!*

The technique may use more electricity than the machine dryer, and requires more time and attention, but it's funnier and more creative and best of all, it works.

Months after designing the program I succumbed to trucking my laundry up the street to the laundromat where I paid seven or eight euros a load to wash and dry it. The novelty of doing laundry at home was no longer amusing and had become far too time consuming. I am happy to sit for an hour or so once a week at the laundromat and read a book while my clothes get clean, and I don't mind reverting to the old way of doing things, the way I've always done laundry: When the wash cycle finishes, it isn't a problem to remove the clothes and put them into a dryer where they tumble deliciously dry without pausing between revolutions.

From time to time, when the weather is bad and I don't feel like going out to read at the laundromat, I use my little washer and the less than efficient, but dependably effective, *Plan B*.

15

WINTER IS COMING

October 29, 2013: I don't know if the 'frost is on the pumpkin' but the jack-o'-lantern's in the window and I'm ready for Halloween!

Before leaving for Kenmare's Halloween Howl kick-off event, I put the jack-o'-lantern I'd carved into my front window. I'd read about the event and other activities planned for the week in a flyer I'd picked up at the market. The celebration begins with a community bonfire in the car park at the end of my street and culminates a week later with a costume parade and trick-or-treating. I was told the kids trick-or-treat through town at all the open shops, restaurants and pubs.

All the windows in town were decorated. There were replicas of bare winter trees, ghosts, skeletons with eyes that glittered, yellow moons, witches on broomsticks, and black cats with arched backs. Spider web was draped in the window corners and over doorways. After dark the town glowed with tiny yellow, purple and orange lights. There was no doubt it was Halloween in Kenmare. The little jack-o'-lantern in my window was my contribution to the town's decor.

On the night of the bonfire the rain had stopped but the evening was damp and cool. The car park had been transformed by volunteers into a spooky and festive assembly point with a stage area decorated with giant cutouts of witches and ghosts and blue and purple flashing lights. Two witches in long black dresses and tall hats circled a huge black cauldron in the center of the stage, and a DJ finished setting up his equipment. Banners and lights strung from power poles and buildings crisscrossed overhead, and orange and black triangular flags flapped in the breeze. The recent rain left a sheen on the pavement, the lights' reflections causing a golden shimmer, adding to the Halloween atmosphere.

Minutes after I arrived I followed the crowd as they moved toward the main street. There may have been an announcement prompting the move, or perhaps some had sharper ears and detected the sound of horse's hooves before I did. Within seconds a headless horseman came charging by, followed by more horses and riders with heads, thundering along, their black capes flying out behind them.

As they disappeared out of town a group of torch-bearing marchers came into view. The torchlight reflected in the wide excited eyes of the children, many in their Halloween costumes. Some of the adults were also costumed. Vampires, ghosts, princesses and witches smiled and mingled with clowns, skeletons, Star Wars figures and the more traditionally dressed among us. People called greetings, waved, clapped, and snapped photos of the passing parade.

The group of twenty or so torch-bearers dressed in long, black, hooded garments marched solemnly by, torches held high, then turned into the car park. The crowd parted to make way for them and they circled around the seven foot high pile of wood, the bonfire waiting to be awakened. In unison they lowered the torches to the wood and the bonfire blazed to life. The flames leapt into the air and the crowd tightened, drawing closer to the blaze.

The faces of all ages glowed and morphed in the shadows and colors cast by the dancing flames of the torches and bonfire, and the flashing lights on the stage. The DJ moved to the music, and smoke machine-produced steam appeared to rise from the cauldron, drifting over the edge of the stage where delighted children danced and skipped and giggled their way in excited circles through the eerie fog. The theme from the movie 'Halloween' filled the air and as the last notes faded away, the animated voice of a local man telling a ghost story came to life, his words booming from the PA system speakers.

The bonfire grew, blazing in earnest, flames reaching toward the sky and shooting sparks high into the night air. A big tour coach passed, slowed down, and stopped while the passengers on the lucky side of the bus pointed and 'Oo-oo'd' and 'Ah-h'd' through the windows. Moments later the engine roared and the coach cruised on out of town.

Kenmare's Halloween Howl opening event and indeed, Halloween festivities in general, are rooted in the Celtic 'Saomhain', a pre-Christian celebration marking the end of the harvest season. One of the traditions involved bonfires and another was going door-to-door in disguise, called 'guising,' reciting verses in exchange for food, obviously a precursor to the 'trick-or-treat' recited by today's costumed children in exchange for candy.

The bonfire event was the sort of experience I was hoping for when I moved to Ireland. The 'spectacularity' factor didn't matter, although it was great. The best part? It was a community gathering with roots in ancient times, put on and attended by locals, people of all ages celebrating together. I felt very much a part of the tradition and although I went alone, I didn't feel alone at all, with both the history and the community around me.

I was immensely glad I was not one of those tourists who had only a fleeting glance through a bus window.

As I walked back to my little Irish home, the damp roadway reflected the old yellow streetlights. Strains of 'Werewolves of London' and the voices of excited children dimmed and faded away. Drifting clouds parted and the moon smiled. It was magical. In the darkness I smiled, too, as I walked past the nineteenth century cottages to my own front door, where my jack-o'-lantern grinned at me through the front window.

◉

On the fourth day of November it wasn't necessary to check the calendar to know winter's cold breath was bearing down on Kenmare. It had changed drastically from the mild weather that lasted well into October. I hadn't experienced winter in Ireland, but it didn't take much imagination to know it was going to be colder and damper than the weather I was accustomed to after twenty-five years in California.

I already knew the old radiators in my cottage weren't very effective but it didn't matter because nothing beats a fire on a cold night. As the daylight hours grew shorter and the temperature cooled, I suspected a nightly fire might become a habit and it did. It was time to stock some firewood to supplement Michael's kindling and Noreen and Paudie's timber.

After trying a sample pack of Megatherm logs, made of recycled compressed beech wood, I placed an order for a half-pallet, forty-eight shrink-wrapped packages of seven logs each. They burned well, were relatively smokeless and made little ash.

My back garden had limited protected space under the over-hang of the roof where wood could be stored out of the rain, but I thought I could manage to make room for forty-eight packages of logs. After the delivery guy made two chest-high stacks in the allocated space and, running out of room, another stack just outside the back door, I was getting concerned.

'So – is that about it?' I asked hopefully. Surely it was.

He paused, took off his hat, and mopped his brow. It was a cool day, but he was sweating; those logs were heavy. He looked at me like he wondered if I was kidding, then shook his head. 'Oh, no – there's more!'

A few minutes later there were two more waist-high stacks of logs in the kitchen and more stashed wherever I could find a spot. Forty-eight packages of those logs is a *large* quantity of firewood. Clearly, it had been a gross error in judgment on my part when I imagined how much space would be needed.

I also had a half-full bag of peat and another containing about twenty pounds of coal from an earlier purchase. After I'd placed the log order, Michael brought me a bag of kindling and the following day Paudie dropped off two feed-sacks of wood from their farm with the announcement, 'Noreen said I was to bring you some timber!'

There was fire fuel everywhere. Two-thirds of the patio was covered. It was stacked in and out of the wood bin, and on top of the patio table. It was stacked in the kitchen and by the fireplace. In the end I even took several packages and stowed them in the upstairs spare bedroom. All I needed was a sign and a cash register and I could have opened a fire fuel shop.

Overkill? Yes, I suppose – but I wanted to be self-sufficient. I didn't want to rely on even very reliable friends and neighbors and have any worry about running out of firewood during the winter. It didn't look as though I would. Even having a small fire every single day, I calculated I was good through at least early spring.

◙

It wasn't but a week or so later when winter arrived – with a vengeance. Temperatures dropped, winds screeched and howled and rain lashed. I was thankful for my overstock of firewood and put it to good use.

One afternoon at precisely 3:45 I realized just how dark and long a winter afternoon in Ireland can be. After several days of I-hope-the-roof-holds-up raging storms, it was quiet. It was one of those rare days when the sun had not shown its face for even a second, not even a hint of the weakest of rays piercing through the flat gray sky. It was as still and quiet as if a thick blanket of snow covered the world, creating that strange muting where the silence presses in on your ears… no cars, no voices, no sounds of people or machines. Even the rooks and jackdaws were silent. I shivered. My immediate reaction was to do something to escape.

I'd already handled all my chores and errands that day, as I normally did by noon, reserving most afternoons for walking, reading and writing. I'd stopped for a cup of tea with the neighbors. I'd walked to the bank and used the ATM machine, and to the post office where I'd mailed a post card to my parents. I'd swept the kitchen floor and started a pot of soup for dinner, cleaned out the ashes from the fireplace, restocked the indoor wood basket, and shuffled the various stacks of wood in the back garden, now secured beneath a large tarp, another handy Amazon.co.uk purchase.

Chores completed, the long afternoon stretched ahead, too dark, too cold, too dreary. I could easily have gone to one of the pubs or cafes and there was sure to be someone to chat with, but I wasn't in the mood. I planned to call my sister, and that always cheered me up, but with the eight hour time difference it was still too early.

Although I didn't normally start a fire until evening, on that day it would not wait. It was the first step toward dispelling the dark and cold that descended on Kenmare that day. I stacked wood in the fireplace and struck a match, the slivers of dry kindling easily igniting, the yellow-orange flames instantly warming the thin cold light of the afternoon. I also turned on the boiler with the hope of coaxing a few molecules of heat from the radiators.

As my final touches, I lit two cinnamon scented candles and made a cup of tea. Like a warm fire, tea always had a way of improving things, too. Shoving the couch closer to the fireplace, I positioned myself and my laptop directly in front of it, feeling the welcome warmth, and settled in to write.

After those first few months of mild weather, the arrival of winter surprised me with its intensity. But on that day I learned I could keep the gloom and cold at bay with the glowing ambiance of candles and a crackling, popping fire. The aroma of soup simmering on the stove mixed with the cinnamon, scenting the air with comfort. I didn't have to budge from my cozy corner to go anywhere at all, and I was warm and content.

While the sun remained ensconced in the grip of the gray sky, trapped by the heavy murkiness, I knew it was still up there and would eventually win out – it always did, and tomorrow was another day. The sound of a rook's cry pierced the quiet, as if in agreement. I didn't even notice when a short time later darkness fell, cancelling out the gray day. The fire crackled, the candle flames danced, my fingers tapped the keys on my computer translating my thoughts to the written word, and all was again right with the world.

I didn't know then, feeling snug and safe in my little corner of Ireland, that winter was only on a practice run and would become more ruthless – much more.

16

THANKSGIVING IN IRELAND

November 23, 2013: Well, it's not Thanksgiving just yet in the USA, but it's the day I've chosen to celebrate here in Ireland. Tons to do – guests coming!

I've always loved Thanksgiving. But it's an American holiday, and I was in Ireland. Still, I thought, as an American, shouldn't I celebrate the day? I decided to host a Thanksgiving dinner for some of my new friends.

It crossed my mind that when it comes to large holiday dinners, I had not prepared many and it was my mother, sister and brother-in-law who did most of the cooking. My contribution to the meal was never more than a pie and a side dish. I roamed around the edges of the flurry of activity during the meal preparation trying to help out, but the bottom line was, my experience was confined mostly to setting the table and helping with clean up. But I felt confident if I kept it simple and did my best to channel the skills of the family members usually in charge, it would work out just fine.

Turkeys are not something one buys in Ireland at just any time of year. They are sold in the supermarkets at Christmastime, more than a month away. A further complication was my diminutive oven, but I had a plan. No problem; I'd roast a turkey breast instead of a whole turkey.

I inquired of one of Kenmare's three local butchers and learned a turkey breast could be ordered, for arrival on the exact day I needed it. Wonderful! The butcher wasn't sure of size, but said it would be large and more than enough to feed the five to seven guests I was expecting for dinner.

The turkey issue solved, I worked on planning the remainder of the menu, keeping it to the basics, the must-have Thanksgiving standards. One of my guests was bringing the pumpkin pie.

I always made chocolate pie for Thanksgiving and Christmas; it was a tradition. It was also easy to make using 'Cook & Serve' Jello chocolate pudding mix poured into a cookie crumb crust and topped with whipped cream. Although a different brand, the chocolate pudding mix I was so excited to have found and purchased online for delivery with the rest of my groceries turned out to be a surprise.

I'd only recently discovered I could do my grocery shopping online and have the groceries delivered for a nominal fee, which was just the ticket without a car. It did, however, sometimes lead to receiving things I hadn't realized I'd ordered.

The pudding I ordered was pudding alright, but not the kind of pudding I had in mind. It was pudding as in *dessert*. I had forgotten the different meaning in Ireland and the UK and when I saw the picture online it looked like a box of pudding mix. When I saw the words 'chocolate pudding,' I pounced. It wasn't pudding mix at all; it was a single-serving chocolate cake.

Gears shifted, the chocolate pie plan was ditched and I made a lemon tart (another mix) topped with whipped cream. The whipped cream I purchased online was also not as anticipated. Again relying on the photo of the item and seeing a tub of fresh whipped cream, I imagined it to be similar in size to a tub of Cool Whip. I needed enough for the tart and the pumpkin pie. Yes, *350 ml* was specified. I often tired of looking up and converting weights and measures so sometimes I didn't. That was one of those times. It was not quite twelve ounces, or about one and a half cups of whipped cream. Fortunately, there was enough to provide a layer across the top of the tart and my pumpkin pie bearing guest brought her own topping.

The day I'd chosen for the dinner arrived. I calculated pots and pans, serving dishes, utensils and the table setting. Pots and pans were limited and I didn't have a pan big enough to cook a large amount of potatoes. I had no serving utensils at all, serving dishes were in short supply, and I didn't have enough plates. Given the overload of kitchen equipment I'd found on arrival it was surprising so much was lacking. I didn't even want to think about the mini-fridge's severe lack of space. It was a cold day so my back patio table helped out by becoming additional cold storage.

The potato cooking problem was solved by cooking the potatoes ahead of time, in batches. Confidence growing after solving each obstacle that arose, I also sliced and sautéed mushrooms and chives to add to the packaged stuffing mix and in a burst of creativity, put together a tomato and cucumber salad I'd never before made, eaten, nor even heard of, but it sounded good to me and like something I could handle without messing it up.

After the initial meal preparations, I walked up the street to the butcher to pick up the turkey breast. It had not yet arrived, so a second trip was required a few hours later. The turkey breast was five kilograms. That's *eleven* pounds of turkey, no bones. This was from a large turkey, indeed. I was expecting a full breast, bone in, but it had been split and each piece rolled and tied like a rolled roast. I wasn't sure how long I should cook them, adding further to the difficulty level of my holiday meal preparation. I asked the butcher and he 'thought' 'about' twenty minutes per pound. That sounded like my style of cooking, but I'd hoped for more precise directions in light of the uncharted territory I needed to navigate.

The butcher gave me a little button device to stick into the turkey. I failed to ask for the correct oven temperature or what the button was supposed to do to indicate the turkey was done.

Carrying that eleven pounds of turkey home in the large plastic bag the butcher had loosely wrapped it in was like trying to hang on to a bagful of large, slippery fish. The sight of me struggling with it was no doubt amusing to anyone who noticed me making my way home.

I salted, peppered and greased the two roasts and shoved them into cooking bags, then, following the directions on the cooking bag package, put them in the oven at 200 degrees Celsius.

After two hours I could smell the turkey so checked on it. It was done, over-done for my taste, despite cooking it for less than the twenty minutes per pound recommended by the butcher. Maybe he had meant twenty minutes per kilogram? The button never changed. It looked the same before and after so I still didn't know what it was intended to do. Doing some research later I discovered the cooking temperature probably should have been lower than the instructions specified.

I'd already decorated the table with a dark brown table runner, an autumn leaf garland with white lights, and burgundy candles, all thanks once again to the miracle of internet shopping on Amazon.co.uk. After I added the Thanksgiving napkins I'd brought with me all the way from the USA, my Irish kitchen table was transformed into the appropriate setting for an American Thanksgiving. Never mind I had to use plastic disposable plates; we did have real glassware and eating utensils.

Noreen and Paudie were the first guests to arrive, bringing wine, a poinsettia plant, a bag of timber and big hugs. My two American friends, Bob and Rose, arrived with smiles, enthusiasm, and pumpkin pie. I'd met Bob and Rose through a forum on an ex pat website prior to moving to Ireland. They'd made the move several months before I did and lived nearby. They shared my love of Irish trad music and we occasionally went out together for music sessions in the pubs.

Sister Mary was the last to arrive. Michael stayed with their father so she could attend. She expressed her pleasure in being included and commented more than once how much she loved Thanksgiving dinner. She explained how she'd celebrated Thanksgiving with some Americans during the years she had lived and worked in Peru. She thought it was a lovely tradition and had missed it. I was glad she was able to come.

Guests settled with a glass of wine or a Guinness, and turkey resting, I turned to the final tasks. I put the peas in the microwave and began making the gravy. I was nervous. I couldn't even remember the last time I'd made gravy. It had to turn out well because what was Thanksgiving without turkey gravy? It could be a tremendous help in hiding such cooking sins as over-done turkey. I had a vague recollection of how to make it. I knew drippings from the turkey were a key ingredient. When I took the turkey out of the oven much of the drippings leaked from the cooking bags, ran across the countertop and seeped under the microwave, but there was plenty left for gravy.

Gravy underway, Noreen kindly took over the stirring while I tended to other last minute details. 'Is it okay, do you think? Is it thick enough?' I asked. 'I haven't even tasted it!'

'It's perfectly fine and however 'tis, 'tis no problem.'

'I think I'll add in a little of this instant stuff because it doesn't look like quite enough to me. Don't tell anyone!' I laughed.

'Sure now we don't care and no one will know. 'Tis fine, perfectly fine.'

I was surprised to discover gravy making wasn't difficult at all, and even more surprised at how good it tasted. It was a victory and a relief.

And so the candles were lit, the guests were seated, more wine was poured, and dinner was served. The turkey was a little dry as I'd suspected, regardless of the arguments from my polite guests to the contrary ('Well, now, we don't care, do we?' said Noreen. 'We just won't worry about it. 'Tis fine.'), so thank goodness for the gravy. The peas could have cooked longer (how does one mismanage the cooking of frozen peas??), and the lemon filling in the tart was over-cooked, but I considered the meal to be at least a moderate success. It wasn't a five star restaurant meal, but it was a home-cooked Thanksgiving dinner. It could have been worse given my inexperience. In between the chatter there were long stretches of serious eating with clinking utensils and glasses raised, sparkling in the candlelight, some requests for seconds, and empty plates at the end of the meal.

We ended up with full bellies and shared stories and laughter by a warm fire. With a diligent eye on the flames, Paudie kept the fire roaring and crackling by steadily feeding it with the bone-dry timber. We ended the evening with a cup of tea while the rain pattered on the roof, the wind swept down the street and howled around the chimney, and the candles burned down to sputtering nubs.

It seemed everyone enjoyed my American Thanksgiving, and so did I. Although far from family and old friends, and in my heart of hearts wishing they'd been a part of the gathering, I knew I was blessed to have folks fast becoming dear friends seated around my Thanksgiving table in my new Irish home.

17

DO NOT PASS GO, DO NOT COLLECT $200

November 28, 2013: Today's Thanksgiving. Really missing family and friends in America.

A few days after the Thanksgiving meal, November was nearly spent. I'd visited by phone with family and eaten the last of the leftovers on Thanksgiving Day. I'd finished another round of scouring the kitchen counter, finally ridding it of the last traces of turkey drippings, and discovered and removed more spatters of whipped cream flung onto the walls by my less than tidy whipping.

As I was cleaning ashes out of the fireplace on the day after Thanksgiving, a small brown envelope poked through the mail slot in my front door. An advertisement, no doubt, but I pulled it out to check. There was a tiny black harp insignia imprinted on the front, but no return address. Curious, I opened it. It was from immigration! The long awaited letter from INIS, seven weeks after I'd applied for permission to remain. How exciting! I was 'official!' Now I really would no longer be just a tourist in Ireland, but a legal resident.

I eagerly began reading the letter. After just the first line my eagerness turned to confusion and alarm. For a moment I just stood there with the letter in my hand. I didn't know what to think. My application had been denied. Denied? *Denied!* I was to leave the country in two weeks. Two weeks! I was stunned. It felt as if I'd been kicked in the stomach and shoved to the ground. It was the one aspect of my move to Ireland I thought I was prepared for and I'd had little worry I wouldn't be accepted. Who would uproot, sell most of what they own, and move to another country thousands of miles away if they thought they wouldn't be allowed to remain? I certainly wouldn't.

This was not part of the plan, not at all. My heart pounded in my ears and a dull ache started in the pit of my stomach, spreading into my chest, and tears burned my eyes, but I blinked them away. I couldn't collapse and give in to tears; I had to think what to do. How could I possibly accomplish a move back to the USA in two weeks?? I couldn't, short of packing a bag, leaving everything else behind, and inviting myself to stay with someone in the USA. Whatever INIS *wanted* me to do, it wasn't realistic. Never mind that I didn't want to leave at all, but doing it in two weeks wasn't happening.

I read more of the letter. The denial was based on my income being too low. I had already been living in Ireland nearly three months so was well aware of how much money I needed and knew my income was sufficient to cover my expenses, but that didn't seem to matter.

Everyone I spoke with thought I ought to fight it, and that's what I did. I wrote a letter of appeal, obtained additional financial documentation and prepared a detailed budget to illustrate I had adequate funds. Having finally determined the local immigration officer's working hours, I made an appointment. A friend told me with a pending appeal I had more time and the two week deadline to leave would no longer be valid. I hoped she was right.

The shock and alarm wore off after a few days, but I was disheartened, like a spent balloon, once bright and cheerful and high in the sky, now a dull, deflated, insignificant scrap on the ground. It was an awful feeling knowing Ireland, my beloved Ireland, didn't want me. But I had to suck it up and carry on. *Mind over matter. Mind over matter.* Christmas was coming, my first Christmas in Ireland. I wasn't going to let INIS ruin it for me.

◙

The evening before my meeting with the immigration officer, I had some friends and neighbors over. We sat around the fire and chatted, the primary topic of conversation the INIS denial. Everyone insisted I simply needed to tell INIS about my passion for Ireland. 'Can't you see what kind of person I am and how much I love Ireland?!' They felt certain that would be the path to approval… The Irish people and the Irish government, like in most countries, are two distinctly different species.

The next morning I set out for the bus stop for the trip to Killarney, my breath turning to white vapor in the cold morning air. I wasn't looking forward to the appointment, but at least the journey was pleasant. The gardens and fields were covered in frost and the sun shone with brilliance in the winter blue sky. In one field the sheep all but disappeared, revealing their presence only when they moved, their wool blending with the frosted grass.

The bus stopped for a ruddy-cheeked lady waiting by the roadside, a lime green scarf covering her head and knotted tightly under her chin. Opening the door, the bus driver greeted her. 'Good mornin', Mary! – 'Tis hardy today!'

Mary stepped onto the bus, the chill air clinging to her, blue eyes bright and cheeks and nose red with cold. 'Oh, indeed! 'Tis fresh!'

In Killarney I caught a taxi to the garda station and was directed to the INIS office, back outside at the far end of the building. I walked the short distance and opened the door, eager to get out of the cold. I looked around at the waiting area which was an enclosed porch, a small concrete block-walled outer room with bare concrete floors. There was no noticeable change in temperature; it was just as cold inside as out.

There was just enough room for four plastic chairs of the kind I'd seen in the Tralee bus station, and a small side table holding a few out-of-date magazines. Through the glass door to the inner sanctum I could see the immigration officer talking on the phone. I was the only person there so saw no need to linger any longer in the cold and uninviting waiting room. As I was about to push open the door, the officer held up his hand in a 'STOP' gesture, no change in his expressionless face.

I complied and planted myself in one of the plastic chairs, wondering that it didn't crack from my weight in the frigid air. It was, literally, freezing. I gazed outside. Despite the sunshine, the lawns outside were still covered in frost.

I sat there clutching my papers, breath puffing out in white clouds around me, realizing what it must be like to be an apprehensive, hopeful foreigner who perhaps doesn't speak the language, and doesn't quite understand all the rules and regulations, waiting for a meeting with immigration in a new country, vulnerable, alone, and far from home. For a moment it didn't occur to me that with the exception of being able to speak the language (well, okay, sort of), it wasn't a *similar* situation, it was *exactly* my situation.

After fifteen minutes in the cooling tank I saw the officer, who had hung up the phone several minutes before, look up from his desk and wave me in. Relieved, I entered, nervous, but all smiles and feigned cheerfulness, only to be met by his still deadpan face under a shock of unruly white hair and bushy white eyebrows. He seemed to be in his fifties, maybe older, doing a job he didn't enjoy. Or maybe he was just having a bad day. At least there was heat inside the office. My fingers began to thaw out.

The officer never once smiled or seemed in any danger of letting it happen, even when I played what one of the Kenmare locals was sure would be my trump card: 'I understand you are from Kenmare!' At first I wondered if he'd heard me. He opened a large three-ring binder of mysterious information and hunched over it, flipping through the pages. The silence lengthened.

Without looking up, he finally responded. 'Yes; I am.'

He snapped the binder closed, still not looking at me. He was the most unfriendly Irishman I'd ever met, after the strange gentleman in the market when I'd been on the hunt for a calling card. I would never have suspected him of being Irish, but his accent gave him away.

I never gave up on the forced cheerfulness, but my efforts to maintain an upbeat demeanor did nothing to help improve his. In the end, however, he agreed with me that it was perplexing why INIS would have denied my application based on insufficient funds when it appeared I had more than the sum they specified. He advised me to send my appeal letter to Dublin at once. I inquired about the date just days away which INIS had set for my departure from Ireland. I wanted to make sure a pending appeal waived the date.

'Don't worry about it,' he said. Easy for him to say. Well, maybe not so easy, considering he clearly was not a talker.

'They won't come looking for me when they don't receive evidence I've left?'

He shook his head in the negative and I think I might have finally seen the barest suggestion of a smile, but I blinked and it was gone. I departed without ever learning his name. I later learned he was just filling in for the regular officer and didn't normally work in the Killarney office. Well, thank goodness for small blessings.

Reaching the outside air and deciding 'fresh' was a lovely way to describe it, I breathed in deeply and felt the tension leave my body. My forced smile faded and was replaced with a real one. I reveled in my freedom, feeling like I had just escaped unjust imprisonment. I squinted in the bright sunshine and hopped into the waiting car of kind friends Bob and Rose, there to rescue me from Immigration, take me shopping in Killarney, and home to Kenmare.

I sent the appeal by registered mail to INIS in Dublin and the wait began. I felt much better then, but my optimism stayed with me for only a few weeks. Like one of the many winter storms that swept through Ireland that year, one day it hit me and weighed heavy on my heart. The country I loved didn't want me and the possibility existed that I would again be told to leave. I felt like a jilted lover. It seemed so wrong, so exactly the opposite of how it was supposed to be, how it had *been*, living in Ireland. Ireland was never supposed to be the source of any anguish for me. I wasn't sure how to handle it.

18

WEATHER REPORT

December 10, 2013: Winter's definitely here. It poured rain all night and into the morning, but this afternoon the sun came out so I grabbed the opportunity to go out and traipse around through the puddles in my wellies.

After my meeting with immigration, my dismay over Ireland's rejection faded a little. I was hopeful, and thankful for my encouraging Irish friends and supportive family and friends in the States. I wouldn't let the decision made by a bunch of bureaucrats, Irish or not, knock me off my foundation. Ireland wasn't rejecting me, it was some jokers sitting behind desks in Dublin. I needed to look at it from the right perspective.

I let my attention be drawn to the wild, quick-change weather we were having as winter clamped its cold steel jaws on us. The west coast is well-positioned to bear the brunt of the winds which gather strength as they come in across the Atlantic Ocean, and during my first winter Kenmare and the entire west coast was hit with a vengeance. The storms that raged day and night often awakened me, the torrential rains pounding and the winds howling, and I'd lay there wakeful and tense, fearful that a tree branch might come crashing through one of my windows and certain, at times, the roof would be blown off.

From mid-December until late February the fierce storms persisted, with infrequent breaks. County Kerry was among the worst hit. While I was fortunate, as were most in Kenmare, damage was widespread. On twelve of those storm days winds were at hurricane force levels with gusts as high as one-hundred miles an hour and rainfall of up to nearly double the norm in some areas. There was flooding, heavy wind damage and the destruction of thousands of Ireland's trees. Property was damaged or destroyed, beaches and dunes were severely eroded, and a portion of Dún Beag, an ancient and beautiful ring fort on the Dingle Peninsula, fell into the sea. The winter of 2013-14 would not soon be forgotten by anyone.

Like everyone else, I tired of the harsh weather that first winter, but overall I came to enjoy Ireland's changeable weather. Not many days pass without the sun popping out, and it seems gloomy stretches without a break of at least one pretty day, except for stormy stretches in the dead of winter, are rare. Ireland is as well-known for having all four seasons in a twenty-four hour period as it is for rain.

Some days the weather is so varied it can be pure entertainment. One morning after a particularly bad couple of days, the rain and wind ceased and a blue sky day dawned, the frosted rooftops glittering in the sun. I couldn't help but feel hopeful we'd seen the end of the terrible storms.

Filled with vigor and enthusiasm, I made coffee and drank it in a hurry, anxious to go outdoors and feel the sunshine. As I gathered my rain jacket (just to be on the safe side) and slipped on my wellies, I watched heavy dark storm clouds bunch together on the horizon. The wind began to blow again and the clouds sailed across the sky like a fleet of black-sailed ships, blocking out the sun. Before I could even set foot outdoors, the clouds opened and dropped their wet payload, and strong gusty winds buffeted the trees. As I watched, the clouds raced away as rapidly as they'd gathered and the sun shone in the blue sky I'd seen a half hour before. There wasn't even time to smile at the returning sun before another storm swept in, swallowed the sun, and battered the land with more heavy wind and rain, this time accompanied by thunder and lightning. It was like trying to pass someone on the street, both moving in the same direction, back and forth, first left, then right, then left. Open door, close door. Wellies on, wellies off, wellies on.

That pattern went on throughout the day and into the night, interspersed with sleet and hail. The number of times the weather changed and the speed with which it changed was astounding. I did little but weather-watch in awe throughout the morning and afternoon. The conditions were simply too severe to consider spending any time outdoors, but were perfect for rainbow sightings. I had the good fortune of seeing a fleeting few high in the sky over my back garden that day.

One afternoon a few weeks later brought yet another sunny day – thank God for those much needed breaks during that terrible winter. Noreen stopped by and we walked the short distance from my place to 'go to the shops' as she would say, to have a look around town and get out of the house in between storms.

I was bundled up in my thick parka, the hood cinched tightly so it didn't blow off, hands shoved deep into the pockets. I felt no warmth from the sun and the cold was piercing, the wind wild. Noreen wore a little tweed jacket, no hat or hood. She had a bright orange scarf loosely draped around her neck, more for fashion than warmth it seemed. She looked stylish, as she usually does, but I couldn't see how she'd be warm enough. But she strolled along as though it was a pleasant spring day and looked at me with more than a little confusion when I remarked on the weather and huddled further into my jacket. Had anyone been judging the weather by watching the two of us, they'd have had to draw the conclusion that one of us was nuts. I'm not saying which one, because I'm not sure that I know. It probably would depend on who you ask and if they're Irish or not.

◻

I was at first surprised by the rain in Ireland. Not by the frequency of the rain, but by its intensity. I thought Irish rain fell softly, like the old Irish blessing, 'May the rain fall softly on your fields...' While there is a fair amount of the soft stuff, there is no shortage of torrential downpours.

'Soft' is but one of many creative ways used to describe the weather. Due to the regularity with which the topic is discussed, it stands to reason a large vocabulary pertaining to the subject is helpful. Knowing a few weather terms provides a welcome conversation starter or makes a fine contribution to one already in progress. I soon picked up the terminology. 'Soft' ('a soft day') is heard often. It means it's raining lightly, but it can be used to make just plain old rain sound better. There are many terms for inclement weather; not so many for nice weather. The reason for that is obvious. A day can be 'grand' or 'fine' or 'brilliant' and no more adjectives are needed. No one gets the chance to use them often enough to make them seem repetitive.

'Lashing' or 'bucketing' means it's raining hard; 'fresh' and 'hardy' both mean cold. If the weather is overall terrible, 'dirty' or 'brutal' or 'desperate' describe it, but brutal and desperate can describe things other than weather. Another word not just confined to describing weather is 'fierce,' meaning 'very,' as in 'fierce cold,' or 'fierce windy' but usually just stated as 'fierce.' No need to point out the obvious; everyone knows what it's doing outside.

The best thing about the weather in Ireland is the appreciation for fair weather, the simple and wonderful joy of a fine day. A beautiful day is not only noticed, it is cause for changed moods and deep appreciation. I can't imagine living anywhere ever again without a climate of four distinct seasons.

In all the changing Irish weather I rediscovered a forgotten childhood joy. Walking in the rain wearing rubber boots. There is something about walking straight through puddles that's fun, satisfying, and liberating! Those designer wellington boots my mother so generously paid too much for because she wanted me to have them in Ireland have proven to be one of my most valuable, trusted, and regularly used possessions. They have a special place by my door and are called into frequent duty, leaving many footprints on the sidewalks, roads and pathways around Kenmare.

19

TRADITIONS

December 17, 2013: It's my sister's birthday today. Wishing I could be there to celebrate with her.

On an early evening walk through town, Christmas was in the air as thick as a snowstorm. Advertising not only the merchandise, but the arrival of the Christmas season, shop windows glowed with lights and greenery, red ribbons and reindeer, Santas, sparkles and snowflakes. Lights strung along the buildings and through the park in the town square further brightened the winter streets. The town was transformed, not a single shop or pub without decoration.

I stepped into the sweet shop to buy candy canes for my Christmas tree and with the jangle of the bell on the door, I was transported back to childhood, to the local five and dime where we bought candy we called 'penny candy' because it cost just one cent. Kenmare's sweet shop was full of what looked like every candy known to man. There were boxes and jars and buckets filling the counter and inside the tall glass case, and row after row of glass jars lining the walls on several tiers of shelving. I was surrounded by every shape, flavor and color of the rainbow. Resisting the urge to buy even more, I purchased the candy canes I'd been looking for and a small paper bag of peppermints after the older gentleman behind the counter asserted 'No one else makes 'em like this anymore! They're the real thing!' I thanked him, he wished me a 'Happy Christmas,' and I left the shop, the bell on the door jingling merrily. I felt certain I was in a Walton's Christmas special.

Outside a car drove slowly down the street carrying its precious cargo, a Christmas tree. On the sidewalk I passed by a mother wearing a bright red scarf, pushing her sleeping baby in a stroller. A young child clutched the hem of her jacket, a hat with reindeer antlers pulled over his ears, his cheeks ruddy with the cold. The mother was softly humming a tune. *I saw three ships come sailing in, on Christmas Day, on Christmas Day…* The baby slept as only babies do, in total peace and relaxation, the little boy skipped along, and mom looked happy. It was a pretty family scene and it tugged at my heartstrings. It was Christmas – and I was far from family.

Ireland felt like home, but America would always be my homeland and I was missing the folks there. There just was no denying it. Keeping in touch by e-mails and phone calls wasn't the same as being there, especially at such times as Christmas. I wasn't lonely in general, but at that time of year I was lonely for them.

◙

The importance of family seemed to grow and become monumental in proportion to everything else that December. It cast a shadow on my merry adventures in Ireland. I missed them and the traditions we shared. In the remembering I could almost feel their hugs – or rather, the absence of them.

It was that evening walk with the humming mother and her little children when I began to doubt whether I wanted to live anywhere permanently so far from home, 'home' being wherever my family is.

It wasn't that I sat around moping; not at all. I had friends and neighbors with whom I socialized and holiday events to attend, but without the family structure to tie it all together, I had to admit life felt a bit too loose and empty just then. It didn't help that I'd been rejected by Ireland. When that fateful letter arrived through my mail slot it had been a huge blow to the happy state I was in.

I've always been a sentimental fool and it doesn't take too much to move me to tears, but it was surprising me how even the quickest, the most fleeting thoughts of family gatherings could catch me, causing a physical ache and bringing tears to my eyes. I blinked them away and carried on, but they were tears nonetheless. I wondered if my time in Ireland might have a quicker end than I'd planned.

I knew there was always the chance when the holidays and dark and cold of winter were behind me, Ireland's springtime magic would pull me back under her spell. I think fear that my permission to remain appeal might fall through was contributing to my sadness. Thinking about the possibility of being forced to leave before I could find out what effect that springtime magic might have on me didn't rest easy on my mind.

The days passed, and with them my melancholy mood. I'd heard nothing from immigration and I was still lonely for family, but it was time to set both aside and enjoy the season, new friends, and my first Christmas in Ireland. It only took a few repetitions of my mind-over-matter mantra, in combination with my younger brother's favorite, *Carpe Diem* (seize the day), to get into a better frame of mind. My first Christmas in Ireland – let the games begin!

On Christmas Eve morning I took a walk just before sunrise. The 'storm of the century' I thought we'd been having, but which had not yet actually hit, had subsided overnight except for the wind which continued to howl. Michael had inquired the day before if I'd been to the pier to see the high waves the wind was causing. I hadn't.

I put on an extra layer of clothes and set out through the very quiet, very cold streets of Kenmare and made my way down to the bay with the wind whistling around me.

It was indeed a spectacle, the wind scooping up waves like a backhoe, then dumping them in the air where they sprayed in huge arcs across the pier. I tried to capture it on camera, with great difficulty and little success, but my mind recorded it vividly. I crouched down against the windward side of the sea wall, seeking some shelter, hoping for the perfect shot, but knowing when and where the water would appear was impossible. The force of the wind was so great I couldn't hold the camera steady and the spray from the waves was threatening to drench both of us. Had my fingers not been freezing even inside my gloves, I'd have stayed longer and continued my photographic efforts, but it was time to head back.

On the walk home the sky spit sporadic hail and the wind continued as did the sun on its upward rise. The strong wind was sweeping the sky of clouds, changing it from pink and gray to gold and winter blue. I arrived back home in sunshine, chilled to the bone, but glad I had braved the weather to see that morning's sights. By that point, I was almost equally glad to be back inside and close to the fire.

In the early evening I heard Noreen's knock-and-rattle at the front door. I opened it and she stepped over the threshold with a big smile, Christmas greetings, and a gift for me.

'Oh, thank you! This is so nice of you! Where's Paudie?' I inquired.

'Oh, he's up the pub!'

'Should we join him?'

Noreen's eyes lit up. 'Will we?'

'Sure – why not? I think we should!'

The rain had stopped again after dumping a fair amount throughout the day, and the wind had lessened dramatically, so we had only some gusts and the cold to contend with on the short walk up the street.

Paudie's favorite pub is a small place, not much bigger than a good-sized living room, its exterior painted bright red, two black Guinness barrels flanking the front doors. We squeezed in among many locals and a few visitors, everyone of good cheer, the warm air ringing with Christmas greetings and frequent laughter above the chattering voices. Paudie smiled when he saw us and found us a couple of stools. We shared a table with a young couple from Dublin, in town for the holiday.

Garlands of greens with red berries and colored lights hung above the bar where men stood shoulder to shoulder drinking their pints of Guinness. The TV was dark and silent, a pleasant and appropriate break on that occasion from the almost constantly broadcast sporting events.

I hadn't been in a bar on Christmas Eve before, but it didn't feel strange. It seemed one of those quintessential Irish experiences. Everyone's first drink was on the house, Paudie said. I wasn't sure if it really was or if he'd paid for my pint. One never knows in Ireland. He could quite easily have been pulling my leg, but on the other hand, it could just as easily have been a Christmas tradition.

Beneath the chat and the laughter, I noticed murmurings about Christmas Eve mass, which soon developed into a louder, pub-wide discussion.

'Bobby!' called a tall, thin man standing at the far end of the bar. 'Bobby!'

A young woman wearing a red Christmas sweater (better known as a jumper) and dangling sparkly earrings nudged the middle-aged bald man sitting next to her, and pointed at the tall man across the room. He turned around on his stool.

'Mass, Bobby,' the man called, 'when is it you'll be goin'?'

Bobby paused, apparently thinking about it.

'Nine, I think?' He swung back around and exchanged remarks with the young woman, then called out again, 'Or would it be half-nine? It might be half-nine.'

This set off the rest of the crowd. What time did mass start on Christmas Eve, anyway? The subject raced around the room like a friendly lost dog looking for its master, enjoying the attention the search was bringing. There were several opinions, no arguments, and more laughter. No one seemed at all worried, just curious. Everyone appeared to know the precise start time on Christmas Day, but the time on Christmas Eve was a mystery.

The general consensus finally boiled down to nine o'clock, half-nine, or ten o'clock, your choice. The jolly confusion amused me given the fact that these folks had probably been attending Christmas Eve mass at the same church for years. I wondered if discussing the start time might be a tradition, just part of the craic.

Two pints of Guinness later, people started to drift out a few at a time, most to attend mass, be it early, late, or on time, others to join family gatherings. Not being Catholic and far from my own family gathering, I bid Noreen and Paudie farewell and squelched the 'Merry Christmas' I almost uttered, replacing it with the customary 'Happy Christmas,' and returned home.

My little Christmas tree glittered in the corner, made festive by the tiny lights, red ribbons and candy canes I'd paired with the few special decorations brought with me from America. After the pub chatter, it was quiet, very quiet. Christmas music, that's what was needed. The beginning notes of an instrumental rendition of 'We Three Kings' took me back to childhood, caroling with my family on Christmas Eve. I stared into the fire and remembered.

Christmas Eve was always the best time. Christmas Day was fun and exciting, but it was Christmas Eve, always Christmas Eve that held the magic. The candlelight church services, the singing, the visitors, the smorgasbord of special treats. Cookies shaped like stars and angels and all manner of 'exotic' finger foods, gastronomic delights such as striped ribbon candy, homemade fudge, crackers that weren't saltines, cheese spread that probably didn't contain any cheese but gosh-it-tasted-great, and potato chips and dip. All there for the taking, available to nibble on anytime you wished (or so my memory tells me), a luxurious departure from the formality of our standard meat and potato six o'clock suppers.

The sharp clean scent of the fir tree mingled with cinnamon, baking pies, peppermint, and fresh-brewed coffee as my sister and brothers and I lay under the Christmas tree looking up through the branches at the lights and decorations, listening to the adults talking. It wasn't what they said, it was the sound of their voices and soft laughter remembering and sharing the old stories. I didn't recognize the concept then, but looking back I can see the comfort was from being in the midst of family, listening to a part of the history which connected all of us. At no other time in childhood did I feel as safe and content. It was magic.

It was a wonderful memory, but it brought such a wave of nostalgia that I had to physically shake it off. I came careening back from childhood into the present, popped some popcorn, put a log on the fire and a Dickens' classic, 'Great Expectations,' into the DVD player. I reminded myself of my many blessings and good fortunes and knew one day I'd look back with similar nostalgia at the sweet memory of the Christmas Eve in Ireland that began with a stormy sea at dawn, progressed to a pint at a pub with friends, and ended by my familiar fire and the twinkle of my own Christmas tree. Life was good.

◉

Christmas morning dawned clear, still cold and windy. The first thing I heard upon awakening were the church bells ringing in the frosty quiet air. It seemed so perfect. I turned on the Christmas lights and Christmas music, lit the fire, and made coffee, then unwrapped the many gifts my dear family spent too much money shipping over to me, among them one of the best: a jar of Vlasic dill pickles!

After dining on bacon and eggs and taking a long and windy walk, I stopped in next door with Christmas greetings for Mary and Michael and Daniel. I accepted the offered cup of tea and chose a cookie from an enormous tin of festively shaped holiday 'biscuits.'

We talked of the storms, sipped our tea, and nibbled our biscuits as the hardiest of the winter song birds flitted about outside the window, flashes of red and blue and yellow, pecking daintily at the feeders, enjoying their own holiday snack.

Back at home I kept the fire going all day as a special Christmas treat, had turkey for dinner (dill pickles on the side), read a book, and nodded off in the late afternoon by the warm fire.

That evening I stoked up the fire to full blaze status, pulled a chair up close, and called my family. As Christmas night gathered around Kenmare, it was Christmas morning in California. I could so easily see my sister's tall tree, laden with decorations and lights, and picture my family taking turns opening gifts as crumpled wrapping paper, ribbons and bows began piling up around everyone's ankles. We talked and laughed together while I sat by the fire, and for a little while, it felt as though I was there with them.

◉

I'd spent Christmas alone and far from family, but the *thinking* about how awful it was going to be proved to be the tough part. It turned out to be a peaceful and pleasant Christmas. The wind persisted with its awful howling. but I had a family who loved me only a phone call away, friends were near, the roof was snug and the fire burned with warmth and cheer. I had *seized the day*. My brother would have been proud.

20

WINTER DOLDRUMS & PLAN B

January 14, 2014: I never would have imagined feeling as I do. I'm really down in the dumps. I don't feel motivated to do anything, really. Even writing seems like too much trouble.

Like the presents under the tree and the decorations in the shop windows, holiday cheer was gone. The festivities were over and the relentless winter storms, short dark days, and my unsettled immigration status again started taking a toll on me. I was deep in a whirling vortex of rain, wind, dark, uncertainty, and sadness. I peered out with lethargy through dull eyes. I was a bit like a discarded Christmas tree lying on the ground next to a dumpster, stripped of lights and decorations but for a single scraggly piece of tinsel blowing in the wind.

I had such a bad attitude I refused to even go to the trouble of trying to talk myself out of it. I was in full hermit woe-is-me mode. I couldn't seem to see a future and that was so unlike me. Where was that dreamy nature when I needed it? The wishful thinking, the big imagination? I was living in the moment, alright, but I didn't care for that moment. I was in limbo and it wasn't a pleasant place to be.

What if I can't stay in Ireland? What will I do? I bristled at even letting the questions form in my mind. It was too hard to think about it.

One morning, still feeling trapped in the vortex, my self-preservation instinct started to kick in. My eyes felt less bleary. I blinked rapidly. Yes, much better. I could see I wasn't at the bottom, but a fair distance higher, inching my way up toward the top. There was light at the end of the proverbial tunnel – literally. We'd passed the shortest day of the year and were now on the downhill side of winter, gaining more and more minutes of daylight each day. There had even been a few consecutive cloudless days of glorious uninterrupted sunshine without wind, unexpected treats that stormy winter. It's amazing what a few pleasant days and more daylight can do for the psyche. It helped me switch gears and pull myself out of the vortex. Enough was enough. I was sick of myself. Hope came up for air. It was time to rejoin life in Kenmare.

I'd received such support and encouragement from friends and acquaintances about my immigration appeal, everyone insisting I shouldn't give up and assuring me it would all work out. Noreen wouldn't even accept the possibility that my appeal would be denied. But it was my sister who was the biggest help. She was a constant source of encouragement. Talking with her by phone, while always enjoyable, really helped lift my spirits at that particular time.

Staying in touch with friends and family in the USA was important to me in Ireland. I am, after all, an American, and I lived in America for sixty-three years. But my sister was the stand-out in the group, the person who always went out of her way to stay in touch. She has regularly jazzed up my mail with funny or sweet cards, sends gifts for every occasion, and care packages when there's no occasion. The effort she makes has given me a strong and steady link to America and family and she's made my time in Ireland unquestionably better than it would have been without her. She isn't just my sister, she's my best friend, and I came to think of her as my true 'American Connection.'

I have no doubt that it was a funny card or a phone conversation with her that was the leg-up I needed to pull out of my dark mood.

It seemed no matter where I went, someone would inquire, 'What's happening with your immigration status?' I tired of saying

I hadn't heard anything and after a while it grated on my nerves. My attitude had improved, I felt some hope, but I was weary of the whole subject. I found myself doing far less socializing.

I decided it would help if I came up with a Plan B for moving back to the USA, in case that's how things turned out. A back-up plan was always good. I'd feel more in control, and I knew myself well enough to know being in control had much to do with my sense of well-being.

It wasn't a well formulated plan, and it wasn't particularly exciting, just various options having to do with timing and possible places to live, but it was *something*. It made me feel like I had at least a small safety net, although its size might make it tough to actually land in. I'd think about that later.

The lengthening days and gathering strength of the sun gave promise of winter's end and with my back-up plan in place, albeit a rickety one, I started to feel less trapped. One day I noticed a fat brown hen join the two red hens already on the hill above my garden. As I watched them, a strong wind began to blow and dense black storm clouds didn't just threaten rain, they guaranteed it. The chickens didn't care; they were calm. They would neither worry nor take any action until the rain started. I remembered an old song made famous by Doris Day, a song my mother sang to me as a child, *Que Sera, Sera* – what will be, will be. I knew in that moment I needed to be more like Michael's hens and just accept what will be. I felt myself relax. A sense of calm replaced my impatience and anxiety. One day at a time.

◙

In the days following my epiphany at the sight of those hens on the hillside I realized I had become a bit of a hermit and more than a little lazy. It was time for a change. Having a Plan B for returning to the USA was one thing; I needed a Plan B for Ireland, another well thought-out program, something like *The Art of Drying Laundry*. Enough with all the self-indulgence, the sitting around staring into the fire, watching old movies on TV, reading for hours, surfing the internet, and eating too many fattening goodies. It was time to get moving, get out there. It was with confidence and great enthusiasm I created yet another Plan B.

PLAN B FOR IRELAND:
5 STEPS TO A BETTER YOU

1.   *Remember telling everyone before you moved how you were going to 'walk everywhere and get in shape!'? Do that for real.*

2.   *See a delicious looking chocolate cake at the market? Look away.*

3.   *Sure everyone's eating chips by the bucket load. That doesn't mean you have to, too. So don't.*

4.   *Wear sweatpants for their intended purpose: sweating, as in from exercise. Do not wear them for the comfortable delight of having an expanding waistband.*

5.   *Go out and do something social at least once a week! Nothing about TV, reading, or writing takes the place of human interaction.*

Now this was a solid Plan B, a plan that could take me places, including out to the pub from time to time as long as I kept a wary eye out for chips and too many pints.

One cold windy night I chatted with bartender Liam and a few other friends, the fire blazing in the corner. It was quiet in the pub as it usually is on winter nights. There were only a half dozen of us there.

'Any craic?' Liam asked as he set a half-pint of Guinness in front of me. I was trying to do better on my caloric intake and had switched from pints to half-pints after formulating *Plan B for Ireland.*

'No, not really,' I said. 'Still waiting on immigration, unfortunately!'

Liam shook his head. 'Ah, the feckers!' he groaned. He dropped my money in the register and closed the cash drawer, then turned to take care of another customer before rejoining our group.

We talked about the weather, of course. *The flooding is very bad in Cork – 'tis desperate! ... Will it snow tonight? ... Remember the year the roads were too icy for cars and old man Charlie rode his donkey five miles into town just for a Guinness? ...The storm will soon pass – 'twill be a fine day tomorrow so!*

We talked of winter holidays in warm and sunny places like Spain. I was asked if it's always warm in California. And when a new customer pushed open the door and walked in, bringing a blast of freezing air, a cry went out to Liam, 'Jayzus, Liam, could you not put another log on the fire?!'

An hour later I stood up to leave, and the subject of my immigration appeal came up yet again. 'But we want you to stay! Surely it's possible?' said one man I'd recently become acquainted with. I smiled and shrugged. If only it were up to the locals.

Farewells were mixed with comments of 'bummer' and 'don't worry' and several more 'the feckers!' and pats on the back. Thanking all of them, I waved and headed for the door. Patrick, a young man I didn't know very well, but liked, followed me.

'Jane, I can't believe you won't be hearing that you can stay! Sure don't we need lovely ladies such as yerself?!'

I smiled but wasn't convinced. 'Well, I hope you're right, Patrick.'

'Jane, you're an angel!' he said, giving me a farewell hug and kissing me on both cheeks. It seemed an odd thing to say and I didn't really get it, but it was cute and I laughed. 'Goodbye, Patrick – see you later.'

'When we were kids my mudder said that to us,' he said. 'And we had to respond, 'I'm an angel.''

I smiled. 'Oh, I like that!' I turned to leave.

He grabbed me and spun me around to face him, hands on my shoulders. He looked me square in the eye, and said again, this time slowly and distinctly, 'You're an angel, Jane!'

And then I got it.

'I'm an angel, Patrick,' I replied. He grinned, gave me another hug, and we went our separate ways.

It was that sort of encounter that strengthened my desire to stay in Ireland.

◙

The lack of activity and the intake of far too many unhealthy calories for too long had me racked with guilt, and *Plan B* included a mandatory provision for getting more exercise. I suited up for a walk on a mixed weather day of sun, light showers and cold. Venturing off the narrow roadway with my new-found vigor and (over)enthusiasm, I climbed up a grassy hill to see what I could see. I was exhilarated and happy; I felt robust and strong. I gazed across the countryside and filled my lungs with the fresh air, pleased with myself for breaking my hibernation and taking the first bold step toward becoming more active.

Starting back down the hill, that 'first step' turned out to be less than stable. My feet shot out from under me on the wet slippery grass like a cartoon character slipping on a banana peel. My ankle turned sharply with a sickening 'pop!' – whether audible or imagined, I can't say. I landed on my rear, sliding down the hillside through the wet grass and patches of mud. When I stopped, I remained seated, shocked, one leg folded under me and the other outstretched and said – no, *yelled* – the F-word which, as I previously mentioned, is not a part of my regular vocabulary.

The first thought in my mind after the pain and shock cleared a bit was to wonder how I would get back home. I didn't feel like I could stand, let alone walk. I then realized I had my mobile phone in my pocket, so if I needed to, I could call for help. That made me feel better. Still… I didn't want to have to call anyone for help.

I convinced myself it was one of those mind-over-matter things, 'where there's a will, there's a way.' I feared if I tried to get up I might slip and fall again. But I couldn't just sit there. I took a big breath and, remaining seated, used my hands to gingerly slide myself down the rest of the slippery hillside while trying to hold my injured ankle above the ground. When I reached more level ground, I maneuvered myself into a position I thought would give me a chance to stand.

I slowly stood up and shifted some weight onto my ankle. The pain was tolerable so I set off toward home. Luck was with me and there was a shortcut near the hill back to my cottage, so it took less than five minutes to limp back.

By the time I got home and removed my shoes, jeans, and jacket, everything wet, speckled and spattered with grass and mud, I was beginning to feel more pain. Later on there was swelling, but I could still put weight on it without causing too much pain as long as I made no sudden twisting movements.

I decided it would be okay, but it was a major annoyance, especially since that original walk was to have been the start of my coming out of hibernation and the injured ankle left me housebound, at least until it healed. Doubling the frustration was the knowledge that had I been in better shape and carrying less excess weight in the first place, I may not have fallen and even if I did, my ankle may have been stronger. Annoyed and frustrated and berating myself for all of the above, I consoled myself by eating M&M's from a care package I'd recently received from my sister. It felt like the right thing to do, but search as I might, I couldn't find any reference to M&M's, pro or con, in my *Plan B for Ireland*.

21

Where There's Smoke...

January 29, 2014: It's cold out there! Having a fire every evening has become a regular part of my routine.

As soon as the weather turned cool, I had a fire going most evenings when I was home. I was always surprised how much I could smell the fire upstairs when I went to bed. I guessed the wood smoke must have drifted up on the warmer air. It was alright, I didn't mind the smell.

One night in late January as I was climbing into bed, I noticed what looked to be a puff of white, a tiny thin cloud emanating from the wall near the floor. At first it frightened me. What was it? Fog? Smoke? It was so faint I wasn't sure of what I was seeing and I wondered if I was imagining it. I couldn't think what it was or where it was coming from. I looked again and couldn't see anything so I turned out the light and went to sleep.

A few nights later there it was again. Not so faint this time; it was definitely noticeable. I realized the bedroom was over the front room and the head of the bed positioned above where the fireplace was. It had to be smoke. I couldn't think what else it could be. But how was it getting into the walls? Were there tiny holes in the chimney? I decided it might have been from the wild gusty winds tormenting Ireland that winter. Maybe the smoke was being forced back down the chimney and the pressure was causing it to seep through cracks in the chimney? I knew nothing of the physics of such things.

I went downstairs to check on the fire, and poured water on the last few smoldering coals. I was beginning to feel alarmed, but I was also tired. I opened the bedroom window and went to bed. I knew there must be some kind of problem, but wasn't in the mood to have the house torn up.

The very next night I saw it again and knew I couldn't ignore it. I needed to investigate further. I moved the bed and the night stand and saw an area low on the wall which was darker than the rest of it. Part of the wood floor below it was black. It looked like it had been burned! My heart rate increased and I shuddered as visions of my bed and my sleeping self going up in flames filled my head. Maybe I had bigger problems than my immigration appeal! It was more than enough to motivate me, and the next morning I reported it to Michael.

Michael came over right away to inspect. Upstairs he looked at the wall and rubbed at the blackened floor. It was not charred, it wasn't a burn mark; it was soot. The dark area on the wall was also from smoke. Better than it might have been, at least it wasn't burned, but still – not good. He said it had to be smoke leaking through the chimney, which should definitely not be happening.

Downstairs he climbed into the fireplace to inspect the interior of the lower part of the chimney. It isn't a large fireplace. Fortunately he isn't a large man. He began scraping the inside of the chimney with a tool he produced from one of his pockets. Michael was always prepared and could fix anything. His scraping dislodged chunks and layers of soot and stone, raining down on him and spilling onto the hearth. That's when the little metal piece fell out, the remains of an over-the-fire hook for cooking pots, from who knows how many years ago? I regret my foolishness in not asking him if I could keep it.

After a few minutes Michael pulled his head out of the chimney, backed out of the fireplace and stood up, black soot streaked across his forehead. Shaking his head he let loose with a few F-bombs, cursing the people who refurbished the place before he bought it. I mentioned the soot on his face, but he waved me off and ignored it. There were more important things to deal with. He said he could see the chimney had not been relined, something he assumed was taken care of during the renovations. Understandably, he was not a happy man.

The chimney had to be relined and it couldn't wait. Michael wondered if putting in a wood stove at the same time would be to my liking? I hated to give up my open fire, but he explained it would be much better for heating. After he told me the stove would have a window where I could still see the fire, I agreed. I knew having a more efficient heat source would certainly be the better choice. Of course, there was also the small fact that it was *his* house, and therefore his choice to make, not mine. But it was so kind – and so Irish – of him to ask my preference.

Michael calculated the job would take a few days. I mentioned I'd been thinking of maybe going to Galway, taking a short winter break – more towards my effort at breaking out of the doldrums – and wondered if it might be a good time to go. He thought it was a grand idea since there would be much dust and disruption.

As he was leaving, he asked about my immigration status.

'I still haven't heard anything,' I said. 'It's been two months since I sent in the appeal.'

He shook his head, muttering 'Those f—ers!' It seemed to be the universal response to my immigration status– and I had to agree.

With a 'Mind yerself, Janie,' the last thing he always said to me in parting, he was gone, soot and all.

◉

While Michael worked on my chimney and installed the wood stove, I took off for a few days in Dublin and Galway. Even without the chimney problem, it was time to get out and about. A change of scene would be good for me and help squelch the last of the winter blues and get my mind off my immigration problems.

In keeping with the good weather luck I so often had when traveling in Ireland, the storms ceased for a few days and the weather wasn't bad at all considering it was late January. In Dublin the sun was shining. After dumping my bag in my hotel room across from the beautiful 12th century Christ Church

Cathedral, I went back outdoors to shake out my train legs, and headed for the nearby River Liffey, the bells of Christ Church ringing out in the clear air. A walk along the Liffey is always a part of any trip to Dublin for me and that day the weather was perfect for it, bright and crisp, the mirror-like surface of the water reflecting perfect images of the clouds and tall buildings.

Over the next two days I went shopping, caught a few tunes in the hotel's pub, heard more music in Temple Bar, and spent a fun evening out with my friend Ciara going to dinner and a movie.

Two days later I hopped aboard the train in busy Heuston Station bound for Galway, stashed my case and settled into my seat. I reached into my pocket to make sure I had enough euros at hand to buy a cup of tea when the snack cart came down the aisle. You can't ride the train in Ireland and not have a cup of tea; it just wouldn't seem right.

I like traveling by train across Ireland. The rolling hills and green fields, trees, cows and sheep streak by the windows like a movie on fast forward. The stops at the stations along the way, sometimes dripping with rain, other times bathed in sunshine, are perfect places for people watching.

Three and a half hours after leaving Dublin the train pulled into the Galway station and I walked the short distance to my hotel at the end of cobblestoned, pedestrian Shop Street, on the banks of the River Corrib. Looking out the window of my room over the racing, frothing river I could have been in the stateroom of a ship at sea. I settled my things and returned outdoors for a closer look at the river. Swollen with the recent heavy rains, it was a gushing torrent close to spilling over the banks. It thundered under the nearby bridge, crashing and churning violently where it met the wide bridge supports, but its rush to Galway Bay was in no way slowed. It was fascinating, even a little frightening, to see the power of it. I tried to capture it in both still shots and video, but knew it was one of those 'you had to be there' things.

I walked along the river toward the sea, my head bent against the brisk wind blowing away the last of the clouds, setting the sun free to blaze in the Galway blue sky. Galway, that city so filled with color, music and energy, never disappoints me. I'm content to wander along the cobblestone pedestrian streets, in and out of brightly painted shops and pubs, listen to street musicians, and just enjoy the upbeat vibe.

On my second day I spent a windy and rainy afternoon taking advantage of the luxury of that warm room with its river view, flat screen TV, hot water at the ready, and lovely clean towels I didn't have to launder and hang outside to dry.

One night in my favorite music pub, Tig Cóilí's, a session was in full swing, different musicians drifting in and out of the pub. Like a walk along the River Liffey in Dublin, an evening at Tig Cóilí's was a must in Galway.

Throughout the evening there were various cries for 'Quiet!' while a patron or two broke into song when the musicians took a break. It was rare anyone other than unsuspecting tourists continued to talk during these solo offerings. Galwegians, even those who've indulged in too many pints, respect their musicians.

One of the session musicians was a young woman from Tennessee, an excellent vocalist and fiddle player. After one set we began chatting after I told her I was enjoying the music. She was bubbling with excitement to be in Ireland, her first visit, taking part in a session. I easily recognized a fellow dreamer.

There was an older guy who swept in from the street, a regular I later learned, his long black coat and black hat reminding me of Bob Dylan. He pulled his guitar out of the case and hopped up on a chair, singing unique renditions of Simon & Garfunkel songs and Eagles' tunes. He also recited poetry and gave loud, passionate rhyming speeches about a woman locked up in prison in Limerick for political activism. He never removed his hat or his coat and when he finished his performance, he departed with the same dramatic swish with which he'd arrived.

And then there was Luke. 'Give us a tune, Luke!' someone cried. The pub patrons took up the chant. 'Luke! – Luke! – Luke!' A handsome young man with dark curly hair stood behind the bar, his white apron confirming the fact that he was the bartender if you hadn't figured that out from his location. The sheepish expression on his face confirmed that he was Luke. 'Luke! – Luke! – Luke!' the chants grew louder, but Luke ignored them and carried on with his duties behind the bar, dark eyes unreadable, pulling pints, running the cash register, wiping up spills.

The chanting was unrelenting and eventually, Luke gave in. He put down his bar towel, removed his apron, came out from behind the bar, and made his way to the musicians' corner. He made no show of it; he just sat down, picked up someone's guitar, started playing, and began to sing. 'Bee's Wing' is an exquisitely beautiful tune, and it was made more so by Luke's rendering of it. His voice was mesmerizing. The music found its way into my heart as easily and gently as early morning mist drifts across the Irish fields. As if the evening had not been special enough, there was bartender Luke with the voice of an angel who, with just one song, made me fall in love with him, never mind he was thirty years younger.

◎

My Dublin-Galway break was what I needed. I arrived back in Kenmare refreshed, with a much brighter attitude. I found my wood stove installed – and wonder of wonders, a small brown envelope with the tell-tale harp insignia imprinted on the front in black ink. Surely it was the long-awaited letter from INIS in response to my November appeal. Like the interminable wait for water to boil if you stand and watch it, I had just needed to take my focus off of receiving that letter.

I picked up the envelope, turning it over in my hands, trying to stay calm, but unable to keep my heart from pounding. My first instinct was to rip it open, but then I hesitated. If it was bad news, I didn't want to know. But that was silly, I had to find out. I opened the envelope and extracted the letter. I slowly and carefully unfolded it, my jaw clenched. *'Please, please, please!'* I silently repeated the wish with fervor, as if I had any power to change the decision already made. My world shrank down to me and that piece of paper.

My eyes squinted at the print trying in some way to see, yet not see. I steeled myself, took a deep breath and held it, then started reading. The first sentence said it all. I had *permission to stay* in

Ireland for the next twelve months. Permission to stay! The held breath escaped, and along with it, the endless weeks of tension and worry. What a homecoming gift!

I laughed out loud at myself, knowing my mind games over maybe wanting to leave Ireland were just that. As soon as I read the letter I never considered for a second whether I would leave or stay. All those questions and doubts melted away like the last patch of snow in winter. No springtime magic was necessary. Ireland wanted me! Small, shapeless, and boring Plan B for returning to the States could sit for considerably longer.

I couldn't have ordered a better scenario for my homecoming. Well, I guess if I'd had a *choice*, in my improved version I would have brought home an older (but only slightly) Luke who would have grinned when he read the letter from Immigration, hugged a younger and prettier me, and twirled me around the room. He would have sat by my fire and composed tender love songs when it was cold and walked with me among the wildflowers when it was warm. He would have smiled at me often, and sang to me whenever I asked, and sometimes when I didn't. He'd promise never to leave, and I would somehow know he never would...

A girl can dream at any age.

22

WHAT'S IN A NAME?

February 18, 2014: Today's my Dad's 88th birthday. I was thinking about the many names he's known by. Some call him by his first name, Charles, others call him Chuck or Charlie and some know him by his middle name. Got me to thinking about the unusual nicknames in Ireland.

It took ages before I stopped wondering about 'The New Shop.' I heard it mentioned several times but could never find it. I figured by the time I finally did, it certainly wouldn't be new anymore. Good prices, nice clothes – but where is it?

One day I learned the actual name of the place is 'Nolan's.' It has only been there for fifty some years, so it's still called 'the new shop.' In the grand scheme of things I suppose it *is* new when compared to the ancient ruins around every corner. Likewise, if someone refers to the New Road, it's necessary to clarify if they're talking about the cleverly named street by that name (again, it is newish compared to many others), or the more recently constructed road which likely has a name, but is also known as the new road, and probably always will be.

Rumor has it that the New Shop is going out of business. One wonders if the new business taking its place will be known as the New New Shop. Or maybe the Really New Shop?

One weekend when Michael's brother, Colin, and Clare were in town, I invited them over along with Noreen and Paudie. Colin told a story he recalled from his childhood. It was tricky enough to keep up because of the accent, but because of all the characters involved I was having an extra hard time.

'And there was Smawl-lan, walking down the road...'

'Excuse me,' I interrupted. 'Did you say 'Smawl-lan'?' It sounded a strange Irish name to me.

He politely stopped and nodded, 'Yes. Smawl-lan.'

'Oh. That was her name?'

'Well, we called her that. Small Anne. She was a small woman, you know.'

No one was amused because it wasn't anything unusual to them; it made perfect sense. Not so accustomed to the rife nicknaming of folks, I thought it was hilarious, but squelched my desire to burst out laughing.

The use of nicknames isn't something foreign to me, but the extent to which they are used in Ireland takes it to another level. The surname 'O'Sullivan' in County Kerry makes names like 'Smith' or 'Jones' in America seem uncommon. O'Sullivans are everywhere in Kerry. There are other common surnames, too, depending on the area. It was only natural for a system to develop which helps distinguish one family from another. Thus, the surname nickname was born.

The hair salon I go to, Morgan's, isn't the surname of either of the sisters who own the salon, nor of their niece. They don't know how or when the nickname started, but doubtless generations back. To further complicate things, the niece's brother, Sean, is known by yet another name. He is Sean Christy (his father's name) Michael (his grandfather's name). There are dozens upon dozens of John Joe Paddys and Michael John Joes and similar names. I had assumed the middle name was actually a middle name, and the third name was a surname, not realizing it was a double surname nickname – sometimes. There's always a chance it actually is someone with three given names preceding their surname. Did I mention it can be confusing?

Michael and his family are O'Sullivans, but everyone knows them as 'Parkers.' It seems when Daniel was a young man he came upon two men struggling to move a large heavy rock. They pushed and strained and sweated, but no luck, it wouldn't budge. Daniel approached, picked up the rock, and moved it.

'Ah, yer' strong as Parker!' exclaimed one of the men.

Parker was a well-known weightlifter/strongman at the time. From thereon, that particular O'Sullivan family was known as the Parkers. At least that's how the story goes.

And this nickname business isn't just casual and frivolous, it's serious. When I place an order for the oil truck to come fill my tank, I need only say I live next to the Parkers. Saying I live next to the O'Sullivans would be of no assistance whatsoever as that would cover a large part of the town, including a number of households on my street.

To further confuse things, sometimes the 'O' is dropped from a name. Noreen and her husband are O'Learys, but her husband is often called 'Paudie Leary.' I don't know why; I don't think he does, either. Even Noreen sometimes calls him that, when she doesn't call him by yet another nickname, Sweetie. I don't mean when she speaks directly to him as in, 'Is it time to leave, sweetie?' No, I mean when she is speaking *about* him, as in, 'Is that Sweetie I see coming down the street?' I suspected for a long time she was being funny, but I wasn't sure, so never dared laugh even though it tickled me every time. It took about a year before I could better read (but not always) the particular twinkle in her eyes that signaled humor.

Noreen entered my name as 'Jane Parker' in her mobile phone. She couldn't remember my surname and I live near the O'Sullivan Parkers and rent a cottage from one of them, so why not? When she told me I thought she was surely kidding and I laughed. On that occasion she wasn't; she was serious.

One of the O'Sullivan Parkers has me listed in her phone as 'Jane Kenmare.'

In the future someone might ask, 'Remember Jane Fadely?' and there will likely be no recognition until, with luck, someone remembers, 'Oh, do you mean Jane Parker?' And then someone else wonders, 'Wait – is that the same woman as Jane Kenmare? *That American Woman?*' There may indeed be some confusion, but eventually, when the fog clears, there might be at least one who will remark, 'Oh, yes. I remember. She was *That American Woman* who lived here for a while.'

23

SPRING APPROACHES

March 3, 2014: It's been a tough winter and I am ready for spring!

The fire burned cheerfully and beef stew simmered on the now familiar hob. On that particular afternoon the rain was being very Irish and falling as described in the old Irish blessing, 'softly on the fields.' It was also falling on the streets, and the rooftops, and on everything else not under cover.

Earlier in the day, Noreen stopped in for a visit. Spring was close, so close we could almost feel it. We took warmth from the fire, but like nearly everyone else we were wishful enough about spring that we found ourselves talking about spring things. We talked of spring cleaning, flowers and planting, what would grow well in containers and what would not. Noreen suggested my concrete garden wall would look nice painted.

'Do you think so?' I asked.

'Oh, 'twould look lovely!' she said with conviction.

It seemed a grand idea. We discussed preparation, sealer, and paint. Noreen said I'd need a couple of weeks of dry weather. Dry weather? A couple of weeks of the stuff?? At first I thought she was joking. Ireland and dry weather weren't often used in the same sentence. But she wasn't laughing and although I checked closely I didn't see any hint of humor in her eyes.

'Wouldn't one day do it?' I asked.

'Oh no,' she said, 'You would need time to let it dry!'

'Noreen. This is Ireland. We're waiting for two weeks without rain??!' I was practically apoplectic.

There was a pause and then she said, 'Well, we had some dry weather *last* summer!'

I laughed. She looked at me blank-faced, then apparently realizing the absurdity of her statement, she began to laugh, too. And that was the end of that particular discussion of springtime, painting, and Irish weather.

The next day on my way back from the post office, I was lost in thought and not taking much notice of anything around me. Half-heartedly trying to assess the probability of rain before I reached home, I glanced up at the sky. Thank goodness for my curiosity. A glorious, bright, intensely hued rainbow, so large and so near it seemed I should have been able to reach out and touch it, arched across the sky. The still snow-covered hills shimmered through the rainbow's colorful translucence, adding to the perfection of the scene. I hated to leave it to dash inside for my camera, but I did. When I returned it was gone, slipping away quietly to wherever rainbows go in their down time. I would have to wait for the next one, and remember to always look up.

◘

A few weeks later on a day that looked as though it was going to extend the four day pattern of sunshine without a drop of rain (was Noreen on to something when she'd talked about two weeks of dry weather??), I decided to paint my garden wall. If it rained, it rained. Surely I'd been in Ireland long enough to realize one doesn't hold off on doing things in hopes of good weather.

I didn't use special outdoor paint, just leftover interior paint Liz had given me, but she convinced me, what did I have to lose? She was right. I'd only be out some free paint and a few hours of work.

The warmth and softness of the air when I stepped outside was surprising. It was wonderful, the kind of day that made you want to just stop, stand, and experience. But there was painting to be done.

While I painted, the birds sang with enthusiasm, sharing my pleasure in the rise in temperature, and I heard voices in the distance I'd never noticed. It was usually so quiet. It must have been because everyone was outdoors gardening, walking, visiting with neighbors, playing with their children, and soaking up the sunshine, luxuriating in the gift of the faux-spring day.

Noreen's idea was a brilliant one. Painting the wall made such a difference. It looked far better than before, much nicer and brighter than the drab gray of the unfinished concrete. I hoped it might last at least through the summer. I planted some bulbs in the ground just above the wall, hoping the chickens wouldn't find them. I could picture how pretty it would look when they bloomed, a row of orange poppies framing the top of the white wall.

Before the painting and planting, I'd made a pot of split pea and bacon soup and left it to simmer on the stove. I went inside to check on it, and when I went back outdoors to do a little paint touch-up, I saw Liz happily working away in her garden. Her husband Frank was in town for a visit so was probably with her father so she could have a break and enjoy the fresh air and sunshine.

She stopped working as soon as she saw me and with a wave and a smile came down the hillside and over to the garden wall. I put down my paint brush and she put down her trowel, and we stood and chatted, relishing the feel of the warm sun.

'How's your dad doing?'

'Oh, he's okay. It's just so hard for him because he's so independent. He wants to do everything himself.' She rolled her eyes and smiled, showing both her admiration and frustration.

'Yeah, that must be tough – for both of you. How's Frank?'

'He's fine. He's watching football with Dad. Isn't the weather just lovely?' She tilted her head back and closed her eyes.

'It sure is! I can't believe how warm it is all of a sudden!'

One of Michael's hens appeared, scratching along the hillside.

'Are those hens digging up your flowers?!'

They had in fact dug up much of what had earlier been planted, but I didn't want to complain about it. The pansies she'd put in soon after I'd moved in had fallen victim in a matter of days.

'Well, yes, but I've learned to use containers for most stuff instead of putting everything into the ground. That seems to be the ticket. I've just put some bulbs in the ground, though, so we'll see what happens! But I like the hens – Michael told me they eat the slugs and snails!' That bit of information had instantly made me an even bigger fan of those chickens.

She rolled her eyes again and we both laughed.

'Will we go for tea tomorrow?' she asked.

'Sure, let's do that! What time do you think?' I knew setting a specific time wasn't the Irish way, but I always tried.

'Maybe after I've made Dad's dinner – around two-ish?' I'd heard '-ish' tacked onto times so frequently by then I was beginning to use it myself.

'Great! Just come on over when you can get away and we'll go.'

She nodded and took off her gardening gloves.

I remembered the soup on the stove. 'Hey – I made soup! If you'll bring a pot over I'll give you some.'

I assured her it was more than I could possibly eat, and there was plenty to feed myself and all of them. I have a bad habit of not measuring when I cook because I don't often use recipes. That's why I like making things like soup. Just use whatever ingredients you wish! But it means I never know how much I'll end up with and, more often than not, it's too much.

'If you're sure you have enough that would be lovely! Dad doesn't usually like soup, but he had some the last time you made it and thought it was nice!' Nice was almost as good as gorgeous so I was flattered.

Liz ran off and returned with a pot. I filled it up with hot soup and she set it on the freshly painted, now dry, wall while we continued to chat. The soup cooled along with the late afternoon air and by the time we both noticed the chill, the sun was setting, the temperature had dropped significantly, and the fog had rolled in and settled in the hills. Evening was about to be upon us; it was time to go indoors. Liz set off with the soup and a wave of her hand, leaving her garden gloves on the wall, perhaps in the hope she'd be able to return the next day to spend more time working in her garden.

'Bye! See you tomorrow about two-ish!' I called, my words leaving small puffs of frosty clouds in the air.

It had been the simplest of days but somehow perfect. Beautiful sunshine, a bit of painting and planting, soup made and shared, a fresh new garden wall, and a long chat with a good neighbor and friend. Life was treating me pretty well in County Kerry, so it was.

回

The painting of my garden wall inspired me. Michael painted my front room before I moved in, but I'd never been fond of the color I thought of as 'hospital green.' With his permission, I decided to repaint. I'd have a painting party! It would be fun, wouldn't it?. My American friends, Bob and Rose, agreed to help as did Noreen.

I arose early on painting day to be ready for my crew. I made sandwiches for later, moved the furniture into the middle of the room and covered it, took the pictures off the walls, and rolled up the rug. Bob and Rose arrived mid-morning, bringing lots of enthusiasm and energy. Bob brought his own special edging brush and bucket, along with floor tarps, miscellaneous tools, and extra paint.

While they finished unloading I turned on the music, playing the special mix I'd put together just for painting. A little trad, a little folk, a little rock & roll. Just something to help keep the blood pumping, jazz up an otherwise tiresome task, and promote a party mood.

We went to work on the walls. There were several small areas where I had attempted to hang pictures using that sticky putty stuff to avoid making holes in the walls, not realizing they were concrete. The putty had been ineffective and had damaged the paint. It stuck for hours or days, then the paint beneath it blistered and the putty fell off, lifting the bubble of paint along with it. It was suggested we'd need to buff up those places before painting.

Using sandpaper and a light touch seemed to be the ticket, but my fellow Americans suggested a wire brush would be the better choice. Under normal conditions, I'm sure it might have been. Here, all it did was increase the problem, causing larger and larger areas of paint to pull away from the wall. What started as dime-sized spots became areas as big as dinner plates, sometimes larger. The more we scraped, the more paint was lifted. It was like a bad dream. A very bad dream. Soon we were using our fingers to pull sheets of paint off the walls as easily as peeling a banana. Instead of several small spots, the areas needing treatment were vastly increasing. There were huge sections of bare wall with more paint just waiting to be peeled. It was dreadful. The mood was going downhill fast and was no one's idea of a party, music or no music.

I had to do something to change direction as the direction we were going looked like a much longer route than I'd planned. I suggested we stop buffing the areas needing treatment and just start painting, deal with it the best we could. It didn't have to be perfect.

Bob felt it was mandatory we continue with the paint removal and Rose agreed. They were certain the new paint would not adhere to the walls in their untreated condition. I knew there was every possibility they were correct, but I couldn't imagine the enormity of the task trying to remove all the paint from the walls. I hadn't planned on a two or three day job, which it was threatening to become.

I made an executive decision. We would stop peeling, do very light buffing, and slap the paint on. If it stayed on the walls, great – and if not, I'd paint again another time.

My helpers, more experienced it seemed than I in the world of painting, weren't happy with my decision, but they proved their friendship by sticking with me. We took a brief tea break and ate the sandwiches I'd prepared that morning. I phoned my other crew member, Noreen, wondering where she was and learned she had several other duties to attend to that day and couldn't come until later. Of course. I should have known. Noreen with an entirely free day to do as she pleased wasn't the Noreen I knew.

Lunch finished, we continued on with the 'party.' After *gentle* sanding, *light* scraping, and peeling only when it was impossible to avoid, we got down to the painting bit.

Bob had a fiddle lesson that afternoon so soon after the actual painting started, they had to leave. Where once there'd been three painters, there was only one, surrounded by open buckets and pans of paint, and rollers and brushes laden with paint. I either had to get that paint onto the walls, or pour it back into the original buckets, then clean the rollers and brushes. One or the other was a must, otherwise I would be left with dried up paint and ruined equipment. I opted for continuing the job and painted as fast as I was able.

By the time Noreen arrived, I'd managed to cover two-thirds of the wall space. I was excited over the progress. With Noreen's help, in no time at all we'd be ready to start the second coat.

Moments after Noreen began painting, Bob and Rose returned from the fiddle lesson. They were convinced a second coat couldn't be applied until the next day. I knew they just wanted to make sure the job was done correctly, but I assured them, with Noreen's support, that the walls were almost dry and ready for a second coat. I then persuaded them to return home since I had Noreen there to help and they'd already put in a hard half-day. I knew they were tired, not only of the painting, but likely of my failure to heed their undoubtedly good advice. I bid them farewell and sent them home with a bag of sweets, some of Paudie's famous timber, and expressions of gratitude.

Disagreements settled, decisions made, shifts changed, and hours of painting behind me, I was beat. It was only seven o'clock but I'd been up since very early that morning. The physical labor and the alarm and tension over the peeling walls had exhausted me. I needed a break. I made the mistake of sitting down, putting my feet up, and opening a Guinness. Noreen insisted I stay there while she kept painting. She was a virtual whirlwind, which did not in the least surprise me. Looking back it's hard to believe, but I was tired enough to do as she said. I continued to sit while we visited and she finished up the last area I'd been working on, then painted the entire second coat in less than two hours. She could paint nearly as fast as she could talk. Her energy was incredible. Now and then I offered to jump in, but she would not hear of it. The woman knew what she was doing; she was a painting machine. I'd have only been in the way.

Liz stopped in, announcing she was present 'only in a supervisory capacity!' She had spent the day caring for her father, cleaning house and cooking. We laughed, and I offered her a glass of wine and a chair. She accepted both. Minutes later Noreen was finished and while she washed her brush and her hands, I pulled out another chair from the table and poured another glass of wine. The three of us talked and laughed and I told the horror story of the peeling paint.

The music continued and a selection of tunes from the Sixties came on, songs we all remembered. It brought back memories for each of us and we shared tales of the funny and mischievous things we'd done in our teenage years. At eleven o'clock, after a busy and productive day which started with peeling paint and ended with chat and laughter, the ladies took their leave and I went to bed. I was too tired to even look at the newly painted front room.

In the morning, a good night's sleep left me refreshed. It was with pleasure I saw the front room looked refreshed, too. The new cream-colored walls made it lighter, brighter, cozier. The painting party may have initially lacked a bit in the 'party' department, but the job was completed. With luck, that paint would stick around for a while. (Last time I checked, it was clinging to the walls with great tenacity. Sláinte!)

24

AN IRISH BLESSING

March 17, 2014: It's 2 p.m. and I'm dragging. Out 'til the wee hours listening to tunes in the pubs and up very early this morning...

St. Patrick's Day 2014 started for me at five in the morning. I'd long thought spending St. Patrick's Day in the town of Dingle, a place steeped in old traditions, would be a great experience. And so it was, but it involved rising very early in the morning.

I roused myself from my bed at a small B&B by Dingle Bay in what felt like the middle of the night. It was time for the dawn parade. I'd be marching with over one-hundred locals and visitors behind Dingle's Fife & Drum Corps through the streets of Dingle in the dark.

The march dates back to at least the mid-1800's and probably earlier. Under cover of darkness to evade the English landlord's ban against such gatherings, the clever Catholics of Dingle defiantly marched through the streets to mass, honoring St. Patrick in the pre-dawn hours of St. Patrick's Day.

I'd long heard of it, but had never experienced it. It was not as easy to take part as you might imagine. The struggle to get out of bed so early after enjoying the craic and the music in Dingle's many pubs the night before was but the first hurdle. The next step was getting to the assembly point, a car park I believe, although it was too dark to make a positive identification. There, marchers milled around talking in low voices until the first drum beat pierced the darkness. The task then was to step out smartly and follow the Fife & Drum Corps along the uneven pot-holed dark streets without stumbling or stepping on someone's heels, or being stepped upon. The expression, 'It's always darkest before the dawn' is true. Still, winter was behind us and we were blessed with unseasonably warm and dry weather. Everyone was in high spirits.

We marched through town to the steady cadence of the drums and tunes of the fifes, lights flickering on here and there inside homes and B&B's along the way, people emerging from their beds to peer into the darkness as the sound reached them. The lucky ones could actually see the parade – if they lived by a street lamp where yellow pools of light shone on the roadway, or at the end of the route where a hint of daylight filtered through the early morning sky.

Some lounged in ground-level doorways wearing bathrobes and others peered from open second story bedroom windows in their nightclothes to watch the procession and wave, and return greetings called out by some of the marchers. The Fife & Drum Corps did their best to make sure the entire town was awake; I'm certain they succeeded. The drummers drummed with gusto and the fife players trilled out shrill, jaunty tunes. It seemed natural for one's feet to move in rhythm with the Corps.

We neared the nineteenth century stone church, the end point for the march, and the darkness took on a glow around the edges, a glimpse of rosy light and a line of deep blue along the horizon announcing the coming of dawn. The timing was amazing. In his long white robes with a large crucifix around his neck, the priest stood waiting for us under a purple velvet sky on the broad steps of St. Mary's. He raised his hands, blessed the crowd in Irish, and sprinkled us with holy water as dawn broke, the morning sun turning the sky to pale azure blue. The Corps struck up another tune, filed up the steps, and followed the priest into the church for the early St. Patrick's Day mass conducted in Irish.

Later that day it was comical how many times I heard the question, 'Did you get up for the dawn parade?' but I took great pride in being able to answer 'Yes! I did!' It was obvious the locals, whether or not they'd joined the march, were proud of the old tradition.

In the afternoon the regular St. Patrick's Day parade was the main event. Trucks and cars sporting over-sized banners advertising local businesses or politicians crept along, full of waving people tossing candy to spectators or playing music; dancing tea cups twirled with red-bearded leprechauns in giant green hats and riders sat tall on skittish horses; costumed people with costumed dogs skipped behind marching school children, and the staccato beat and lilt of the Fife & Drum Corps pierced the air once more. It was good fun to watch and see everyone enjoying themselves, especially the children, but it was a St. Patrick's Day parade you might have seen in Anytown, USA. It couldn't compare to the experience of the dawn parade.

It may not be something everyone aspires to, but I'm pleased to be a member of what I consider a fairly elite group: Those of us who have marched in the dark with Dingle's Fife & Drum Corps and watched dawn break on St. Patrick's Day as holy water and a priest's blessing in the native tongue of Ireland rained down upon our bowed and humble heads.

It was a great privilege to have taken part in that tradition. It was more than a unique experience, it felt like something that surely must be good for you, too.

On my way back to Kenmare, I gazed out the bus window at the blue sky, the brightening green of the fields, and the new buds emerging on the bushes and trees. Winter was gone, spring was gathering strength, and I was so glad to be living in Ireland.

25

THE IRISH ATTITUDE

March 20, 2014: I love the Irish sense of humor and the sometimes unusual way they look at things. I don't think I'll ever stop being intrigued and entertained.

Describing the Irish as talkative and friendly is common, and true, but far too flat and drab. There is a complexity that goes much deeper than that, a hard to define mix of appreciation for life, optimism, quick wit, an ever-present sense of humor, and fierce independence. Yes, that's a generalization. But when you run into people with those traits as often as I have, generalizing seems appropriate. I thought of it as the *Irish Attitude*.

During my first visit to Ireland I'd noticed the way most people walk on the left, rather than the right. It was the same in Kenmare. I decided to ask Noreen about it; surely she'd know why. I thought maybe since everyone drives on the left side of the road, they walk on the left, too. Was that it?

Noreen snorted at my foolishness and said, 'We walk wherever we want!'

Later that day I realized jaywalking fell into the 'walk wherever we want' category. Except during heavy tourist season, I'd never seen anyone use the crosswalk on Kenmare's main street. There was only one in the entire town. In the beginning I used it unless it wasn't practical because I was too far from it, but even then I stuck with my schoolgirl training and crossed carefully at intersections only.

Noreen and I were window-shopping, midway down the street and a fair distance from both the crosswalk and the street corners. Directly in front of us two garda officers stood in the middle of the road talking to someone; it appeared to be a traffic or parking problem. Noreen grabbed my arm to pull me into the street to cross to a shop on the other side. Traffic wasn't a concern; the streets weren't yet flooded with tourists so a car cruised by only occasionally. But what about the garda? I pulled back, thinking jaywalking right in front of them wasn't the brightest of ideas.

'Isn't jaywalking illegal in Ireland?' I whispered.

'Oh, sure, 'tis!' she nodded, then immediately stepped off the sidewalk into the street.

I hesitated, unsure of whether to follow. I saw that she had stopped right in the center of the road and was *chatting with the garda*. She then continued on to the other side of the street. I couldn't believe what I was seeing. Following her lead I casually crossed the street, giving a polite nod and a smile to the garda officers as I passed them. It was plain the only possible consequence to jaywalking in Kenmare in the off-season would be getting bumped by a slow-moving car. There certainly was no risk of a ticket or arrest for any kind of violation and from thereon I was an avid jaywalker.

Noreen and I finished our afternoon by having a cup of tea. She mentioned she and Paudie were startled awake that morning just after six o'clock when they heard someone come into the house.

'Oh, my gosh! You're kidding!?'

'No, no…' She waved me off and continued. After deciding it was their neighbor, they went back to sleep. *What?* I wondered if I was misunderstanding. When they arose, she said, sure enough, there was their elderly neighbor sitting quietly. They gave her tea and breakfast, then went on about their normal routine. After a bit, the woman got up and wandered away. Noreen stopped talking and sipped her tea, gazing out the window.

'What??' I said. It was an odd story; surely I was missing something. I was getting fairly good at understanding the Kerry accent, but maybe I'd failed this time. 'Weren't you shocked?'

'Oh, no, not a'tall!' She waved the air with her hand. 'It happens all the time!'

I wasn't sure that changed the oddity factor. 'But isn't it frightening to wake up and hear someone in your house?'

She agreed it could be unsettling, but she hated to be inhospitable. They didn't want to ask the 'poor crayter' to stop doing it. She was their neighbor. She caused no harm.

'Why don't you just lock your door?' It seemed blatantly obvious to me it would solve the problem.

'Oh, we never do!'

Obviously it was an Irish hospitality thing that was beyond me.

We finished our tea, Noreen went on to other business, and I walked back home.

There'd been workers on my street for two days, resurfacing the roadway and as I approached my place, I saw they were working very near it. Their bright yellow hats and vests gave them high visibility. There was no one directing traffic, no 'Caution' or 'Men Working' signs, but then it was a quiet street and this was rural Ireland.

As I got closer I saw hot asphalt had just been spread directly in front of my door, blocking my way. What to do?

Standing on the opposite side of the street, I shouted at the closest worker, trying to make myself heard above the noise of the paving machine further up the street. 'Excuse me? That's my house.' I pointed across the street then gestured with open hands, palms up, as though to say 'What shall I do?'

He smiled and shrugged. I wasn't sure if he didn't understand what I was getting at, couldn't hear me, thought I was kidding, or just didn't care. I stood there and waited, hoping one of us might come up with a solution for my safe passage over the hot, sticky surface.

He looked at me, and then at my front door, and then at the road. Then he understood, or gave up on coming up with a solution. He whistled and shouted to the other worker running the paving machine, then waved his arms wildly to get his attention. The rumble of the machine made it impossible for conversation at that distance. Seeing that he'd gained his co-worker's attention, he pointed to me, the road, and my front door, then repeated the sequence.

The worker on the paving machine was amused; he threw his head back and let out what was surely a belly laugh if we could have heard it. He stepped down from the machine and turned to face us. Then, as though standing on a stage, he performed an exaggerated pantomime. Holding his arms bent at the elbow and out from his sides as though walking through waist high water, or holding them above a tutu, he did a few quick and dainty hopping skips on his toes, flashed a wide grin and climbed back onto the paving machine. The first worker turned to me, smiled, and shouted, 'Go quickly!' And so, I did.

◙

A few days later I took the bus to Killarney to do some shopping. On arrival I contemplated which direction I should go to find a particular department store. I didn't really know just where it was. Even though getting directions in Ireland is a little like the time concept – it can be abstract and vague and is perhaps more a reason for conversation than for actual instructional purposes – I decided to take a chance.

I stopped a lady passing by. She was perhaps in her fifties, of small stature, and looked pleasant and approachable. She wore a beige rain coat, had a yellow umbrella under one arm and carried a large matching vinyl tote bag.

As soon as I said, 'Hello! I wonder if -,' she stopped and gave me a quick, bright smile and her full attention. She had a face that looked as though she smiled often. I asked if she could tell me how to get to the store and she seemed very happy to provide the directions I needed, in due time. There was first the mandatory discussion of the weather.

"'Tis a lovely day, isn't it?'

'Yes, it is! I hope the sun stays with us!' I said. We both looked up and squinted our eyes against the brightness of the sun.

'Sure now the rain is gone. We won't be havin' anymore today!' she said with Irish optimism and a huge grin.

I smiled. It seemed it would be not only pointless, but rude, to mention how easily and quickly the Irish weather could change. And not saying anything might help us move on to the topic of directions.

'You've chosen a lovely day to be walking around Killarney!' She raised her face to the sun again and closed her eyes for a moment before looking at me again, still smiling.

'Now, it's directions you're needin', is it? Let's see… if you just go up this street, this one here (gesturing) by the church – see the church?' I nodded, yes, I could see the enormous church directly across the street. 'And turn right at the 'T' and you're nearly there. Just go a ways down past the smaller shops and you'll find it. It's not far.'

That sounded simple enough. I would have liked to know how many blocks, but I knew better than to ask. I thanked her and just as I was about to head out in the described direction I realized she wasn't finished.

'Or, if you wish, you could go through the car park up this way,' she pointed in the same direction as before, but I was unable to see a parking lot, 'and take any lane to your left; that will lead you to the same street.'

This didn't make sense and I was confused, but it felt good that at least I understood the words she'd spoken and hadn't needed to ask her to repeat herself as I so often found myself doing. I smiled, thanked her and decided I'd ask someone else. But she continued.

'Now you can't miss it if you just go up the street - just follow it around until you come to the 'T' – now it's a fair ways up there, but just keep going and when you get there, turn right and you'll see Quills. Go a little further and there you'll be. But really it would be quicker, I'd say, if you cut through the car park,' she again gestured in the same direction, 'and take any lane to your left and you'll come out on the same street.'

I didn't want to point out the inconsistency of going *right* via the street or *left* via the car park and still end up at the same destination… But I decided since she was making such an effort to be helpful I might ask for the street name where the store was located. I figured that would be a good tool to have in my arsenal when I later had to stop and ask someone else for further directions.

'The name of the street? Hm-m-m… you know, I don't know!' she said, and laughed. 'Isn't that funny?'

I smiled as though it was.

'Now I live in Dublin you understand and I'm only here visiting, but I lived here, I did, I lived here for years, and I'm here all the time and you know, I just never noticed the name of the street! Isn't that funny?' She laughed again. 'But you needn't worry. If you just…' and she launched into the two sets of conflicting directions once again, her narrative varying only slightly from the prior recitations.

Well, it was, after all, a nice day for a chat. The rain had indeed passed, the sun was shining in a clear sky, and we both seemed to have time. To my surprise, I found the store by following the first part of her directions and disregarding the alternate route. But isn't it funny? Should anyone ask me, I don't know the name of the street it's on, either. Funnier still, I don't feel the least bit anxious about it.

26

WELLIES & OTHER GREAT INVENTIONS

March 28, 2014: Sunshine continues but it has turned quite cool again!

I'd put it off for many weeks but it could no longer be ignored. The day had come. After breakfast do not turn on the computer, do not leave the house, do not pass go, go directly to jail. I mean kitchen. Go to the kitchen. Go directly to the kitchen!

It was time for The Defrosting of The Fridge, an unpleasant chore, but one I'd allowed to grow to over-blown proportions not only in my mind, but in reality because I'd put it off for so long. I really, *really*, didn't want to do it. But the guilt I was feeling over my procrastination was becoming more disagreeable than the task, so it was time to slay the dragon.

I had no Plan B; I didn't really even have a Plan A. I was venturing into unknown territory. Of course I'd defrosted a freezer before, sometime in the far distant past, but never one buried deep in the tomb of a tiny fridge located at knee level.

Imagine if you can, a woman in her sixties, not particularly slim, after indulging in all the Irish potatoes, bread, and sweets one seems to meet around every corner in Ireland. Her sleeves are rolled up and the front of her shirt is wet. She holds a table knife in one hand and a wooden spatula in the other. She stands in her kitchen, her feet encased in wellies, surrounded by puddles made by melted ice. More chunks of ice float in the puddles. It isn't a dragon she fights, but a more formidable opponent: the dreaded iced-up, defiant, definitely-not-frost-free fridge.

The freezer section of the appliance I called my refrigerator was laughable, about the size of a small shoebox – a child's shoe box. The fridge was made for college students or folks on vacation; it wasn't intended to be used in real life, right? Perhaps. Nevertheless, whatever the intent of the designer, this particular unit landed in a real life scenario – *my* life.

The amount of ice in and around that little freezer section was astounding. It took two and a half hours and nearly more chipping and scraping than I had the strength and stamina to do. The ice had grown and wasn't just coating and filling the freezer, it had morphed into a small glacier (small by glacier standards). It covered the inside wall of the fridge on the side where the freezer was located, and down behind it, and underneath, coating the drip tray which was frozen solid and immoveable. Ice covered all areas that had any proximity to the freezer. Even so, the amount of ice I removed seemed out of proportion to the amount of surface space that existed. I had no idea where it all came from. Slaying a dragon would probably have been quicker and easier, although a wooden spoon and a table knife wouldn't have been my weapons of choice.

In the end, the fridge was ice-free, the kitchen floor was flooded, the sink was packed with frozen food and chipped ice, and the rest of the refrigerator contents were in a box outside during what remained of a cold dry spell. Everything cleaned up and returned to its rightful place, I calculated that I had at least maybe a week or so, before the iceberg would begin to form again. All part of the craic of living in a nineteenth century Irish cottage.

I think the saying, 'the greatest thing since sliced bread' really ought to be 'the greatest thing since frost-free freezers'!

I was, once again, thankful for those wellies, but I knew if I ever got a frost-free fridge, that might just be the possession that trumped the wellies.

◙

Liz came over during the ice clearing and was appalled at what I was having to do. A few weeks later, on her suggestion, Michael took pity on me and bought a new frost-free, nearly full-size refrigerator for the cottage. I was thrilled – and did not have to come up with a Plan B for fridge defrosting because slaying the ice dragon would never be on my chore list again. As much as I liked that new fridge, and oh, I most certainly did, after much consideration the wellies retained their place of greatest invention and most valuable possession.

27

CHANGE IS IN THE AIR

April 19, 2014: The evidence of spring is everywhere and we'll soon be in full bloom in County Kerry!

The abundant sunshine of March continued and brought little doubt we were on the edge of springtime. And then one morning in early April I awoke to find spring had arrived in all its glory; it was everywhere. Flowers bloomed, winter's dormant ivy rejuvenated itself and while still cool, the air had a noticeable softness. There was a chill in the evening worthy of a good fire, but the days were filled with sunshine and the hint of warmth.

Throughout the terrible winds, heavy rains and freezes of the winter the violas I'd planted in my window box shortly after arriving in Ireland never stopped blooming, so they became my flower of choice. I planted more of them in pots and on the hillside above my garden wall, on either side of where I'd earlier planted the poppy bulbs. As I settled the violas into their new home I was excited to see tiny green shoots poking their heads above the rocky ground – the poppies were sprouting; they'd survived the hens!

One pretty day I was tending to my container garden when I saw Michael on the hilltop. He was wielding a hoe, working to get the soil ready for planting. We started talking about the weather and how nice it was to see everything beginning to bloom. At one point he fell silent, tipped his head back, eyes closed, face toward the sun, and sighed. I was learning this was a favorite position of the Irish when the sun shone. I suspected one day I might well be doing the same thing.

'Someday,' Michael said, 'I'm just going to sit up here and read a book.'

I told him he ought to do that and reminded him there's no time like the present.

He laughed and said 'Ah, can't do it, Janie. Can't stop moving,' and smiling, bent over his hoe again, turning his attention back to the earth and the task at hand.

回

About a week later I set out for a late morning walk, full of enthusiasm for the bright spring day. I was surprised to find the air temperature finally agreeing with the calendar. Up to that point it had not been warm enough to go without a jacket. On that day, in a bold move, I removed my jacket for the first time that season. The freedom from the confines of outerwear made walking a different experience. It reminded me of being at Girl Scout summer camp, one of several giggling nine-year-old girls shedding our clothes at the water's edge and plunging into the lake for the first skinny-dipping of the summer, the glorious freedom of swimming naked at dusk, the water smooth and silky against my skin.

I felt light as I strolled along Kenmare's sidewalks. I took long deep breaths of the spring air, the clean smell of freshly cut grass and the light perfume of wildflowers adding a sweetness to it, its softness caressing my face as lightly as the gentle touch of a lover. The fragrance and feel of the warm air was glorious, but I was distracted by another change. Something had happened to the sidewalks and the streets. Something was different, and it wasn't just the air temperature.

With the coming of spring, so, too, came the tourists. In droves. I'd been told it would happen, but I wasn't prepared for it. It started around St. Patrick's Day, but it was just a small trickle, not enough to have much of an impact. But during Easter week it appeared the floodgates had opened. The streets of Kenmare were no longer mine.

The wide quiet sidewalks and empty streets were gone. I could no longer step out into the street and cross with little need of more than a quick glance for oncoming cars. I could no longer walk wherever I wanted at whatever pace I chose. The sidewalks had narrowed, filled with people and dogs; the streets were suddenly owned by a steady stream of vehicles and cyclists. Caution was required. Great caution. Gone were the days of easy strolling, the kind you could almost do with your eyes closed.

Change wasn't just in the air and on the streets, it was in the color of Kenmare. Green was on a rampage, decimating the brown of winter, and flowers didn't just bloom, they rioted – in gardens and window boxes, hedgerows and hanging baskets, and with robust enthusiasm from tiny fissures in rock walls. Wherever they could take root wild daisies, daffodils, and bluebells flourished. Rhododendrons bloomed, violas, geraniums, and petunias spilled from pots.

A picture of spring had been painted with a full palette of colors and it was a masterpiece. In shades ranging from pale to bright, the blooming colors mingled with the greens of the grass, ivy, moss and trees, the gray of the old stone walls, the bright yellow sunshine, and the white of the wispy clouds in a sky so blue you could get lost in it if you gazed at it for too long.

In accompaniment to the color and warmth, birdsong arose in a chorus. Birds who could sing warbled their songs with clear, perfect pitch, and those who could not trilled their cry with more sweetness and certainty, overpowering the haunting, harsh voices of the rooks and jackdaws, and disrupting their domination of the telephone wires and tall evergreens where they'd once gathered in winter, sulking and scolding.

People, cars, cyclists and happy dogs wandered their way through the scene, blending with it and creating a day that can surely be found pictured in the 'S' volume of an encyclopedia under 'Spring,' subheading 'Spring Comes to a Small Town in Ireland.' And there, if you look closely, you will see me in the corner, just as I reach the outskirts of town, on the sidewalk next to the stone wall where tiny purple flowers snuggle in the soft moss and curling ivy, dressing the old wall in handsome Easter finery.

Soaking up the sunshine and spring beauty, I thought again of how lucky I was to live in such a place, while most of those I was sharing 'my' sidewalks and streets with would have but a short time to enjoy it. I once was one of those tourists. It was still strange to me, even after several months, that I was a settled-in resident of Kenmare. How could I begrudge visitors some space? I couldn't, of course. It was time I acted like a more responsible and generous citizen of Kerry the Kingdom.

28

FROM THE PIG'S BACK

April 28, 2014: What a fantastic music-filled weekend! I was in hog heaven!

Kenmare's traditional music festival, Féile Neidín, is a weekend long event. Musicians gather for sessions in the pubs, buskers young and old appear on street corners, and dance, music and instrument making workshops are held. Despite the less than ideal, gray, damp weather that descended on us that weekend, people flocked to town and there was a festival vibe in the air.

My proximity to town and all the events made it easy to wander about, coming and going as often as I wished. I had no worries with parking or any of the other logistics involved for those who lived out of town. Heaven!

Music in the pubs is not unusual for Kenmare, but this was on a larger scale and one didn't have to wait until ten o'clock at night as is so often the custom in Ireland. The tunes started mid-afternoon Friday and continued on until late Sunday night.

At one lively session with friends Bob and Rose, we were lucky enough to find a table near the musicians, a real treat given the full-house conditions at most of the pubs. Fiddles and guitars were plucked and tuned and minutes later the jigs and reels filled the pub and drifted out into the street; fiddles, Irish accordions, bodhráns, concertinas, pipes, banjos, and whistles rising and falling, tickling our ears and commanding our feet to tap the floor. It was wonderful and we couldn't stop smiling.

After one especially rousing set a local man who was standing near our table leaned over to us and with a wide grin said, 'You've landed on the pig's back!' We returned his smile and politely nodded (as one becomes accustomed to doing when you are not Irish and either cannot understand the words being spoken to you or are unfamiliar with a particular expression, as in this case). It took a minute before we realized that the expression was akin to 'hog heaven' and no time at all to decide it was an expression worthy of adoption.

All weekend the music went on, weaving along with the locals and the visitors through the streets and pubs of Kenmare. Afternoons and early evenings found entire families in the pubs, even some of the youngest entranced with the music, the instruments and the musicians. I watched and listened, too, as fiddlers fiddled, wielding their bows, coaxing spirited, quick tunes from their fiddles, then melting into melodies soft and sweet; the occasional beat of a bodhrán, strum of a guitar, and trill of a tin whistle joining in here and there, and the unique mellow sound of Irish accordions blending with the other instruments. Occasional mournful fiddle solos and sean nós (old style) singing touched the heart, bringing even the loudest and most talkative pub patrons to silence and sometimes moving all to tears, or at least the threat thereof.

The ever-elusive, enchanting and complex uilleann pipes appeared on Sunday night along with a sighting of the actor John C. Reilly and excited rumors that Colin Farrell was also drifting about somewhere in town, both in Kenmare to film their new movie, 'The Lobster.'

Those lucky enough to have bought a ticket attended the Liam Ó Maonlaí concert at the Carnegie, in my opinion the jewel in the crown of the festival. Having some familiarity with his music, I was already a fan and bought my ticket confident I'd enjoy the show. And, oh, I did. Mr. Ó Maonlaí's performance was spectacular and the intimate setting of the small one-hundred and forty seat local theater enhanced the experience.

Barefoot, he walked onto the stage and sang and played. He sang in Irish. He sang in English. He sang blues and traditional Irish and folk and world music. He played guitar, bodhrán, harp, banjo and kalimba, and he played the piano like I've never heard it played before. He caressed, cajoled, pounded and tickled those keys making it sing like a living thing.

He sang a rousing rendition of 'Kansas City' as though born to the blues in a little shack the other side of the railroad tracks in Memphis. He sang a couple of Mali tunes as he plucked his kalimba and we were transported to a tiny dusty African village where children laughed and played in the sunshine, and he sang 'Lakes of Ponchartrain' and 'Saudh Ni Buruinnealadh' like no one else does.

He interacted with the audience by explaining some of the Irish song lyrics and joining in a bit of banter in Irish with some who spoke the language. He had us humming rhythmically on a few tunes at his command, teasing us into thinking maybe we were special, different than other audiences; maybe we had a tiny but precious connection to the performance and the man.

He whistled and whispered, cracked jokes and crooned, hummed and hollered, sang and smiled and shared, a pink scarf around his neck, his curly hair falling over his forehead and into his eyes, one bare foot slapping against the stage in rhythm with the music, living in his own intricate world of beautiful lyrics, feelings, melody and rhythm – while we watched his heart and soul and talent in admiration and enchantment, maybe even a little envy, knowing we were seeing but a glimpse of his complex world, and feeling privileged to see it.

The concert ended with a standing ovation and Liam Ó Maonlaí bowing deeply several times before exiting the stage on his silent bare feet with a wave and one last smile.

The man at the pub was right: I had indeed landed on the pig's back. The weekend had danced and flowed with people and pints, tunes and tea, conversation and laughter. It was enough to make me giddy, and it did. It was a feast for my soul, and I dined with gusto.

Walking home late Sunday night I looked up at the clear and moonless sky studded with winking stars. It was beautiful, the icing on the weekend's cake. I started counting my blessings until I realized there was no need: I had only to look up. They surely numbered as many as the stars that glittered in that beautiful Irish sky.

29

THE PIED PIPER OF KENMARE

May 2, 2014: The craic was mighty at the pub last night! Good chat and laughs with Kieran and a funny encounter with an entertaining writer from New Zealand.

One evening I was having a pint and a chat with my house-painter friend, Kieran. He'd been giving me an animated and interesting synopsis of a novel he'd just finished reading, a story set in World War I, when we were brought back to the present time by the entrance of a friend of his.

Ned was youngish, tall, with dark eyes framed in black spectacles, and a baseball hat compressing his curly dark hair, bits of it sticking out in the back and on the sides. He was from New Zealand, in Kenmare on an extended holiday, waiting for his book to come out. A book, huh? My writer's ears perked up like those of a guard dog on alert. Ned was charming and funny so even without the publishing a book bit I was intrigued.

Ned was an enthusiastic talker and launched into a number of stories, but after he used up some of his nervous energy he wound down enough to be able to sit down and have an actual conversation.

I learned he was a burned-out former science teacher. He told me his first novel was due for release in a few more months and he was in Ireland writing and doing research for his next book. When he learned I like to write he asked me what I'd been working on. I told him about a few pieces and mentioned a blog I wrote for friends and family about my time in Ireland. He was interested in hearing more about the blog, wondering if it could be turned into a marketable book.

Ned seemed to bubble over with things to say, his enthusiasm spilling over onto his audience, his sense of humor ever-present. He was also a good and thoughtful listener. He was another one who made me laugh – and that was how our friendship began. That evening turned out to be a precursor to a fun and different summer, a time when, for some reason, I stepped outside myself more than I normally do, and lived a sort of second young adulthood, a unique experience for someone at the age of almost sixty-five.

Ned offered to take a look at some of my writing and in the coming days sent me excerpts from his book to help me decide if he was worthy of judging my work. I was most impressed. It gave me more confidence in his critiquing skills, but less confidence in my own writing skills. Still, perhaps there was something I could learn from him. In any case, I couldn't think of a single reason not to develop a friendship with Ned. Even if it led to no assistance with writing, who among us can have too many kind friends who make us laugh?

In the weeks to come I realized everyone knew him, or so it seemed. In a few short months he had become something of a local celebrity. He was a pied piper, especially with the females. His sense of humor, kindness and quirkiness came together in just the right way. The baseball cap he was never without, except on colder days when it was replaced with a knit hat, covered most of his wild curly hair but didn't hide his intelligence and engaging personality. He was a tall, thin beacon of smiles and light and everywhere he went, laughter went with him.

He so often said nice things. While I was growing accustomed to this in Ireland, especially from Irish men, my first reaction was to assume he was not being genuine. I imagined he was just playing his pied piper role and sprinkling me, as one of the multitude of admirers – oh yes, he had many – with standard-issue blanket flattery. But I decided it wasn't important. He was saying what he knew made me smile.

Ned had what he and I came to refer to as a posse; a gaggle of young women who appeared and gathered around him whenever he was in town. He likely told them what they needed to hear, too. Ned cared about people; he wasn't the type to reject anyone he thought was a good person.

I suppose deep down I was envious of those girls. Not that I wanted to be one of the posse, not at all. I rather enjoyed being separate, having my own niche. But they made me painfully aware of the fleeting, finite nature of being young and how far away I was from it.

Despite our age difference, we developed a friendship, the Kiwi writer and the retired American lady. Ned and I discussed writing and romance and adventure, food and drink and childhood. We talked of both the expected and unexpected sometimes peculiar ways of life and people. He once used a one-euro and a two-euro coin to represent two love interests and their attributes, lamenting the fact they were each in their own way perfect, yet lacking. I took note that there was surely some meaning behind his choice of assignment to the lower and higher value coins, but after hearing his opinions on both I told him I thought he needed to begin a quest for a third coin, the one whose imperfections would be neither a detraction nor distraction. I think he agreed.

He was a heavy drinker, but I discovered my original assessment of his drinking persona was correct. Even after he went beyond the number of pints he should have had, he never became surly or sloppy. But I hated to see it happen and hoped it was a phase rather than a lifestyle. I knew eventually, if he kept it up, he'd begin to lose himself and the beacon of smiles and light would dim, turn dull, and disappear. I didn't want to hear someone had walked into a pub looking for him and found nothing left but his baseball cap perched on a barstool. I'd seen others lost to the dark side of alcohol. I hated to think it could happen to him.

I knew from the beginning that Ned would only be in Kenmare a short while before returning to New Zealand. It was easy to use that knowledge as an excuse for the wild summer that ensued. A summer of too much drinking, eating the wrong things, and staying out too late, living as he was: like a crazy twenty-something, instead of the almost-forty year old he was and the senior citizen I knew very well I was. Ned was feeling younger than his years, and he made me feel younger than mine. Besides the fun and friendship he brought to my life, I put a high value on the help he was giving me with my writing. I didn't want to miss any time with him.

30

MAY DAYS

May 30, 2014: I have spent the day in complete couch potato mode. I feel guilty because the sun has been shining and I know I should be outdoors, but my energy is gone. I've hit the wall.

Everyone I knew who planned to take a holiday in Ireland in 2014 had chosen the month of May to visit Kenmare. During those few visitor-filled weeks the pace was much faster than my generally low-key, frequently solitary lifestyle. The time was packed with greetings and goodbyes to old friends and new, travels and tour guiding around Ireland, tea and talking, picnics, pints, and pub tunes, and nights of too little sleep. I was, as the old saying goes, burning the candle at both ends.

But it was worth it. Ireland showed its best face to my visitors and I was thrilled to be able to share it. We enjoyed the green hills and the bright May flowers, Kenmare's scenic main streets, inviting pubs and shops, and tours through the surrounding countryside.

The green was out in a multitude of shades, deepening in hue with the onset of the warmer weather. At times the landscape looked unreal, so brilliant was the green and so intense the hues of the flowers. Gorse blazed yellow-gold across the fields, bluebells, purple lilac-like butterfly bushes, and pink foxglove bloomed and grew around every corner, splashing the earth with color, and ivy's curling dark green tendrils rapidly climbed trees, walls and buildings as though racing against one another.

In the towns and villages, the sun brought the tourists from near and far and the locals from their homes to linger at sidewalk tables outside of pubs and cafes, or to walk, everyone enjoying the warmth and light and thrill of the it's-almost-summer sunshine.

Sunshine is revered in a place like Ireland. It is not taken for granted. Every opportunity to enjoy it is relished.

Kathy and her husband from Oregon were my first visitors, in Ireland on a golfing trip. Best friends as teenagers, Kathy and I hadn't seen each other since then. She'd found me on Facebook a few years before and we'd exchanged a steady stream of messages, remembering old times and excited to be in touch again.

We'd seen photos of each other so had some sense of how the passage of time had left us, but when I opened the door and saw her standing there, I wasn't prepared for how well she'd aged. She looked amazing, but then she'd been attractive and slender as a teenager, too. Best friend though she was, I'd often been envious, wishing I had her pretty face and long slender legs. I guess I was still wishing.

There was no awkwardness in the meeting at all. We talked and laughed together easily, as we had so many years before, getting ourselves into trouble for being giggling chatterboxes during class. Her husband was a pleasant and easy-going guy and didn't seem to mind our reminiscing.

We spoke of their passion, golf, listened to Irish music, dined on pub food, and reminisced about the good old days before they departed for points south and east to play more golf and continue their loop around SW Ireland. I felt certain that should our paths cross again we'd pick up where we left off.

Next up was my Canadian friend, Deb, a lady I'd met on my first trip to Ireland, my fellow 'Ireland Addict' as she once called us. Our mutual enthusiasm for Ireland had connected us instantly. I imagine no matter how little we might see one another, we'll always have that connection. She was the perfect person to share my new town with and I was very proud to do just that.

Kenmare was buzzing, on the cusp of summer. In advertisement of Pink Ribbon Week, a breast cancer fundraising campaign, garlands of pink bras in every size and style were strung across the street, zig-zagging back and forth from the eaves above one bright shop front to another. To the unfamiliar eye, unaccustomed to more neutral colors, the buildings of Kenmare, as in many other towns and villages, might at first appear garish. But once the eye adjusts and registers the entire scene, one can see how they blend with and enhance their natural surroundings. In winter, I'd seen the welcome cheer those colorful buildings brought to the dark days and bleak landscape.

Deb is an avid and able photographer so I knew she'd enjoy some of my favorite nearby walks. Together we walked along the river to admire the spring flowers, stopped at ancient sites, and visited the open air market, a photographer's paradise with its many colors and textures.

The market was bustling with people. Brightly patterned scarves blew like flags in the breeze, cobalt blue hand-crafted mugs and beaded earrings gleamed in the sun, red and pink balloons bobbed from strings. Blocks and wheels of yellow and white cheeses vied for space on a crowded table, deep vats of dark brine were filled with an exotic variety of olives. Jars of honey sparkled like liquid gold. The smell of brewing coffee reached us and as I always did, I automatically took a deeper breath, inhaling the scent as it mingled with the other spicy and sweet aromas filling the air.

While we wandered and admired our surroundings, we talked of old times and future plans, and in the evenings raised a glass (or two) before it was time for Deb, too, to be on her way to continue her trip around Ireland.

I'd no sooner waved goodbye and bid her 'Slán!' than my Pennsylvania friends, Jan and Tony, arrived. More than twenty-five years ago Jan and I had worked together at an engineering firm in Pennsylvania. Tony was our boss. I ended up quitting to move to California; she ended up marrying Tony. We had stayed in touch and I know they'll always be dear friends, no matter time or distance.

With them I toured into West Cork and around the Beara Peninsula, and made stops by the roadside to photograph and remark upon the different vistas, chat with strangers, and wander through castle and church ruins. We talked of Irish weather, the nerve-challenging, twisting roadways, and the virtues of tea (Jan's drink of choice) versus pints of Guinness (Tony's). I enjoy both beverages so we made a compatible trio.

We traveled on narrow country roads through hairpin turns, gasping at the sudden appearance of oncoming vehicles or stray sheep. We drove up, over, and down the always magnificent Healy Pass, stopping at the summit to listen to the silence and admire the view, and wherever else we wanted to pause to enjoy our surroundings. We talked with a friendly Californian couple touring Ireland on motorcycles, and iconic bachelor farmer Sean, who once wandered along the roadside on foot with his dog, but now travels in style in a beat-up blue Toyota, creeping along the steep mountain road, pulling over for a chat wherever he sees someone stopped along the roadway.

We stopped at a friend's home for tea served in pretty cups, and went for a shell hunting wander on Ballydonegan Beach, watching the waves crash on the black rocks, and the tide pools fill and drain with the ebbing tide.

One afternoon we drove into the woods of Glengariff Nature Reserve and had lunch on a wooden picnic table in the warm still air as the sun filtered through the verdant canopy of leaves, covering us in patterns of light and shadow. We talked as we unpacked cheese and crackers and fruit and ate to the tune of birdsong in the otherwise quiet forest. It sounds idyllic, it looked idyllic, it felt idyllic – until the blasted midges, who mistakenly thought they were invited, arrived and we were driven back to the car, allowing them to have our table and whatever crumbs they might scavenge there.

And then there was Gougane Barra. Ah, Gougane Barra! I'd stayed at the Gougane Barra Hotel on my first trip to Ireland and always looked forward to returning. I couldn't wait to share the hotel and the beautiful surroundings with Jan and Tony.

There is something about Gougane Barra. The moment we stepped out of the car I felt myself taking a slow, deep breath. Two sheep scrambled across the road and up the hillside, followed by a black-faced lamb. The breeze rustled the treetops, the birds sang, and Gougane Barra Lake lapped lazily against the shoreline.

At the hotel, the gracious proprietors, Neil and Katy, were the delightful, cheerful hosts they always are, but they seemed to go even further out of their way this time to welcome me back and make my friends feel as though they'd been there before, too. Their hospitality and humor, the well-kept old-world charm of the hotel, attentive staff, serene lake views and the delicious, elegantly presented food created, as always, an experience which leaves you wishing to stay longer and knowing you'll return some day.

Gougane Barra is part of a Gaeltacht, an Irish-speaking region of Ireland. On arrival I said hello to Neil in Irish, as I always do. It was a bit of a game with us.

'Dia Dhuit!'

'Dia dhuit! Conas tá tú?' he asked, 'Hello! How are you?'

'Tá mé go maith!' I answered, 'I'm fine!'

His eyes twinkling with devilment, he said something further in Irish and my only response was laughter because he went beyond the limit of my Irish skills (a cúpla focal – a couple of words) – and he knew it.

We arrived ahead of check-in time so our rooms were not ready. Tall, thin, witty Neil, who handles front of house, offered us tea and showed us into the library bar where we sat in overstuffed armchairs. Tea appeared within minutes and Neil sat and talked and joked with us while we drank it, as though he had all the time in the world and nothing more important to do, but he most certainly did. He just had a way of making us not realize it just then. After our tea interlude, he helped carry our luggage up the stairs to our waiting rooms.

As a single, I am accustomed to being put in a small room somewhere, often lacking a view and generally nothing special. I didn't pay the price for a premium room, so was bowled over when I opened the door to my room, the one I later learned they call 'The Crow's Nest.' It was wonderful, a real treat, although I admit to feeling guilty for not offering to trade rooms with Jan and Tony. They had a nice room, but no room rivals The Crow's

Nest. On the end of the hotel, on the top floor, across the lake from St. Finbarr's church, it has panoramic views from big windows on two sides of the room, windows that open to let in the fresh air and birdsong. Even from the shower, I could look out across Gougane Barra Lake. I wished for another day just to sit in that room and gaze out the windows.

When I thanked Neil for giving me such a special room his eyes lit up and he smiled.

'You deserve it!'

Spoken not only like a true Irishman, but like the caring, thoughtful and savvy host he is.

That evening, when we entered the dining room for dinner, there was another surprise. I didn't have to give my name; the server knew who I was and took us at once to our reserved table by the front window overlooking the lake. I suppose it would be a small thing to some, but I am not accustomed to such special treatment. I was impressed.

Kind Katy supervises the kitchen and does much of the cooking. She came out to make sure everything was to our liking and to chat with us for a moment in her quiet smiling way. I told her how much I was enjoying my meal and Jan and Tony exclaimed over their selections. Neil stopped by more than once to continue with his joking and laughter that is so much a part of the place.

It was a delightful dinner in that dining room overlooking the lake, with tea lights flickering and small vases of delicate wildflowers adorning the tables. It's a place that makes you heave a big sigh and sit back and relax and enjoy the moment, where conversation and laughter flow as easily as the Guinness and the tea.

The next morning after a leisurely and delicious breakfast we checked out and said our goodbyes to Neil who followed us out to our car. Rarely seen outside the kitchen except for her brief forays into the dining room, busy Katy also appeared. The very fact that they were taking time from their duties, time I was sure was very precious, for thanks, hugs and farewells added to the special experience of our time there. It was, as always, hard to leave such an easy, welcoming place. I was happy to have the chance to share it with my friends, the newest members of the Gougane Barra Hotel fan club. I knew I would return, and they vowed to do the same.

◙

Throughout those weeks in May, nearly every day the sun was with us, shining on the colors of the land and sparkling on the sea while the gleeful serenade of birds, the bleating of sheep and young lambs, and the breeze rustling through the leaves of the trees and hedgerows provided a natural symphony. If butterflies had a song, it would be lovely and they would have been singing it. Instead, not to be outdone, they showed off the intricate delicacy of their patterned wings, spreading them with grace and fluttering to gentle landings on fields thick with wildflowers.

While the stimulation and activity of those busy weeks in May caused me to collapse on the couch when they were over, it was a wonderful time. I didn't know then that within a few more days, spring would become summer, the social whirl would really kick in, and I'd spend nearly three months on over-drive. I wouldn't just be burning the candle at both ends, it would be an entire candelabra. Those few weeks in May would be fondly remembered not only for their beauty and the company of old friends, but for the easy, gentle pace I wouldn't recognize until much later.

31

FAT FRIDAY & WALKING MEN

June 10, 2014: Finally got to go to Strawberry Field Pancake Cottage. It was great and I look forward to returning!

One of the first beautiful mornings of summer began with a taxi ride through the country from Kenmare to the Strawberry Field Pancake Cottage. It was a day of food and fortunes, blue skies and twenty-sixth birthday greetings. There were five of us including Dierdre, the birthday girl, who had kindly invited me to join them.

The place, the setting, and the food were all first class and I was in cheerful company. It would have made me happy to spend the entire day there. Or longer. The views across the land were of the glossy calendar kind, the forty shades of green blanketing the valley and rolling hills, the black silhouette of the mountains standing out in sharp contrast against the blue sky. Behind us tall evergreens towered on the steep hillside and their faint scent rode on the breeze, filtering through the clear air. The sun lit up the landscape and warmed the world, and the pristine puffy whiteness of the clouds looked like a Monet painting. All was quiet but for birdsong and the faint drone of hard working bees.

We dined outdoors on a wrought iron table, eating pancakes the size of dinner plates. We shared seven kinds, both savory and sweet, each one a circular work of art. The lemon and strawberry was my particular favorite, but they were all delicious, made more so by the beautiful weather and views. Lazy chat and tea from cast-iron teapots encircled with Celtic knot designs followed the pancakes. Relaxed and lulled by the good food, the sun's warmth, and the sweet music of the birds, our chatter soon slowed and then subsided. Before we drifted off to sleep we roused ourselves from our pancake and sunshine trance and left the table to have a look inside.

The dining room and adjoining gift shop are charming and spotlessly clean. The colors and décor, along with a large wood stove, leave no doubt it would be a cozy spot for dining on cooler, wet days. I made a mental note to return in winter. Deep-set rectangular windows overlook the outdoor dining area, framing the views we'd enjoyed while we dined.

The dim low-ceilinged gift shop is small, but shelves and tables are laden with merchandise. On the back wall two windows are portholes to the lush, forested hillside and on that sunny day allowed in enough extra light to better explore and inspect the goods. Wind chimes and other unique trinkets hang from the walls, the ceiling, and the window frames, and fill every square inch of surface in the room. Tiny 'Strawberry Girl' necklaces, antique plates, tea light holders made from clay flower pots, wrought iron wine racks and trivets, and metal garden stakes topped with – what else? Strawberries. A trip to the toilet calls for a camera because who could resist taking a photo of the red walls and strawberry design imprinted toilet seat and lid?

Back outdoors we walked around the grounds, across stretches of green lawns under the evergreens, reluctant to leave the place. A small abandoned stone out-building set in the corner of the side garden captured my attention and my imagination. A tangle of overgrown fuchsia bushes obscured one side of the building, the deep red blooms making it look like a summer Christmas tree. The weathered wood door of the building faces out over the valley, toward the spectacular view.

My mind jumped into over-drive. I imagined restoring the old shed, turning it into a one-room haven with a wood stove for warmth on chill days, a deep, soft easy chair for reading, and a bed piled high with bright pillows and down quilts for sleep. I could see the stained glass sun catchers hanging in the windows, bookshelves full of books lining the walls, and the lanterns ready to be lit at sunset. It was a picture that took no effort; it popped into my mind ready for immediate occupancy. And a kitchen and bathroom? I had that covered. I'd dine on pancakes and use the strawberry-themed ladies' room.

I noticed everyone else had walked on, so I pulled myself out of my reverie.

One of the invited guests that day was Ned, but he'd decided last minute to take off hiking and camping with a friend who had arrived from New Zealand earlier than planned. It was summer in Ireland; who could blame him? I had the pleasure of meeting his friend before they left. He was a friendly, fit, and good looking man, and, at fifty-five, much closer to my age than most of the single men I usually meet. Not that it mattered since the day after I met him he was off walking in the hills of Ireland somewhere.

Full of pancakes, tea and well-being, we headed back to Kenmare. Wanting to stay outdoors in the glorious weather, we sat in the sunshine in the town center park and toasted Dierdre with the Prosecco we'd not been allowed to open at the restaurant. Two of the girls dashed across the street to the little market for snacks. Had there been sheep in front of the market that day, the park would not have been a fragrant place to be. But there weren't any, and the park was a perfect, easy spot on that sunny, early summer afternoon.

Once settled on the grass, we noticed a small camper van parked on the street, the side back door open, lace curtains tied out of the way and 'Gypsy Breda' emblazoned on the side. On the sidewalk in a plastic lawn chair sat a little white-haired lady in a straw hat. Meet Breda. Two of the girls went for readings and were amazed at the things she knew, and moved to tears by some of the information given to them. I didn't go see Breda that day, but thought maybe someday I would.

After the day melted into late afternoon and we all drifted off to our respective homes, we met up that evening at a local pub as planned, a habit that would become a regular one that summer. As if the seven kinds of pancakes we had started off the day with, and the crisps and ice cream some of the girls had eaten in the park was not enough, we moved on to yet another table full of food that evening.

We decided to share several starters. Our little table was filled edge to edge with food – more than enough for five. Problem was, there were just three of us since two of the five had to work that evening. People were staring. We giggled, but only for a few seconds, before launching into the food. I am pleased to say I was not among those who indulged in the midday crisps and ice cream. I do have my limits. Those limits did not, however, keep me from over-indulging in the morning pancakes or the evening wings, wedges, pizza and nachos.

The night ended with meeting yet another interesting man. Mandy, the young Scottish lady I'd met soon after moving to Ireland, joined us later in the evening and brought a fellow Scotsman to our table.

'So, how long have you known him?' I said, shouting directly into her ear because of the noise in the pub. I assumed he was her significant other, or maybe just a friend from home.

She turned and grinned at me, looking mischievous. In her thick, difficult to understand Scottish brogue she said, 'About four minutes!' and burst out laughing.

Mick was in Kenmare just passing through, traveling around on foot. A forty-something free spirit, he was taking a break from his IT career in Edinburgh and was in Ireland to walk. He worked as a volunteer at the Buddhist center on the Beara Peninsula for room and board and when he could get free, he walked. It was incomprehensible to me, but he'd walked that day the nearly thirty-five miles to Kenmare.

Mick was talkative, cheerful, and had a good sense of humor. On the last round of drinks it was my turn to buy. He was concerned with time as the hostel where he was staying locks the doors before the pubs close.

'I'll soon have to leave or they'll be locking me out,' he explained. 'And I have to be up early in the morning. Going to Killarney, I think.'

So after the thirty-five mile walk to Kenmare he was going to walk another twenty-plus miles to Killarney. I didn't even want to think about the number of miles he'd have to then walk to get back to the Buddhist center.

'Just a half-pint this time, please!' he said.

When I returned with the drinks and handed his glass to him he said, 'Oh, they're all going to know I'm a tourist now, won't they? A real man would never be caught in a pub with a half-pint!'

While that may have been true, being caught in a pub with a nice young man who made me laugh worked for me.

Perhaps I would see him again sometime, the next time he was out walking. I thought I might one day ask Gypsy Breda about that. Possibly a better plan was to start walking more myself since it seemed that was where all the men were. Given the amount of food and drink I'd been consuming, it was probably a good idea in more ways than one.

32

LIFE & DEATH

June 17, 2014: Today was an unusual mixture of sadness and beauty and blessings. I won't soon, if ever, forget it.

Another beautiful summer morning was in progress. Just a week after the day of frivolity, eating pancakes, lazing in the park, and drinking pints with the Scottish folk, I stepped out of a taxi in front of a pretty, solid looking, mid-nineteenth century stone church in the country, surrounded by lush green foliage, well-groomed lawns and tall evergreen trees. The sun was brilliant in the deep blue of the sky, large white clouds intermittently passing by and creating dancing shadows and uncertainty as to whether sunglasses could be stowed away or should be kept at hand.

It was a lovely spot for a wedding, but that was not the occasion on that day. I entered the nearly full church and found a seat, waiting for the Catholic requiem mass to begin which would recognize and mark the passing of a man.

I knew him as Daniel, but everyone called him Danny. He was ninety-two years old, a life-long resident of Kenmare, and my neighbor. And he was the father of my dear friends, Michael, Colin, Liz and Mary. I knew what a deep impact his passing would have on the family.

I remembered sitting in his kitchen drinking tea on a winter's day and watching with him as the birds flocked to the feeders hanging outside his window. You could read the interest and pleasure in his eyes. When the weather was nice they'd help him outside so he could sit under the trees in the soft air, hear the birds, and watch Michael's hens milling around.

Not long before his passing I'd found a little bird carving I thought he would like and bought it for him. I was told he loved it. I regretted not having spent more time with him. His passing soundly disproved the popular saying, 'There's always tomorrow.'

Sitting on a slippery polished wooden pew in the old church that morning, sunlight filtering through the tall stained glass windows and casting rainbows on the floor, I learned it was the same church where Daniel was married in 1946, the same year my parents were married. Listening to the words being spoken, prayers offered, and songs sung in memoriam and celebration of his life, I felt sad for those grieving for him, especially his family. I wished, as one does, for something to say or do to help, knowing nothing could. As the service progressed, I don't suppose I was the only one also saddened and overwhelmed with thoughts of loved ones here and gone and by selfishly thinking of my own mortality.

I fought tears and watched with deep empathy as the casket was slowly and carefully lifted and born down the center aisle and out of the church by Danny's sons and grandsons. The rest of the family followed, taking slow sedate steps, faces set in mask-like composure, eyes filled with a deep sorrow. They all so loved that man and his passing was an end of an era.

Some of them had devoted their lives to him in his last few years, providing the care he needed to stay where he wanted to be: in his home of seventy years. It was a wonderful gift they'd given him and said so much about them, and about the kind of man he was.

As the procession continued, I yearned to reach out and comfort each of them, these people who'd become so dear to me. As Mary passed near I could not help myself. Even knowing it surely was not appropriate behavior for the time, I gave her a quick squeeze on the shoulder and one of her hands closed lightly over mine, her solemn tear-filled eyes looking straight ahead.

Outside, we stood aside in mute respect as the casket was put inside the hearse, and watched it pull away as a single bird crowed loudly. We followed behind, a long line of cars winding at a slow pace down sun-dappled country roads, making our way to the Old Kenmare Cemetery. The cemetery is an old place of tall trees and stone walls and graves old and new, some covered over with long grass and wildflowers, others manicured and adorned with fresh flowers. It isn't a place that feels of death, but rather of spirituality and peace.

Danny was laid to rest next to his wife, on the northwestern edge of the cemetery with an open view across the bay to the hills beyond, a pastoral scene. As his daughter-in-law sang a song, the last clouds in the sky drifted away leaving a clear expanse of blue. The bright sunshine glittered on the sea's surface, warmed those who came to pay their last respects, and illuminated the blanket of flowers covering Danny's final resting place.

The service over, I walked away from the gravesite toward the line of trees and the promise of shade by the high stone wall on the outskirts of the cemetery to wait for Noreen, my lift back to town, still chatting with those who had not yet left. As I stood in the shady breeze reflecting on the day, the trees swayed and sighed overhead and the birds joined in an especially melodious serenade – not for me, but for Danny, of course. I would not often hear birdsong again without thinking of him.

A large crowd of mourners had already gathered at Liz's cottage by the time Noreen and I arrived. Tables and chairs had been set up in the open outdoor space between Michael's place and Liz's, and food and drink was being collected and arranged. Noreen ran down the street to her cottage for more tea cups and I passed my patio table and chairs across the garden wall to add to the mix, and grabbed a bottle of wine and some paper plates before joining the crowd.

In a short time a sumptuous buffet feast was ready and the tea and the Guinness and the wine flowed. The family must have been cooking day and night. If you couldn't find something you liked, you didn't like to eat. As the feasting and drinking began, so, too, did the chatter, and the mood began to lighten. It was as though everyone took a deep breath, exhaled in unison, and the sadness lifted. Shoulders relaxed, smiles appeared; everyone was talking and laughing, remembering Danny and catching up on news and gossip. It was the first time I've ever seen anyone drinking both wine or Guinness and tea, but I saw many doing it that day and it would not be the last time. The English have notoriety as tea-drinkers, but I was surprised to learn the amount of tea consumed in Ireland far exceeds that of England. It is a mandatory part of every social gathering. And on that occasion, a cup of tea in one hand was not the slightest barrier to holding a glass of wine or a pint of Guinness in the other.

What followed was nearly eight hours of wonderful kinship and celebration. We sat or mingled under the cloudless Irish sky, on an unusually warm day, enjoying the sunshine and fresh air, wandered in and out of the kitchen, eating and drinking our way through the afternoon. And then we ate and drank some more. We hugged, chatted, told stories and jokes, and laughed until our faces hurt. Second cousins were introduced to third cousins-once-removed, neighbors to old friends, old friends to new.

I helped clear and wash plates and glasses so they could be used again and again, watched one of Danny's artistic great grandchildren draw a picture, sympathized with another one who fell down the hill and scraped his knee, and was endlessly teased by Liz's Frank because I drank his Guinness thinking it was mine. And of course, in between I sipped a cup of tea.

When most folks had left, leaving only family behind, I felt it was my time to leave, too, and began my farewells. Liz insisted I stay and without waiting for an answer poured and handed me a glass of wine and pulled out a chair. 'Jane, you must stay. You surely can't miss the bread and cheese?! Please! Sit!' It was more a proclamation than a question. I sat.

Yes, there was to be more food. A platter of assorted cheeses, crackers, bread and olives appeared from nowhere, along with more wine. The cheese was followed by a box of chocolates passed around until every piece was consumed. This, then, was the third stage of the day, after the service and the initial feasting, and I realized in looking back that without it the day would have been less complete.

The scene became more intimate as the afternoon waned, the sun lower in the sky. Fewer voices spoke more softly, and intertwined with the laughter I could hear the music of the birds in the still air, birds I was certain had been singing all afternoon. I felt like I'd been transported to a faraway make-believe land, maybe sitting on the terrace of an Italian villa in a foreign film, the Irish and English accents the only sign that I wasn't, and the fact that Danny's children were all there at the same time the only reminder he'd passed. No one needed to sit with him; we were all sitting with Danny on that day.

The companionship, sunshine, wine, rich food and emotions of the day wrapped around us as though, along with Danny, we hung suspended together in a soft, benevolent hammock, a slice of time apart from the real world for just a little while.

I felt so blessed to be counted as a friend by this family.

It was a remarkable day. I wished the occasion had not been someone's death, but perhaps it is only then that we remember to truly celebrate life. I thought it must have been the kind of day Danny would have loved, and I liked the thought of that. He will live on through his children and grandchildren and the generations to come. And his birds, and the generations of birds to come, will never stop singing for him. May he always rest in peace.

33

WORLD CUP FEVER & LADIES' DAY OUT

June 25, 2014: I've been writing like a maniac! Ned has created a monster! Thank goodness for World Cup games — at least it gets me away from the computer and out of the house.

World Cup 2014 was a special occasion in Ireland, another chance to watch sports. The Irish do love their sports. I saw more soccer in 2014 than I'd seen in my entire life. Far more. It was irrelevant that Ireland wasn't playing in the World Cup. The World Cup games sprang to life in any pub with a television and during the finals the atmosphere in town was similar to that of a festival. Ned, a huge soccer fan and an Aussie Rules football player was at the pub for every match. I joined him for most of them.

The USA was playing in the World Cup and I sported my red, white and blue scarf and American flag pin for those games, not so much because I was madly into whether they won or lost, but more to show my pride in being American. I wanted them to win, but I wasn't all *that* invested. It wasn't very Irish of me, nor American either, I suppose, but I just don't normally get too worked up over the outcome of sporting events.

Because of the time difference the games were often on late in Ireland. The night of the exciting USA *vs.* Belgium match the pub closed on us an hour before it was over. Many of us hurried on to another pub which stays open later than the others, albeit there are times when everyone is asked to be quiet. It's amazing how fast everyone falls silent. You can hear a pin drop while the barman stands and peeks through the crack between the double

186

doors, his open hand raised behind his back in signal for the silence to continue. Pub patrons freeze, like children with their hands in the forbidden cookie jar surprised by mom coming into the room.

After the yellow-vested garda have walked by on their rounds of the town the barman's hand drops and he turns around, the signal that the danger has passed. It is my belief that how closely the garda listen and what they decide to hear depends entirely on their mood, but I'm just speculating. At the all clear, the action continues where it left off.

On the night of the World Cup USA game we gathered in the beer garden behind the pub in front of the big screen. It seemed everyone was supporting Team USA and the atmosphere was upbeat during the tied-up game. A tie was all the USA needed to make the quarter-finals. I confess that by this point, I was starting to become far more invested in it.

Five minutes remained on the clock when the back door of the pub opened and the yellow reflective vests of every garda officer in Kenmare (all three of them) shone in the lamplight. They didn't have to say anything, they just gestured for us to leave. They would entertain no requests for 'Just five more minutes!'

We filed out onto the sidewalk in an orderly fashion, lamenting the timing, but feeling sure of the outcome of the match. Several people left, already celebrating. Most stayed behind, including Ned and I, cupping our hands to the glass to peer through the window and watch the final few minutes on the small TV in the front of the pub. There we watched with disbelief as Belgium scored in the last thirty seconds, defeating Team USA.

The number of people who came to me in the days following to express genuine regrets and heartfelt sympathy caught me by surprise. But this is Ireland. It was assumed the outcome mattered a great deal to me.

In between World Cup matches and pub hopping, Ned and I met a few times for more review and discussion of my latest writing efforts. After learning more about me and my life and various adventures such as my days working on the Trans-Alaska pipeline, he was convinced I should write a memoir, not just about Ireland, but covering more of my life. It seemed it would take years. Even with his encouragement I had considerable reservations, but decided to give it a try.

I follow directions well. In the days after, I wrote of picking beans as a kid, high school boyfriends and corresponding shenanigans, and a wilderness canoe camping trip in Michigan, with more stories banging around in my head, clamoring to be put onto paper. I wrote and re-wrote upon arising in the morning and stayed with it the entire day, sometimes into the night – on those nights I wasn't out carousing with Ned and company. Knowing it couldn't be good for me to sit at the computer all day, I needed to come up with a more balanced approach. I promised myself I'd do that, just as soon as I finished writing that day, or maybe the next. One never knew when writer's block could take over...

In just those few short months of mentoring, Ned increased my enthusiasm for writing and gave me hope that perhaps I could get a book published someday. I found a different sort of rhythm and style. What had always been a pleasant pastime became a growing obsession. Ned created a monster; I couldn't stop writing. I wrote page after page of stories for the book he suggested was in me. Begin at the beginning, he said, and just keep writing.

I think part of the obsession, my sense of urgency, was caused by knowing Ned would leave soon. Before that happened, I was desperate to get as much written as possible and get his feedback.

All of us who became friends with him feared he'd one day just disappear, leave without saying goodbye as he had indicated he would prefer to do, despite our strongly voiced opposition to such an idea. 'I'm not good at goodbyes,' he'd told me. Who is, Ned, who is? I had no doubt it's what he'd do if not for his kind heart. But I was confident he would suffer goodbyes rather than disappoint us, those who were having a hard time imagining how it would be without him.

I knew I'd miss him when he was gone, but would never regret meeting him. The inspiration he gave me, the way he boosted my confidence, and the good memories he helped create would stay with me long after he'd given me a final big Kiwi hug and departed for his homeland with his baseball cap jammed onto his head, setting out for the next adventure, the next laugh, the next chapter in the Amazing Adventures of Kiwi Ned.

▣

A few days after the disappointing World Cup match I accepted an invitation to join an outing with Noreen, Liz and Clare. It came along at the right time, successfully tempting me away from the pattern of writing all day and carousing half the night. I supposed at some point the lifestyle I'd developed over the summer with its excesses of writing, drink, pub food, and late hours would catch up with me. A break from it could only be a good thing. A relaxing day with prolonged breathing of fresh air was the very thing I needed.

On a warm summer morning we took off on our ladies' day out, a drive around the Beara Peninsula. It is an area I've toured on several occasions and always enjoy it. One of the nicest things about the Beara is that it's less traveled by tourists than the Iveragh Peninsula (Ring of Kerry) and Dingle Peninsula and I don't recall ever seeing any large coach tours. I don't think most of the roads are wide enough to accommodate big coaches.

The day was filled with fabulous sights old and new, conversation, companionship, and laughter, and no shortage of sweet, fresh air. The sky was a water-color painting, a study in blue and white, just enough fair weather clouds to keep it from becoming too warm. As incredible as it sounds, 'too warm' can happen from time to time in Ireland.

Driving along in Noreen's car we stopped wherever we wished, at beaches and viewpoints, pubs and markets. In Castletownbere we visited MacCarthy's Bar, made famous to some by Pete McCarthy's book, *McCarthy's Bar*. I'd been there before, read the book, and thought it well worth a stop. In MacCarthy's you can have a pint while you shop for milk and toilet bowl cleaner and a wide assortment of other items displayed in the glass case near the register and on the high shelves that line the walls. The old burnished wood of the interior, the heavy highly polished bar, and the walls crowded with quaint old signs, photos and newspaper clippings leave no doubt it's a true old-time Irish pub. The ladies enjoyed the visit.

In the colorful and neat village of Allihies Noreen slowed the car to look for a likely place to have lunch. A newly painted pub caught everyone's eye. The bright red façade and hanging flower baskets flanking the front door, pink and purple geraniums and petunias spilling down the sides, gave it an inviting look. Given that the name of the pub was the same as her surname before she married, Noreen decided in seconds it surely was the place to go, and parked the car. We laughed about it, but she was right. My fresh crab sandwich on brown bread was delicious with a glass of Guinness, and the ubiquitous bowl of a generous portion of you-know-you-shouldn't-be-eating-these chips.

After lunch we made our way to Dzogchen Beara, the Buddhist retreat center perched on the far southwestern tip of the peninsula high above the sea. A drive deep into the forest brings you there, the turn-off sign nestled in the lush greenery and tall stalks of purple-pink foxglove growing by the roadside. The center's facilities are housed in several buildings, places for lodging, classes, and meditation, and there is a small café and gift shop. We weren't there to meditate or take a class, but to enjoy the spectacular setting and beautiful grounds.

In the café, we sat overlooking the sea, enjoying coffee and a mouth-watering chocolate raspberry bar split between us while we breathed in the bracing sea air drifting through the open window. I filled my lungs with it and felt it on my skin. It was delicious, surpassing even the chocolate and the coffee, and I couldn't get enough. I was like a traveler emerging from the desert and drinking my first pure, cool water after many parched, dusty days.

A small many-windowed lounge room awash in light is attached to the cafe. The space is filled with flowered sofas and bright cushions. Overgrown geraniums spill from the window ledges. A door leads outside to a wooden stairway winding down the hillside with landings at different levels where seating areas made private by the surrounding trees and flowers face out to sea. I wished for time to try out each one, not for their intended purpose of meditation, but simply to drink in the surrounding nature and scenic views. But then, isn't that a form of meditation?

After coffee we inquired about the walking man from Scotland, but he was busy in the woods setting up tents for an event that afternoon. We perused the goods in the tiny shop, shelves packed with polished stones, photos, books, jewelry and incense, then wandered around outdoors. In a sheltered glass case among flowering shrubbery the ladies lit prayer candles not because they are Buddhists, but because they are Catholics and probably saw it as being no different than their own religion's practice of lighting prayer candles.

We walked about, enchanted by the forest, the flowers and the peace of the place. The views of the water and coastline are far-reaching and dramatic, the kind which make you want to keep looking and never move on, explaining at least part of the reason for the multiple seating areas on that hillside above the sea.

Noreen and Clare strolled on ahead while Liz and I slowed, chatting and stopping to admire and identify the flowers growing among the tall pines. Liz knows her flowers. I didn't, but was trying to learn. We were examining some roses when we noticed a sign among the foliage, MEDITATION GARDEN - SILENCE PLEASE. We fell quiet and I followed Liz through the opening in the thick hedge. I hadn't taken two steps before I collided with her, stopped in her tracks. She whipped around, eyes wide, grabbed my arm, and scampered me back to the pathway.

'There are people in there meditating!!' she hissed.

We hastily tip-toed away from the meditation garden, realizing that before entering we'd been chattering like monkeys with nothing between us and the meditators except trees and shrubs... We continued on the path to the cliff edge, stifling giggles, trying to stay quiet, like silly schoolgirls thrown out of class for talking too much, then convulsed with helpless laughter.

The Buddhist center was wonderful, but there was more to see on the Beara Peninsula, so we hurried along to catch up with Noreen and Clare, then the four of us headed back to the car.

Down the road we stopped at a small market and Clare and Liz went in to buy snacks. Noreen and I chatted while we waited, enjoying the warmth and relaxation of the day through the open car windows. I remembered a story Eric had recently told me and thought Noreen would enjoy it.

Eric was helping Paudie clear some underbrush and the mosquitoes were eating them alive. 'Is there a particular time when they aren't so bothersome?' inquired Eric.

'Oh, there is,' Paudie said. 'When they aren't hungry.'

I laughed as I had when I'd first heard it, but Noreen didn't. She looked perplexed. 'Moss-kee-toes??!' She'd never *ever* heard of a single mosquito in Ireland, *never ever* heard anyone *ever* mention them! Not in all her life had *anyone*, not a single person, mentioned moss-kee-toes, well, except maybe once someone had said something, but she paid no attention because she knew there were *no* moss-kee-toes in Ireland. She'd heard of midges and bottle flies, yes. And of course she'd *heard* of moss-kee-toes, she knew about the people who wore nets to keep away from the moss-kee-toes, but *not* here, not in *Ireland.*

'What do they look like?' she asked.

Describing the appearance of a mosquito isn't so easy. 'Um-m-m... let's see...smaller than a fly, bigger than a gnat.'

'What's a gnat?'

'Sort of like a midge, but they don't bite.' I kept trying. It was like a game, *'sounds like...'* 'Well, let's see... You can hear mosquitoes if they get close to your ear. They make a high-pitched buzzing noise. And when they bite you it leaves an itchy bump.' I ran out of descriptors.

'Is it like the doctors, maybe?' she asked.

I wasn't sure what she meant. 'No, no, it isn't something serious, you don't need to see a doctor for a mosquito bite.'

By the time Clare and Liz climbed back in the car, both of us were laughing. Noreen knew mosquitoes by another name, *The Doctors.* 'You know, because they inject you with something, like going to the doctors.' We were both relieved to have solved the mystery.

Back on the road I noticed goat-like creatures, not knowing at first that they were sheep without their thick wool coats. It was shearing season, Noreen explained. It was also summer. Oh, my, was it ever! I'd seen Ireland in fall, winter, and spring, but it was my first summer. Except on the top of the rocky Healy Pass, flowers bloomed everywhere. Summer made spring seem shy, a water-colored memory. Summer was loud, bold, vivid; drenched in intense color.

Multi-hued hydrangeas grew in dense clumps of snow white, lilac, blue, and pink; massive bushes laden with rhododendrons towered far overhead; foxglove, wild roses, and red and purple fuchsias blazed. Ferns, tall grasses and tangles of blackberry bushes formed a thicket of green behind the floral colors. Trees heavy with foliage leaned across the roadways, meeting overhead to form shady tunnels. I always felt like I was on an amusement park ride on those roads, a man-made adventure like Disneyland's Jungle Cruise or when the car rocketed around the winding narrow curves, another Disneyland favorite, Mr. Toad's Wild Ride. Knowing it was real made it that much more magical.

Liz and Noreen grew up in the area. Throughout the day they provided interesting and sometimes touching narration, pointing out cottages, ruins, mountains and lanes which have played a part in their lives, and telling the stories those places brought to mind.

Liz remembered when she was a little girl and she and her older brother Patrick stayed with her grandparents in a remote cottage on a rocky hillside while her mother was in the hospital giving birth to another sibling. She was miserable and hated that it was always her, never her brother, who had to do the dishes, and she was terribly homesick. She'd sit on the side of the mountain with a heavy heart and ask, 'Where's Kenmare, Patrick?' and he would point into the distance and say 'Over the mountain.' Though a short distance by car, to young Liz it may as well have been the other side of the world.

She recalled a story their mother told them about her own childhood, of how she'd had to walk the great distance over the mountain, barefoot, to get to school. Even by a fit hiker today the journey would take several hours. When they later saw a picture of their mother, a young girl in fashionable clothing wearing a wristwatch - a luxury at the time - they asked her why she had such nice clothes and a watch, but no shoes?...

Noreen showed us where her mother grew up and many homes where this cousin or that lives - or once did - and where Paudie went to school. As we began our descent from the mountain pass, the fog closing in, we stopped to look at the view. Noreen pointed out her home and the land where their sheep roam, the same home where she was raised and still lives with Paudie. Far below in that deep valley among the trees, it was a miniature dwelling nestled among the steep grass-covered hills dotted with stones and boulders, a misty abstract landscape in shades of black and green, a perfect Irish picture postcard.

My small contribution to the day was helping with navigation. 'Looks like you need to stay on R575,' I said, looking at the map. 'But I don't see any markers on the road so I'm not sure how we'll know.' Laughter from everyone. 'Oh, you've found us out, Jane!' After living in rural Ireland for close to a year I suppose I should have realized finding road number signs on the road which corresponded to road numbers on a map was an unrealistic expectation. At least we didn't come across any of the directional signs mischievous children have turned to misguide unsuspecting drivers.

It was a lovely ladies' day out and I couldn't have been with three more enjoyable companions. It was another of those days that prompt blessing counting. It was also a day that made me think again of the need for finding a better balance. I was reminded of how much I was missing by the habit I'd developed of restricting my movements from bed to computer to pub and back to bed. I chastised myself for almost forgetting how much else is out there.

The next day was the 4th of July, Independence Day in America. I hunkered down to spend a rainy day writing, no backyard barbecue or family picnic on my schedule. But I was not so caught up in writing and summer adventures that I had forgotten the significance of the day and it tugged at my patriotic heart. I displayed my 'God Bless America' garden flag and two small American flags in my front window. I wouldn't be celebrating with family or friends, eating hot dogs and hamburgers, listening to patriotic music, or watching fireworks, but I flew my country's colors in celebration and announcement of my nationality and my patriotism. It felt important to let people know that even though I was living in and loving Ireland – I was, and always would be, a proud American. God bless the land of the free and the home of the brave!

34

THE GOOD, THE BAD, & THE UGLY

July 14, 2014: Yesterday was a tough one. Kiwi Ned finally took his leave, as I knew he someday would. Didn't make it any easier, though.

The day had come for Kiwi Ned's departure. Many of us had grown accustomed to having him here; he'd become such a part of the fabric of the place. We couldn't see how the summer's fun would continue without him and of course, it wouldn't, not in the same way. I'd miss having him as a writing buddy, too. In retrospect it sounds overly dramatic how much emotion his leaving evoked, but somehow, in just a few short months some of us had forged tight bonds. I never figured out how it happened so quickly, but chalked it up to the amount of time we'd spent together during those months, the magic of Ireland, and a special summer in Kenmare.

To mark his departure we had a party and a night out pub-hopping; an evening of laughter and tears, hugs and reminiscing. The night started in Dierdre's front garden, festooned with crepe paper, balloons and fairy lights. Shortly after dark, Dierdre and another young local woman, barefoot and giggling, began a step dancing demonstration on the lawn. Realizing grass wasn't the best dancing surface, they moved out the gate into the roadway. It was a small side street with little traffic, but a car approached as soon as they started dancing. So much for Irish dancing that evening. But I was in for a surprise. Rather than laying on his horn or yelling at them to get out of the road, the driver stopped his car and watched the show, his headlights providing stage illumination for the two laughing and barefoot Irish dancing girls.

The evening ended for me after some pub-hopping took us to The Hour Glass, Kenmare's disco bar, a place I didn't think I'd ever set foot in, but where, surprisingly, I had a good time. We all danced together under the bright, pulsing lights, so dazzling and dizzying you could see little else. At one point a young man grabbed me and started swinging and twirling me around, saying 'The young ones don't know how to dance like this anymore!' When he finally released me I caught a glimpse of his face on the edge of the dance floor, slightly out of the direct brilliance of the blinding lights, and had to laugh. He couldn't have been much over thirty. It was one of those things that just seems to happen in Ireland.

I made my way home after nearly an hour of wild dancing, shortly after one in the morning. I don't know what time the rest of the group called it a night, but I'd heard about other evenings that stretched into dawn. I guess my age was showing.

The next day several of us met up again for the final send-off at one of the local pubs. The bus would arrive in just under an hour. The closer the leaving time drew, the quieter and less the talk. The atmosphere was the opposite of what that summer had been; awkward and uncomfortable as goodbyes naturally are when no one's looking forward to them. I knew it was exactly what Ned had hoped to avoid, but he just had to endure it like the rest of us.

One of the young ladies looked serious and another alternately laughed and cried, like a wind-up doll gone haywire. Most of the men were quiet, seeming unsure of just how to handle the moment, one of them looking perplexed, as though he didn't really understand the solemnity of the occasion. Others fiddled with phones, glanced at the clock above the bar, stared into the depths of their beer, or attempted nervous chat. Ned was mostly quiet and so was I. I felt his tension as he drank a last pint of Guinness at his favorite pub.

At ten minutes before the bus was due, we all trooped outside for a group photo, the tension eased for a moment by having something to do. A group hug spontaneously formed. The mood lightened as we stood facing each other in a tight circle, then it grew serious again. No one spoke. There was some nervous laughter and a call for 'speech!' – and finally Ned, the man who loved to talk and always had something to say, struggled to speak. 'I think this is the first time I have nothing to say,' he announced. Some laughed, some cried.

There were twelve of us, five men and seven women. Together, we walked the short distance to the bus stop, not wanting to give up any of the remaining minutes. We must have been a sight as we milled about, crowding the narrow sidewalk, moving like ants after our happy summer ant hill was disturbed. He had not even left, yet already it seemed we didn't know quite what to do with ourselves. The natural rhythm of things was disrupted and we hadn't yet figured out how to get in step with a new one.

The bus arrived and in a rush, the final round of hugs and farewells commenced. Ned and I hugged and I wished him luck, managing to say 'Write me!' before I couldn't say anything more. He didn't say anything funny. He didn't say anything at all.

He climbed aboard the bus, his usually smiling face solemn, and we watched as he found a window seat and sat down. I knew he was looking forward to the release of his book and to seeing old friends and family, but he didn't want to leave Ireland. Like the rest of us, he didn't want that easy summer to end.

A couple of the girls blew party horns, the silly noise lessening the strain and prompting a few giggles. The bus moved out slowly, Ned looking at us from beneath his baseball cap, peering through his black spectacles and the bus window. He raised a hand in farewell and we waved back, and kept waving until he disappeared around the corner.

We stood there a few seconds, staring at the empty place in the street where the bus had been, then together we turned and resolutely marched back down the sidewalk in a changed Kenmare, wishing we didn't have to feel his absence quite so much.

Ned's departure left us all feeling a little orphaned for different reasons. We each had our own unique relationship with him, but he'd been like the Papa Bear, the patriarch of our little clan. He was a presence, a force, in Kenmare. The void left by his absence not only in town, but in our individual lives would be with us for a while. I'd miss his writing help and those few months of feeling younger than my years.

I knew we'd long be remembering and telling stories about Ned and that crazy fun summer of friendship, excesses, and laughter.

◙

About two weeks after Ned left, I treated myself to a mini-holiday. I knew it would help me change gears. Months before I'd bought a ticket for a show at Siamsa Tíre, the National Folk Theater of Ireland in Tralee. As a fan of traditional Irish music and dance, it was something I'd long wanted to do. I could easily travel there by bus and decided to also include a stay at Inch Beach on the Dingle Peninsula and make a four-day trip of it.

I'm sometimes asked how it is to be without a car. Those with a car can't quite imagine it and I understand that. I once had a car, too, and spent a great deal of time in it. But I've done just fine without one. While it can be limiting, it never has really been a problem. I take the bus, the train, and in a pinch, a taxi. Mix it up with some patience and a sprinkling of helpful friends with cars now and then and you're in business.

My small boutique hotel in Tralee, the Park Georgian, was on a broad avenue lined with Georgian buildings made bright by the colorful doors. It was an easy walk from the bus station and near the theater. My room was small, as rooms often are in historic properties, but it had character. There were tall almost floor-to-ceiling windows, a view out over the street, a pretty chandelier, period-looking wallpaper and the original decorative moldings around the high ceilings. And at fifty-five euros for the room and breakfast, the price was right.

As in all lodging in Ireland, electrical outlets in the bathrooms are non-existent. I think there's a law against it. Oddly, there are outlets for 'shavers only.' Can one not be electrocuted with an electric shaver just as easily as a hairdryer? I don't get it, but that's the way it is.

Most places have a mirror near an electrical outlet elsewhere, but not in my room at the Park Georgian. That meant drying and styling my hair without benefit of a mirror, requiring frequent trips running back and forth into the bathroom to look in the mirror and assess my progress. It was difficult and time consuming, and greatly increased the chances for a bad hair day.

After the delay caused by the hair dryer situation, I arrived in the dining room for breakfast rather late. A young woman was starting to clear everything from a buffet table in the quiet, and empty, dining room. When she saw me and I asked if I was too late, she smiled and said 'Oh no! Please sit down!' and offered me a choice of tea or coffee. She then brought me a pot of coffee in an ornate silver pot, and handed me a menu with another smile.

After taking my order and turning it in to the kitchen, she returned and started up a conversation about where I had been and where I might like to go, and inquired, 'Are ye' enjoying yerself?' (That is a very Irish, often heard query and one I always liked. I've often wondered whether it's taught to Irish children, like learning to say 'please' and 'thank you.')

It was a lovely start to the day. There's something luxuriously wonderful about drinking coffee from a pretty silver pot, in an old, high-ceilinged Georgian-era dining room, while being waited on by a cheerful and chatty Irish lady.

The entrance to Tralee's Town Park with its rose garden was across the street. Although I'd had the one brief visit while waiting for my bus to Dingle on that earlier weekend trip, I hadn't realized what a large and impressive garden it is. I was amazed by the variety, colors, and beauty of the roses and other flowers blooming there. I wove my way in and out of the flower beds taking photos of large bushes heavy with purple and pink and white hydrangeas, and seas of roses in nearly every color of the rainbow. Beds of buds in palest pink, vibrant orange, deep reds brilliant yellow, and purest white swirled around me. Just when I was sure I'd found the perfect rose, I'd see the next one – and on and on it went. It didn't matter that it was a gray day; that only intensified the garden's spectrum of rich colors.

I'd noticed some large plants near the entrance to the garden, plants I'd seen elsewhere in Ireland. I thought they were called *Giant Rhubarb*, but I wasn't certain. Noticing two groundskeepers working nearby, I approached them to inquire.

'Excuse me? I was wondering what these plants are called?'

The two men looked up from their work and smiled. One shook his head and shrugged. The other said, 'Sorry, we don't know.' He gestured up the pathway, 'But the gardener is right up there. He'll be able to tell you.'

I thanked them and walked on. I heard a loud machine that sounded like a chainsaw and then saw the man who seemed to be the gardener. He was using an electric trimmer to tidy shrubbery along a fence behind a bed of snow white roses. Nearby, there were more of the large plants I'd seen by the entrance. His back was to me and the noise was too loud to try to get his attention. I waited, hoping he might pause, turn off the machine, or turn around. A minute later, he powered down the machine to a low murmur and stepped back to inspect his work.

I was ready. 'Excuse me?'

He turned toward me, a muscular, middle-aged man wearing dirty khaki work pants, a small paunch visible beneath his thin white t-shirt. He stood waist-deep in roses, the hedge trimmer buzzing in his right hand. On that humid afternoon sweat dripped from his face, and blood dripped from his left hand. Narrow red rivers flowed from the upper part of his forearm onto the back of his hand, tattooing it with an intricate, red, crisscross pattern before dripping onto the ground. I was startled by the sight and wondered if I should mention he was bleeding, but it seemed profuse and visible enough he surely already knew.

'Hi! I was wondering if you could tell me the name of those large plants.' I pointed to them. 'Is it Giant Rhubarb?'

I tried not to stare or wince as a few drops of blood landed in perfect ruby spheres on the velvet petals of a snowy rose. I thought of Sleeping Beauty.

'No, no, 'tis Elephant Ears. They look very much the same, though.'

'Oh, thank you! They are so prehistoric looking, aren't they?'

He nodded his head, a quick dip, and smiled, but didn't say another word, just returned to hedge trimming, sweat pouring off his brow and the blood dripping from his wounded arm of no apparent concern. A common hazard of gardening with machines? All in a day's work, I supposed.

I think it might have been the only time in Ireland – except for that strange day soon after my arrival when I was on the calling card hunt – when a simple question didn't turn into a full-blown conversation, both with the gardener and the two men I'd spoken with earlier. They must all have been very busy, working to keep that beautiful garden looking so lovely.

◎

That evening I arrived at the theater early, so had time to walk around the grounds, just on the edge of the rose garden. It was cool and breezy, welcome and refreshing after the day's high humidity. In the shady forest steps away from the theater I admired the tall oak and beech trees alive with twittering birds singing their evening songs, then wandered across the gently sloping expanse of green lawn surrounding the building. The entire perimeter of the grounds was lined with more beds of multi-hued roses. Hanging baskets of pink and purple petunias flanked the stone walls leading to the theater's entrance, giving a cheerful welcome to visitors.

As I so often did when encountering something extra-special, I called my sister to report on the scene and express my excitement about the upcoming show. We talked as I strolled under the trees enjoying the refreshing air and the light scent of green and roses. I wished she was there with me.

As show time approached, more people arrived and clustered in groups in the lobby and just outside the entrance, lingering as long as possible in the pleasant, cool, evening breezes.

I couldn't have been happier with my seat in the fourth row, near center. It would be perfect viewing and I congratulated myself for buying my ticket well in advance. It was almost curtain time.

The last few stragglers found their seats and the theater began to grow quieter – until a large chattering group of people walked in. Judging from their accents I guessed they might have been German, but I can't say for certain. There were thirty or forty of them and it appeared to be a tour group. I thought it thoughtless, rude even, for anyone, especially a large group, to be arriving so late after everyone else was settled. Perhaps there'd been extenuating circumstances. I wondered what their story was. Traffic? Bus break-down? One thing was certain: they were loud, but maybe that's just because there were so many of them. I was trying to give them the benefit of the doubt rather than get annoyed.

I stood up to make room as several filed past me to get to their seats. As the last man passed, I started to sit down, but couldn't. The man had stopped abruptly, right in front of me. I couldn't sit down; there wasn't room. Awkward. He started waving his ticket in my face and telling me I was in his seat. I quietly assured him I was in the correct seat, but he loudly demanded to see my ticket. Okay, now I was annoyed. I dug it out and showed it to him. He produced his own ticket. We'd been assigned the same seat.

Rather than being polite and exiting the row to find someone to help him with his ticket, or even offering to do that, this gallant gentleman stayed where he was. I could neither exit the row nor sit. I was penned between him and my seat.

Much rapid conversation went on between the man and some of the others, in what I presumed to be German. A large, round Spanish-sounding woman I guessed must be the group's leader, probably a tour guide, stood in the aisle waving her arms and interjecting comments and questions in English. All of them looked at me as though *I* was the offender. It wasn't just annoying; it was embarrassing to be a part of such an unpleasant scene. My heart rate was rising and likely my blood pressure, too.

The chaos brought an usher to see what was going on. The tour guide and the man trying to claim my seat began arguing with her. I let that go on for all of about five seconds until I saw a slight opening which allowed me to dislodge myself and escape to the aisle. When I glanced back down the row, I saw the man was already planted in my seat. A gallant man, indeed. I stood in the aisle while the usher went to the lobby to see what could be done to sort out the problem.

The usher returned and apologized for the double-sale of the seat and explained that the tour group had arrived late to purchase tickets and in the rush before curtain time, an error was made and one of them was issued a ticket for an already occupied seat. Yes, I knew that. It was my seat. Seeing that the man had taken firm ownership of the seat in question, the usher asked if I would mind sitting in the empty seat on the aisle one row back. She could obviously see I was the more cooperative patron and therefore the easier person to move. Lights dimming and curtain about to go up, I couldn't see that further argument would be helpful. I sat. She thanked me and told me to have a drink on the house during intermission. The curtain opened and the show began.

And what a show it was. It was sung entirely in Irish. There was no program to help one understand what was being said, but I didn't have too much trouble figuring it out. For someone unfamiliar with Irish history and customs it might have been more difficult. Even knowing it was wrong to do so, I couldn't help hoping that was the case for the man sitting in my seat. The show portrayed the traditional activities and customs of the old days covering each of the four seasons, stories woven together beautifully and seamlessly through harmonious music and expressive dance. I enjoyed it immensely, and the curtain came down too soon.

I took advantage of the courtesy drink and enjoyed a delicious Irish coffee during intermission. Aside from the rough start with the seating issue, it was a wonderful evening. It is a show I would enjoy seeing again and perhaps I will. But should the situation arise, I'm quite certain no amount of free drinks will entice me to give up my seat.

◍

From Tralee I traveled by bus to the small, quiet village of Annascaul on the Dingle Peninsula, the closest stop to Inch Beach, arriving about noon. I tried a few pub doors, all of which were locked. My plan was to get a cup of tea and call a taxi to take me the last few miles to Inch Beach. Seeing an establishment up the street, the Anchor Inn, I went in that direction and was relieved to find an open door. I entered and found myself in a charming little café, empty except for one young man, busy sweeping what looked like an already spotless floor.

I hesitated in the doorway.

'Are you open?'

'We are,' he said, 'but only for coffee or tea right now.'

'Perfect! That's exactly what I'm looking for! May I have a cup of tea, please?'

'You may, surely,' he said, nodding his head and gesturing toward one of the tables.

He disappeared and I sat down at the offered table. Within minutes he brought me a steaming hot cup of tea. We chatted for a moment and I learned he was the proprietor. I asked if he knew of a taxi service in the area. He shook his head in the negative.

'Where are you going?' he asked.

'Inch Beach.'

'I can take you if you don't mind waiting a few minutes while I take care of some things upstairs.'

Well, of course I didn't mind. I was once again amazed at the kindness of the Irish, the willingness to help. I thanked him and told him I was in no hurry at all and whenever he was ready I would be, too.

I drank my tea, and after several minutes he came back downstairs and I heard a door slam toward the back of the building. Seconds later a car pulled up out front and he hopped out of it. I went outside and he met me at the door, grabbed my bag, and took it around to the car trunk (although I'm certain he thought it was a boot, not a trunk). I reached for the car door handle on, as always, the wrong side of the car. 'Wrong side!' he called out with a smile. Although living in Ireland long enough to know better, I consistently tried to get in the driver's side. I couldn't seem to break the habit.

We set out on the short drive to Inch. When we arrived he pulled into a turn-out off the narrow two-lane highway overlooking the sea, across the road from my hotel. I thanked him and asked how much I owed him. He said 'Oh, a fiver to cover the petrol.'

'Are you sure that's enough?'

He nodded. 'You're grand.'

I paid him, thanked him again, and crossed the highway to the hotel as he did a U-turn, waved, and headed back to Annascaul.

I was looking forward to the enticingly described '*sea view room with balcony!*' which I'd paid extra for as a splurge. My heart sank when I opened the curtains of my room. I was overlooking the sea alright, but from the ground floor. And there was no balcony, not even a private patio. The area directly outside the windows was a common area. If I opened a window, I could literally reach out and touch people walking by, children playing, and a gardener with a noisy edging machine. So with the drapes open, there was no privacy – and, of course, no sea view if they were closed. Still, for the few minutes here and there when I bravely pulled them back, the view was outstanding. If only I hadn't minded feeling like a monkey in a glass cage at the zoo.

I mentioned the problem to the woman at the front desk, but she seemed to think I was in the right room and said, 'it's not possible' I would have booked a room with a balcony. Showing her the evidence of having done so after she demanded my receipt didn't help. And she seemed not to understand the privacy issue at all. I must mention here, in case there's any doubt, the woman was not Irish.

I was uncertain whether the issue was with the hotel or the booking agency. I decided not to press it further just then. I hadn't planned to spend much time in the room, anyway, and given the lack of privacy would be doing little more than sleeping there – with the windows locked and the drapes drawn.

I'd been to Inch Beach before, but only for brief stops. It is a beautiful broad beach almost two miles long, the kind of beach where you must kick off your shoes no matter the weather and stroll along the water's edge. The multitude of hues and patterns caused by the play of light on wet sand and the ebb and flow of the water is striking. I'm always reminded of an animated glass container of sand art, the shadows and colors all changing at the whim of the sunshine and clouds, creating a picturesque, shifting panorama of sea, sand and rolling hills.

It was a sunny summer day but unfortunately, along with the summer season comes the commercialism of surf school signage and trailers and the regular arrivals of the big coach tours and their crowds of people. The wild beauty and peace of the place suffers from such intrusions. The off-season is a much better time to be there, but it is such a special place it's impossible not to find enjoyment in it, whatever the season.

On the last day after checking out of my room, I ducked into the café on the beach to escape the wild winds. The bell on the door jangled as I pushed it open, but otherwise the place was quiet. The weekend was over and that seemed to have cut back on the crowds. There were only two other customers. A young couple sat at one of the tables, voices low, heads close together. I had an hour to kill before my bus to Tralee, an hour I'd planned to spend walking on the now fairly empty beach, but the winds were simply too strong to make that a pleasant activity. Reading a good book in the ocean-front café seemed a nice alternative and I was happy to find it so empty and quiet.

I settled in with a cup of tea at a table by the front window, opened my book and began reading. From time to time, I glanced at the view across the beach to the waves sparkling in the sunshine and the distant green hills, enjoying the beauty and peace of the morning.

My nerves jolted and my head jerked up from my book when the café door burst open and a large, noisy tour group poured in to the café, shattering the morning's serenity. Oh, no. Not again! After the theater incident, I was a little sour on tour groups. I admonished myself for having a bad attitude and tried to ignore the noise and confusion caused by the milling people. It was, after all, a public place. I couldn't claim it as my own.

Tables soon filled up inside the café. It was a big tour group, indeed. Being a paying customer, I didn't worry about taking up a table for four; there weren't any smaller tables. I returned to reading my book but seconds later was interrupted by a lady with an American accent, I assumed from the tour group.

'Are these seats taken?' She gestured to the two chairs on the other side of the table.

I hesitated, then decided there was no harm in letting her sit down, and maybe she just wanted the chairs, anyway.

'No, I'm not using them,' I said, and continued reading.

Within seconds two more women swooped in like seagulls to a fisherman's bait bucket and sat down in the empty chairs across from me. Dang. The original woman stood next to the chair beside me, the chair wedged between my wheeled bag and the table. The chair holding my over-stuffed backpack. I ignored her and kept reading – until she asked me to move my backpack. At that point, I realized they intended to take over the entire table, so I gave up. I gathered my things, abandoned my tea and left, but not before I said, 'Did you notice there are tables outside?'

'Yes!' the woman said brightly, and sat down, either missing my point or choosing to ignore it.

There were no protestations at my departure. I don't think they had the slightest idea of the rudeness of their intrusion.

I moved into the attached pub and continued reading, then went out to the highway to wait for the bus, watching as yet another tour coach pulled up. I love Inch Beach, but by then I was glad to be leaving.

The bus arrived, I boarded, sat down and thought about my little holiday, about how nice it was that I'd come across the usual Irish hospitality during my trip, but how it had made the encounters with the thoughtless seem that much worse. I was out of practice with that sort of thing after living in Ireland for almost a year. I made a mental note to restrict my traveling to the off-season as much as possible as that surely was the key.

It came to me on that bus ride home that there should be an 'Irish Hospitality School, an intensive course on how to be kind and thoughtful for those who needed it.. Or a test everyone has to take to get through customs. And there would be no separate lines for 'EU' and 'Non-EU' citizens, everyone in the same line. Pass, welcome to Ireland! Fail? Go directly to Irish Hospitality School – or back from whence you came. Your choice.

35

TO MARKET, TO MARKET TO BUY A FAT PIG

August 15, 2014: Tomorrow is Kenmare's Fair Day. My wellies are waiting beside the door, along with my camera, ready to hit the streets first thing in the morning!

For months I'd been hearing about Kenmare's Fair Day, held annually in late summer and often called *The 15th of August*, the name matching the event's date. Opinions varied; some loved it, some hated it, but there was little in between. It evoked enough emotion and had enough controversy associated with it I knew for certain I would attend because good or bad, it was sure to be an experience not to be missed.

The festival is a sort of country fair in the middle of the town and has been held annually every summer for a couple of hundred years. It was once primarily animals for sale and trade, along with a few stalls selling items such as apples and shoes. It was a time for people to get out and socialize, see folks they hadn't seen in months or perhaps even a full year, since the last Fair Day. It was an important occasion, a special event. This was particularly true in earlier days when people lived further apart and didn't have the luxury of hopping in a car and going into town regularly.

As all things do, over the years Fair Day changed. Apples and shoes were joined by more shoes, more produce, items made by craftsmen and artisans, and the occasional carnival game of chance. With farmers' greater mobility and other places to sell animals, the number of animals brought to the fair decreased over the years.

Today, a large contingent of Irish travelers is visible. A traveler is the Irish version of a gypsy, nomadic people of undetermined origin. They are a close-knit group with their own ancient culture. There are an estimated 20,000 of them in the Republic of Ireland, most living apart from the rest of the country's population. Prejudice against them is deeply ingrained and many see them as thieves and troublemakers. I haven't enough knowledge and familiarity to know how much truth there is behind the prejudice, but like all prejudices I know it is a mistake to paint *all* people with the same broad brush.

On Fair Day a growing number of traveler stalls offering cheap plastic toys and trinkets and mass quantities of mostly used tools and equipment have all but pushed out the craftsmen and artisans, many of whom don't want to associate with the traveler element. Garda and shopkeepers are kept busy by traveler boys who appear to run free in the town with no adult supervision, most just having fun, but some caught during or after the act of shoplifting. Many of the little boys are rowdy, some just cocky, others argumentative and belligerent. Most of the traveler women and girls apparently either stay home or keep lower profiles.

On the eve of Fair Day I had dinner with some friends at one of the more upscale restaurants in town. Five little traveler boys ranging in age from about six to ten marched brazenly into the small, candle-lit and intimate dining room, a place where you could reach out and touch the tables next to yours. We knew they were travelers because no other Irish boys of their age group would be running loose at the time of the evening without an adult, nor behaving in that manner.

Three of the boys hopped up on the only three bar stools in the restaurant, in front of the small, busy, multi-purpose counter where diners are greeted and can wait for their table if necessary. It is also where food is set out for pick up by the wait staff. The three boys sat swinging their legs, kicking the stools, and talking and laughing while the two youngest scuffled around punching each other and being obnoxious. All of them were in the way and disrupting both diners and staff. Their behavior wasn't outrageous, but it simply was not the place nor the time for it.

During the initial confrontation with one of the servers who asked them to leave, one of the older boys loudly and repeatedly protested, 'But miss! He's disabled, miss!' pointing to the fit-looking lad with a smirk on his face sitting on the stool next to him. It took several minutes of coaxing by the wait staff and then the chef before they left. I thought how sad it is that it takes only the poor behavior of a few to give an entire group a bad reputation.

The traveler issue aside, the 15th of August is still an occasion in Kenmare, and the town's busiest day of the year. It is a time for the locals and those from further afield to come out and mix and mingle, and you can feel the excitement in the air.

I arose at 7:00 am. for better photographic opportunities, before the crowds gathered. I hadn't seen that hour of the morning since the first few months after I arrived in Ireland. After nearly a year, it was a good two hours before the time my feet hit the floor on most mornings.

The morning was one of those fine Irish summer days I'd seen often, but never took for granted. Puffy cumulus clouds blazed white against the deep blue of the sky while a few smaller, gray rain clouds periodically danced past the sun. I threw on a rain jacket and stepped into my trusty wellies and was out the door. The wellies were more for the deposits left by the animals on the streets – I'd been forewarned – than the possibility of rain.

I walked the short distance to the end of the street to the town square. Most of the stalls were already set up. I use the term 'stall' loosely. Many were nothing more than a rectangle delineated by lengths of chain or rope laid out on a section of the street next to the curb, the goods arranged on the ground, sometimes on a tarp or old sheet, others sitting right on the pavement. Some were more traditional stalls, with canopies and shelving and display tables.

The town was fairly quiet except for the sound of the animals. A growing cacophony of clucking, crowing, mooing, whinnying and quacking reached me, becoming louder the closer I came to what I thought of as 'animal lane.' There, rows of colorful caged poultry lined the street; turkeys looking a little confused, hens puffing out their feathers and stretching their wings, roosters trying to out-crow each other, ducks milling and quacking. Other cages held rabbits and one was full of yellow ducklings. In another cage tiny, weeks' old pure white kittens I felt certain were too young to be away from their mother mewed and pushed against one another for warmth. The owners of this assorted menagerie sat in lawn chairs near their animals or clustered together in groups, talking.

A dozen muddy cows looking too thin stood dumbly packed together on one side of the street. Nearby a young boy in a baggy faded red sweater, loose brown trousers, and knee-high wellies leaned on a tall stick, both his clothing and posture mimicking that of the man standing next to him.

Across the street two donkeys stood on the sidewalk tied to a shop front. They brayed in loud complaint as three small ponies were led from a truck and tied up near them. Further on, a teenage lad unloaded horses from a beat-up trailer, and nearby, another stuffed hens into already full cages.

In the middle of the street a man paraded a handsome tall brown horse with a white face, taking advantage of the space and quiet of the morning to display his steed.

Early in the day a group of adolescent boys sauntered by me, taking exaggerated strides too long for their legs, chests puffed out, foolish grins on their faces. 'Well, hello Miss!' they said. Spoken too loudly and brashly to be a polite greeting, they were just taunting, looking for trouble. I'd never seen any of the children of Kenmare behave in that manner, so assumed they were travelers. I ignored them, knowing it was best not to engage. I didn't feel they were any real threat, so I wasn't afraid. They were just showing off for each other. Besides, they were young, it was broad daylight, and there were plenty of people around.

Later I watched one garda officer marching two reluctant and uncooperative boys of maybe eight or nine years of age down the street in the direction of the local market while they protested with loud, bold indignance, 'But it's mine! I own it! I didn't take it!'

But Fair Day is more than kids looking for trouble, a variety of cheap and tacky goods for sale, and the occasional scene that'll tug at your heart, like the tiny white kittens missing their mother, or the man carrying a full-grown, trusting Jack Russell terrier in his arms, offering it for sale for the price of eight euros. Fair Day is a mostly happy, colorful, chatty sort of day.

By midday the sun blazed in a clear sky and the streets were alive with people, young and old. Neighbors, families, old friends and new, meeting and greeting, talking and laughing. Babies dozed in strollers, toddlers rode on fathers' shoulders high above the crowd, and older children stayed close to their parents. Farmers in their old wool jackets and wellies stood in groups having a chat, others inspected animals or produce.

A merchant gave a spiel about the quality of his rugs, and the Speedy Peeler guy demonstrated the miracle of his veggie chopping machine, reducing vegetables to slim strips or tiny cubes of their former selves, slivers of potato and eggplant and cucumbers piling up around him and the occasional random piece veering off and shooting into the crowd.

Bushels of giant carrots and parsnips were stacked high on makeshift tables or in the back end of vans with their doors thrown open; racks of hoodies emblazoned with CALIFORNIA waved in the wind. There were three-euro scarves, row upon row of boots, books, DVD's, CD's and even cassette tapes. I wondered how many of the younger generation were curious as to just what those cassettes actually were, and realized even CD's would soon likely become curiosities.

Loads of utilitarian mostly metal items like automobile grills lay in the street in piles or in orderly lines, along with lawnmowers without handles, filters for industrial ventilation systems, impressive chain saw and power drill collections, and rusty nuts, bolts and unidentifiable parts for unknown machines.

Unsuspecting tourists trying to drive through Kenmare sat in bumper to bumper traffic, inching along, surrounded by the crush of waving, chatting, smiling festival-goers who filled the streets like busy and contented bees in a field of sweet summer flowers. Most looked surprised, amused, or interested.

Kenmare's Fair Day is an old tradition and a not to be missed experience. With the sun shining and the street corner buskers playing music and the flower baskets spilling over with bright flowers, it is a good place to be and one of those Irish experiences I felt lucky to have. There is something for everyone. A pint in a pub, tea or coffee at one of the sidewalk tables. A pause to listen to the music or visit with a friend. A browse through the goods, the purchase of a book or a scarf or any tool you've likely ever imagined. A slow wander to look at the colorful chickens, the cute bunnies and ducklings, the cows, goats, bored donkeys and patient ponies. But do keep a sharp eye for piles of animal dung, adolescent traveler boys oozing testosterone who enjoy revving up unsold chainsaws just for the noise and power and macho appearance of it, and the younger ones racing around the town in a state of excitement over their festival day of freedom, who might fancy something that doesn't belong to them and perhaps, in their heightened state of invincibility, walk away with it. But by all means ask those youngsters if they'd like to have their picture taken and they'll stop their puffed up bravado and boasting, relax into their true child-selves and pose like little angels, their sweet smiles and rosy cheeks belying the mischief they've just been up to and will no doubt continue on with once you've snapped the picture. It's all part of the color and the craic of Fair Day in Kenmare.

36

PLACE YOUR BETS!

August 27, 2014: Off on another excursion in the morning, this time to see horse racing on the beach!

Glenbeigh, on the Ring of Kerry, is a small, sleepy place. Something between a village and a wide spot in the road. But on the weekend of the Glenbeigh Festival & Races there is an explosion in the population and activity level. 'Sleepy' no longer applies. I was there for that festival and looking forward to seeing the horse races on the beach, races that have been held since 1924. It seemed to be one of those very Irish things I should do, and it sounded interesting and fun.

Among the traffic, horse trailers and people, I counted three pubs, a deli/take-out pizza place, a couple of B&B's, a combination petrol station and convenience store, a church, and two hotels. I threaded my way through the melee to one of the hotels, the old Towers Hotel, where I'd be spending the weekend.

My room was a beautiful corner room on the first floor, which is actually the second floor if you're American, but in Ireland – perhaps all of Europe? – the first floor is known as the ground floor, making the second floor the first floor. The room had tall, deep-set windows on two sides, the window sills wide enough to sit on. From my room I overlooked the street and could see across to a glimpse of Rossbeigh Strand in the distance, the beach where the horses would run, and beyond that, the mountains of the Dingle Peninsula.

I'd hoped to hear trad music in the hotel's pub that evening. I was out of luck with the music, but there was a cheerful local man who seemed pleased to make my acquaintance. He had a nice smile, was good-looking, and appeared to be of my generation. A retired garda officer, he was friendly and talkative.

I asked him if he was married. He was a little vague on the subject, but indicated he did have someone waiting for him at home. I didn't see that as problem and figured we could still have a friendly chat, but soon learned I was wrong. With his next breath he inquired as to whether he might buy me dinner. I missed a few beats, not really believing what I was hearing, thinking I must have misunderstood. We'd only met two minutes before and he'd just told me he wasn't single. I inquired if his wife would be joining us. No, she wouldn't. He repeated the invitation, this time with a definite flirtatious tone. It was *me* he wished to take to dinner, he emphasized with a wink. I politely refused with a thank you.

He looked exaggeratedly crestfallen and proceeded to compliment me – at length. I was surely the most beautiful lady he'd seen in a long while, I had lovely eyes, I was obviously a genuinely kind person. He didn't seem to know he was diluting the value of his compliments with his excessive flattery and wasn't making the kind of impression he was probably hoping for.

He introduced me to several friends as the love of his life. I laughed – the first time he said it. Would I open the door if one day he showed up in Kenmare? If you bring your wife along, I replied. His eyes widened. Oh, no, that isn't what he was asking. 'Would you not open the door if I show up on my own?'

'No, I'm sorry, I wouldn't.' He was not daunted and continued on in this vein, his words interspersed with hiccups and apologies and gestures toward his pint glass. He didn't seem inebriated, but continued to repeat himself and persisted with his fantasy of meeting me in Kenmare. This wasn't quite the friendly, pleasant, easy chat I'd hoped it would be.

I tried ignoring him and struck up a conversation with the person sitting on the other side of me. He didn't give up. He tried a new angle. Had I ever stood on the beach at Rossbeigh Strand to watch the setting sun? No; I hadn't. 'Oh, 'tis a beautiful sight! 'You must see it! Will we go?'

I forced a laugh and said, 'Not tonight.' I was trying to diffuse the situation, keep it light, but it wasn't working. He pursued the topic of the beach sunset for several more minutes, then circled back around to Kenmare like a dog on the trail of a rabbit.

'Don't be surprised when you see me! It's your door I'll be knocking on one day – just wait! And we'll go out, we will, and paint the town red! You'll open the door now, will you not?'

'Sure. If you bring your wife,' I said through gritted teeth. For the third time. Or was it the fourth? He frowned and sighed. So did I. He seemed not to notice.

I enjoy flattery as much as anyone else, and it is often the way of many Irish men, but this wasn't the teasing banter I was familiar with. It went far beyond, and was uncomfortable and annoying. The fact that he was not single made it even more so. I realized the only way to end it was to take my leave. I excused myself, much to his loudly voiced dismay, and retreated to my room.

Meeting men didn't seem to be a problem in Ireland, but meeting the right ones was no less difficult than anywhere else, I supposed.

◫

From my room I could look down on an outdoor seating area which wrapped around the street side of the hotel. A geranium-filled terrace enclosed with white wrought iron railings and creeping ivy, it was charming and picturesque. I didn't know that was only its daytime and early evening persona. I slept in fits and starts that night as that pretty terrace became a haven for the drunks with nowhere to go when the pubs closed. The terrace party went on until, at last check of the clock, five-forty in the morning.

Yawning, I mentioned the all-night gathering to the lady at the front desk when I went down for breakfast, not so much as a complaint, but more as something I thought the hotel might want to know about. She just smiled. It was, she explained to the clueless American, 'festival weekend.' I guess she thought those two words said it all and I suppose they did. It was indeed festival weekend. The hotel and the streets were crawling with people. Thankfully, the annoying man from the night before seemed to have disappeared or was well lost in the crowd.

In the hotel dining room I ate a full-Irish breakfast that would leave you prepared for a winter in hibernation, complete with the white and black pudding I always pushed aside, bacon, sausages, beans, eggs, grilled tomato, toast and more toast. I at first thought it strange that potatoes are rarely included in a full-Irish breakfast, but decided they are purposely omitted because they're so much a part of every other meal.

After breakfast I called for a cab to the races, the only taxi service in town, one driver, one car. I called at just the right time and was lucky to get him. His name was Sean and we chatted on the five minute drive to Rossbeigh Strand.

'I was hoping to hear some trad music last night, but there wasn't any,' I said. Sean was a young man, probably in his twenties, so I knew he probably wouldn't share my taste in music, but I was just making conversation about something other than the weather.

'Oh, 'tis trad you like, is it?'

'I do, yes! Very much!'

'Tomorrow morning! At the pub across the street!'

I wasn't sure what he meant. Music on Sunday morning? Trad music?

'There'll be trad music then?'

'Oh, there will, there will. Me and the lads will be playing music for a few hours before the races start!'

So Sean wasn't just the only cab driver in town, he was also a musician.

'That's great! What time?'

'Right after mass!' he said with a big smile.

We reached Rossbeigh Strand and he stopped the cab. I paid him, stepped out onto the sandy roadway and waved as he roared off back toward the village. It was windy and cloudy, but occasionally the sun broke through, so there was hope for a fair day.

I was excited to be there, so really wasn't concerned too much with the weather. I'd been to a horse race only once in my life and it was certainly not on a beach nor was it in Ireland. I was fascinated by everything I was seeing.

From where Sean dropped me off, I walked in on the narrow paved roadway running parallel to the beach, leading into the race site. It was lined with parked cars and food trucks, more food trucks than I would have imagined could be found in the whole of County Kerry. You had your ice cream truck and several selling burgers and sausages; fish and chips trucks, and trucks specializing in coffee and tea. There were trucks selling crepes, trucks advertising 'Best Ices!' and those selling cold drinks, hot dogs, and bags of crisps. In between the trucks were a few tacky souvenir stands where overly optimistic vendors hawked their mostly made of plastic wares.

Reaching the end of the food trucks I could see the long beach, a broad smooth stretch of sand and water framed by green hills, strewn at one end with seaweed left behind when the tide receded. A bulldozer worked to maneuver the sea's discarded vegetation into piles, clearing the route the horses would take. A trainer walked a lone horse along the beach at the other end, near what I'd later learn was the finish line.

Straight ahead a giant wooden cut-out of a horseshoe about eight feet high, emblazoned with the words GLENBEIGH FESTIVAL & RACES stood in the center of a ring fenced in with white rails. And then there was the area which, if it had a name, would surely have been called 'Betting Alley.' Between a line of food trucks and the beach, a narrow path was lined on either side with bookies. Digital signs above each stand showed the odds for the horses. You could bet on horses with names like *Squeeze Your Knees, Pocket Rocket, Good Times Ahead* and *Top of the Morning.* As the minutes counted down to the next race of the day, the bookies began calling out like carnival barkers, urging the growing crowd of people to place their bets.

The ring with the giant horseshoe served double-duty as warm-up ring and the winner's circle. I was surprised at the young age of most of the handlers and jockeys. A number of them were without a doubt under the age of fourteen and several looked to be as young as ten or eleven.

The area around the ring, between the road and the beach, had previously been the sandy top of the dunes. After the unfortunate massive erosion caused by the winter's awful storms, most of the dunes were gone. Instead of sand it was a giant rock pile, loose rocks trucked in to form a sea break. It wasn't gravel; these were large stones of varying sizes, none so small as a piece of gravel and some larger than a fist, a treacherous surface for walking. What was left of the sand dunes and beach grass provided the far northern boundary of the race grounds, where the horse trailers were parked. Pathways for the horses leading from the trailers to the winner's circle, and down to the beach, were clear of rocks and covered in a mixture of freshly poured damp soil and sand.

To view the races from the flats of the beach, it was necessary to make your way down the steep and unsteady hill of stones – if you dared. Most spectators stood atop the rock pile at the edge, above the beach, and, as each race ended, moved from their viewing point back to the winner's circle to watch as the winners were recognized and the jockeys and owners interviewed, then made their way back to the viewpoint across the ankle-breaking stones, for the next race. Climbing repeatedly up and down the rocks to and from the sand was only for the very young or those with goat-like tendencies. I didn't fall into either of those categories.

I watched the trainers walk slender long-legged horses around the ring as they were announced before each race, some of them straining to control the often skittish animals, then lead them down the sandy pathway to the beach, the young jockeys dressed in their bright silks now sitting astride their energetic steeds. An ambulance parked on the sand reminded us of the danger in this sport.

Reaching the sand, the jockeys took the horses at a slow gallop far down the beach to the left, past the spectators and almost out of sight to the starting point for the longer races. And then they were off, soon charging past us, running along the beach where the waves met the sand, then out of sight again and back around, crossing again in front of us, closer to us this time, racing for the finish line. It was thrilling to see them skimming across the wet sand, the waves in the background, the dull thudding noise of their hooves audible above the wind and the sound of the sea, little sprays of sand kicking up and trailing behind them. It was every bit as exciting as I had imagined it would be. The weather had turned windier and colder but I wasn't distracted from the action on the beach.

The announcer's voice blared over the loudspeakers, a steady commentary undoubtedly full of all kinds of information, but what he said most of the time could as well have been Greek – or more appropriately, Irish. But no, it was English, the Kerry accent, poor sound system, and the wind creating a whole new language which most of the time I was unable to translate. Luck was with me during one race, though, and I was able to understand him as he called out the names of the horses approaching the finish line, Sandy Cove and Pocket Rocket vying for first place, his voice becoming louder, higher pitched and more urgent as the race came to an exciting end. *'And it's Sandy Cove and Pocket Rocket and here comes High Definition and it's Sandy Cove and Pocket Rocket and High Definition in third and it's Sandy Cove inching ahead and it's Sandy Cove in the lead followed by Pocket Rocket and High Definition and it's SANDY COVE! IT'S SANDY COVE IN FIRST PLACE!!'* (Cheers and applause.)

As the races wound down, by late afternoon I was starting to feel the chill and tiring of the rocky scramble back and forth so decided to call it a day. I telephoned Sean for a ride back to town, but he was sorry, he couldn't collect me just then. He was in Killarney, a good thirty miles away. Oh. If I wanted to wait, he said, he could be there in an hour. I didn't think I had any other option since he was the only cabbie in town, but he asked that I call him if I found another lift.

I sat on a big rock at the entrance to the beach parking and watched cars come and go. I contemplated sticking my thumb out versus biding my time for an hour. I would have started walking but the narrow road back to the village had no shoulder so it didn't seem a safe thing to do. I'd been caught on a road like that in

Ireland once, and I wasn't in the mood for the ditch diving and periodic walking through brambles and nettles I knew would be required to escape oncoming cars. As I ruminated, a car pulled up near me with two women in it. One of them got out and headed toward the nearby public toilets. She looked to be around my age and perfectly normal and approachable. I wasn't sure what 'normal' meant, really, but that was my gut reaction. *Now's your chance. Just ask!* I took the plunge.

'Excuse me? I wonder, are you heading back to Glenbeigh?' I was uncomfortable asking but decided nothing too terrible would come of it. I hoped I didn't look like a vagrant; I hoped her gut reaction might be similar to mine and she'd see me as normal, too.

'Glenbeigh?' she asked.

I nodded.

'We are!' she said, smiling.

I explained the taxi situation and she told me to hop in the car, they'd be happy to take me back to the village. Sean was a bright guy after all. I phoned him to let him know I got a lift, then enjoyed chatting with the two pleasant women, sisters from Wales who now lived just beyond Glenbeigh, out for a day at the races. I could easily picture my sister and I having a similar outing, and I thought how much fun we'd have had if she'd been there.

◻

The next morning after breakfast I took a cup of coffee outside and sat down at one of the picnic tables outside the hotel's pub. It was a soft day, a fine, nearly invisible mist dampening the air. I had no idea what time mass was or when it would be over, but the hotel sat on the village square and I had a clear view of the church to my right and the pub Sean had mentioned to my left. I was ready.

I drank my coffee, listened to the banter between a few jockeys, trainers, owners and their friends, and chatted with Bob and Rose who'd arrived to join me for day two of the races, just as the sun began shining through the mist.

It wasn't long before the church doors opened and people started emerging, wandering into the street, many going into the pub. It was ten o'clock in the morning. And sure enough, as promised, a short while later my new buddy Sean appeared, guitar in hand, and the rest of 'the lads' – another guitarist, an accordion player, and a guy on bodhrán. They took up their places on a picnic table on the sidewalk beneath the pub's awning, and the trad tunes began on a gray misty morning after mass.

Festival banners crisscrossed the street, flapping in the breeze, and the one yellow-vested garda officer stood in the middle of the main street through the village, ready to direct the flood of traffic. On the Ring of Kerry, Glenbeigh has a steady stream of traffic during the tourist season, even without the festival. As the morning progressed, traffic increased and continued unabated, so the view of the musicians was sometimes blocked by giant tractors and combines and horse trailers, but it was all part of the scene.

The jigs and reels played on and a few adults and several children danced, others talked and laughed, and some dodged passing cars to run back and forth across the street when they spied familiar faces. The garda waved traffic through, trying to keep it moving, but unperturbed when the occasional car stopped in the middle of the roadway to have a chat with him, and others slowed down to gawk at the crowded square or call greetings through car windows. It was a grand way to start day two at the races – or any day, for that matter.

The weather wasn't cooperative that day, turning colder, windier and wetter when the music ended, but it didn't matter. I'd gone to the Glenbeigh Festival & Races to see horse racing on the beach. I lived that experience and more. I hadn't just seen horses racing across the sand, I'd also met a guitar-playing cabbie and two Welsh sisters, mingled with race officials, bookies, and spectators, and admired the views. I drank tea from one food truck and treated myself to an American-style hot dog from another, both enjoyed in the brisk sea air. I survived the over-attention of a bold Irishman, and heard trad tunes on a Sunday morning after mass, drinking coffee in the mist, while trucks hauling horse trailers creaked and clanked down the road to the beach, jockeys joked with trainers, people laughed, and children skipped and danced to the music in the town square. Another grand Irish adventure!

37

But It's August!

August 31, 2014: I had a fire going last night! In August!

I went to bed one night at midnight after darkness had fallen on a long summer's day only a few hours before, and woke up the next morning to the steady patter of rain on the roof. Not so unusual; I was in Ireland. But after the rain continued for nearly two weeks with only minor breaks, the gloom and cooler temperatures had me wondering if summer was over. I had even lit the fire one evening to ward off the chill. The *fire.* As in, it was cold and I needed heat. Just an odd evening, I told myself. A fluke. It would pass. It was still August.

All spring and summer it had been gloriously sunny and warm. It surely couldn't just become fall overnight? An Irish friend told me, 'Autumn begins in August in Ireland!' I laughed, figuring it was a joke, but I was starting to question that assumption.

The rain and wind followed me home from Glenbeigh and by the time it reached Kenmare it picked up speed and intensity. Getting ready to go to the market the next day I zipped up my raincoat, pulled up my hood, and put on my wellies, the boots which had sat undisturbed in a dark corner all summer except for their outing on Fair Day.

Soon after heading up the street I ran into Mandy and we stopped to chat, but the wind and rain soon sent us hurrying along on our respective ways. Yes, it was August, but this was not the way of summer.

I rounded the corner into town and the rain lessened, but persisted, swirling in a fine wet mist around me. Cold drops dripped steadily from the edges of shop awnings. If you were fool enough to be without hood or umbrella, they'd find the top of your head or the back of your neck and drop with pinpoint accuracy, running down a secret pathway beneath your clothes, dripping down your back in icy streams. But still… the calendar, the number of tourists, and the flowers blooming everywhere were all firmly on my side. They gave me hope my supposition might be correct; it was still summertime in August as it had been my whole life.

As I walked back home I caught a glimpse of a pair of wool slippers in a shop window, but I averted my eyes, pretending I never saw them. I continued on as the wind picked up and the clouds raced across the sky from the Atlantic Ocean, carrying the rain away to points east, and the sun burst through with warmth and light. Yes! Yes! I knew it! I unzipped my jacket and pushed back the hood, turning my face to the sun, smiling, luxuriating in the certain knowledge that summer had not yet gone.

I didn't reach home before another cloudburst hit, nearly drenching me before I could gather my jacket around me, and the rest of the day stayed very un-summer-like, cool, dark, and stormy… Nevertheless, the calendar said August.

Then one morning the day dawned clear and the sun shone all day. I was relieved to know I'd been right; it was still summer. Something was niggling at me from the back of my brain, though, something I'd forgotten. When my sister called me that evening she reminded me it was my one year anniversary of moving to Ireland. Ah, yes! That was it. My calendar still said 'August,' but that was only because I was a week late in changing it to 'September.'

And that's when I finally gave up on summer. Yes, the sun was shining, but it was autumn's sunshine in autumn's sky I saw that day. Without my knowledge or permission summer had tiptoed quietly away, all under the cover of those few weeks of gray skies and rain. It wasn't that I didn't like autumn. I just felt sad knowing summer had gone and I never got to say goodbye.

It seemed like overnight many of the tourists had left and passage along the streets and sidewalks was easier. So I should have noticed; I should have known. But like the wool slippers I'd seen in the shop window that rainy day, I had looked the other way.

Funny how knowing that it was September finally allowed me to see through clearer eyes and notice the sky was a paler, cooler shade of blue and the sunshine thinner, more diffused. Even on warmish days the occasional scent of a peat fire escaped from chimneys riding on thin tendrils of smoke, and the landscape had a fuzzy, golden glow. The flowers which had been such a bright part of the landscape since spring were beginning to droop and disappear, and the first fallen leaves swirled along the ground.

Fall is such an earthy and hardy time of year, and I've always loved it, but that fall was bringing with it a taste of melancholia. It had been my first summer in Ireland and it was still so new. I wasn't ready for it to be over. Like a passionate love affair coming to a sudden end, I had not yet come to know summer as well as I wanted, had not yet taken full advantage of being in the arms of those glorious, sunny, soft, flower-filled, color-splashed, brilliant green and blue sky days. I'd miss them.

I wish I'd known. Sometimes farewells are important. I would have liked to say goodbye to sweet summer. I'd have then been better able to turn away and open my arms wider to enfold autumn's humble glories.

38

IN THE DARK

September 20, 2014: Big game today – Kerry versus Donegal! Up The Kingdom!

On a sunny summer-like autumn afternoon I was at Hallisey's waiting to pay for my purchases. I don't recall just what I bought, but the visit stands out in my mind because of an encounter with the cashier that day. It was a few hours before the All Ireland Football Final. As a meteorologist stated in his weather forecast that day, it was 'a lovely day for football.' It was, indeed. The World Cup was big news, but the All Ireland Football Final reached another level of enthusiasm and interest. Something like the Super Bowl in the USA.

Gaelic football is a sort of cross between soccer and American football, minus the padding and constant pile-ups. County Kerry was playing for the championship against County Donegal so, of course, enthusiasm was highest in those two counties.

Hallisey's, indeed all of Kenmare, was quiet. Most people were either at home or in their favorite pub waiting for the match to begin. The lucky few were in Dublin at Croake Park ready to watch in person. I planned to watch, too. Whether or not I was particularly interested seemed quite beside the point.

Following the usual custom, I chatted with the young man ringing up my purchases at Hallisey's, which probably included some trinket from my favorite shelf. He wore a green and gold Kerry jersey and a big grin, excited about the topic of the day, the upcoming match. I didn't know much about the game or the athletes, but did my best to keep up my end of the conversation by making enthusiastic vague remarks or agreeing with him.

I paid for the things I bought, put my change in my pocket, and ended the conversation with a cheery 'Well, win or lose, it will be exciting to watch!'

He gave me a long, hard look. He wasn't smiling anymore.

'No,' he said solemnly. 'We *have* to win.'

Sports are not a joking matter in Ireland. I knew that; what had I been thinking?! It was embarrassing and terribly un-Irish of me! Apologizing for such a thoughtless, silly remark seemed like it would make it all the more awkward, so I said nothing. With a nervous giggle I collected my purchases and scurried out the door.

Later, after removing the foot I'd shoved into my mouth at Hallisey's, I was in the beer garden of the same pub where we'd bid Kiwi Ned farewell in July. The match was about to start. I sat with the rest of the excited crowd in front of the big screen TV to cheer Kerry on to the championship. Up The Kingdom! Kerry Abú!

There was something else on my mind besides football that day. Kiwi Ned's book had recently been released, but was only available in New Zealand and Australia. I'd arranged with his publisher to place a bulk order for copies for myself and Ned's other friends in Kenmare to save on shipping costs. I'd sent the list of names to Ned so he could autograph each copy and paid for the order in advance. Everyone would pay me for their copy by the time the books were received. That was the plan.

You know what is said about the best laid plans. Getting reimbursed didn't turn out to be an easy task in some cases. Payment deadlines were set and re-set, lists posted at the local pub with 'Paid' and 'Not Paid' columns. People had been contacted with inquiries and reminders. The money was trickling in, but it was becoming a pain trying to collect it.

Sitting there waiting for the match to start, I scanned the crowd knowing many of the folks who'd ordered a copy might be at the pub that day. Soon after the match started I spied someone from the 'Not Paid' column. I knew who he was, but didn't really know him. He had never been friendly to me, although everyone says he's actually a nice guy. I'm sure he is, but I always found him to be somewhat surly and therefore, intimidating.

I'd sent him a text message after he'd missed the payment deadline, asking him to please leave his money at the pub for me. He replied 'OK.' But he didn't leave the money.

I waited until half-time to talk to him as I wanted nothing to add to his possible dislike of me. Or maybe I just put it off because I really didn't want to do it. Not only did I have to approach someone I knew in advance probably wasn't going to be friendly, but I had to ask him for money! It was especially awkward since I'd already sent him a text about it. But it was now five days later. I needed to take a more aggressive approach and get the money collected.

I casually strolled over to where he was sitting, trying to hide my nervous awkwardness. He could have been sitting with people I knew, that would have helped. But he wasn't.

With a forced smile and an overly bright chirpy-sounding voice, I said, 'Hi! So sorry to bother you, but might you be able to pay me for your copy of Ned's book?'

He didn't say anything, he just looked at me. Oh dear. I cowered, and followed up with a quick, 'If you don't have it today, no problem.' I wanted to turn and run, but somehow that didn't seem like quite the right thing to do since I'd just asked him for money. I had to stick it out and wait for some kind of response.

He continued to glare at me, stone-faced, without smile or greeting. 'Didn't Susan pay you?'

I missed a few beats as I was trying to figure out what he meant. Yes, Susan had paid me – for her copy. Susan was one of the barmaids at the pub and had been helping me with collections. I'd just spoken with her. Had she collected from him and forgot to tell me?

'Um... well, she paid me for *her* copy!' I was sweating now.

Looking disgruntled, he reached into his pocket and pulled out a twenty euro note. 'I don't see the sense in having *two* copies!' he fumed. He wasn't happy at all. I was disheartened. I'd hoped maybe I just had the wrong impression of him and he would actually turn out to be friendly.

I was confused and really did not understand what he was so annoyed about, but just wanted it to be over.

'Oh, no problem at all if you've changed your mind and don't want your copy. Thanks!' I blurted in a rush, and fled without taking his money.

Back inside the pub I stood at the busy bar waiting to talk to Susan about it. We'd gone over the list together on the date the money was due. We'd looked at each name and I'd asked her for an opinion on who was good for the money. She believed everyone on the list would pay within a few days. We were past those days. The man I'd just confronted was someone she'd identified as one who would definitely pay – and on time.

While I stood there pondering the whole situation, I figured out the recalcitrant gentleman who didn't want to pay, or didn't want his copy – I wasn't sure which – must have some connection to Susan. It was the only explanation. Were they related? Maybe he was her brother? A close friend?

Susan approached with a bright smile. I told her what he'd said and asked if they were related. She laughed.

'Oh, no, we're not related! He's my boyfriend. We live together.'

I guess my mouth was hanging open because she laughed again. I had no idea at all. I'd been around both of them for more than a year. It must have been a new thing.

'What?? How long have you been together?'

'For six years,' she said. Oh, my.

But that still didn't clear it up for me. His name had been on the list. She knew his name was on the list. She'd said he'd pay.

'Was he not supposed to be on the list??'

She rolled her eyes and laughed. 'Well, I wanted my OWN copy!'

I finally understood the confusion was between the two of them. He had intended to read her copy of the book; she'd added his name to the list thinking they should each have their own copy.

'So... what shall I do? Take him off the list? Have Ned sign one copy to both of you?'

'Sure,' she said with the ever-present Susan smile. To me, she had always seemed the exact opposite of the man I had just learned was her significant other. She was always pleasant, upbeat and friendly. Well, I'd end up with an extra copy of the book, but I was relieved I didn't have to worry about any further efforts to collect from him.

I returned to watching the match and decided to give up on any more collecting that afternoon. Communication had not been my strong point that day. But an hour later those communication skills did not fail me as my voice joined the others in cheering for County Kerry as they beat Donegal and secured the All Ireland Football championship!

I thought about the cashier at Hallisey's and chuckled to myself, knowing all thoughts of my poorly phrased remark earlier that day had surely been forgotten and wherever he was watching the match, he was proudly wearing that green and gold jersey and a big smile. I didn't see Mr. He's-Actually-A-Nice-Guy again that afternoon, but hoped Kerry's win had brought a much-needed smile to his face, too. (In fairness, I had a chat with him many months later and was pleased to find out he really *is* a nice guy and doesn't seem to have an aversion to me. I guess it just took him awhile to warm up to *That American Woman*.)

Up The Kingdom! Kerry Abú!

▣

A couple of days after Kerry's victory I was heading back home about nine o'clock after the Sunday night trad session at my favorite pub, musing over the darkness, thinking how it didn't seem that long ago that it would have still been daylight at that hour. Just before reaching my street, I noticed the black front window of the Atlantic Bar. Always lit up, that night it wasn't. Odd. It wasn't closed; the door swung back and forth as people drifted in and out. I guessed they were having problems with the window lighting.

I continued on and turned the corner onto my street. It seemed darker than usual. I looked up to see there weren't many stars that night and no moon at all. I guessed it was cloudy because on clear nights the sky is ablaze with stars. Without a bright moon, the street is a shadowy avenue, but on that night there wasn't enough light to make any shadows. I thought again as I had before how an extra street light or two would be nice. It was then I realized none of the street lights were on. Strange. But it explained the darkness.

I wasn't afraid of anyone accosting me or anything like that, but it was so dark it was unsettling. It was impossible to see where I was walking. I wondered why the street lights were off. Taking slow, tentative steps I moved along the sidewalk, the only light bulb offering any illumination the one that finally came on in my head when I realized the electricity was out. Not a single light was visible anywhere; the entire street was pitch black.

The sidewalk is more uneven than the street and darker, too, so I moved out into the middle of the road and used the faint shadow outlines of the houses on either side to keep my bearings. It helped me move in the direction of my cottage without running into any buildings. I hoped there was nothing in my path. For years I'd carried a small flashlight in my purse, but on the one night I needed it, I didn't have it. It fell off my keychain months before and I never reattached it.

As I crept along I imagined how it would have been walking home after dark before there was electricity in Kenmare, on an unpaved street. There would have been obstacles, many of them. Horse and cow dung, stones of varying shapes and sizes, muddy ruts and rain-filled holes, perhaps a random horseshoe, or a chunk of turf fallen from a wagon. I actually didn't have it so bad.

Nearing my cottage I was excited to see a welcome glow. A single candle burned in the window next door in Liz's rental cottage. I fit the key into my front door by feel and pushed it open. I don't know what I expected, but there was nothing there but darkness. The 'can't see your hand in front of your face' kind of dark. Did I dare try to enter and risk falling over something while feeling my way around in search of a light source? I thought better of it.

I knocked on the door where the candle glowed. The door opened a crack. A man and a woman stood close together, a flashlight illuminating their faces. When I greeted them they relaxed and opened the door wider. They were French and apologized for their limited English. I didn't care what language they spoke or with what kind of accent, they had light! We were able to communicate enough that they understood I lived next door and had no flashlight.

The woman kindly followed me over and aimed her flashlight into my front room so I could find matches and a candle. When the candle was lit I thanked her and she left. I hunted for more candles and my own flashlight. Fortunately, I have many candles, and I remembered I had a small rechargeable camping lantern I'd recently charged, thinking I might use it in the back garden.

After the candles were lit the front room felt cozier, the flickering light dancing on the walls. I could have started a fire in the wood stove but was afraid it would get too hot on that warm September night. I called my sister in California to report on the latest adventure, but probably more to reassure myself I wasn't as alone as I felt in the dark and silence of that night. We remembered together the fun we'd had as kids whenever there was a power outage. Using flashlights, something normally reserved only for camping trips, was a treat. And the whole family gathered to talk and play games and eat sandwiches by candlelight. It isn't the same when your family consists of one person.

I hadn't eaten before going to the pub so I was hungry, but peanut butter and crackers was the best I could do. I ate and went to bed and read by the dim light of the lantern. No, it wasn't the same as when I was a kid, but it was okay.

I arose the next morning craving my usual cup of coffee but the electricity was still out. A shower would have been nice, too. My boiler runs on oil, but surprise! It has an electric starter. My range is electric, too. Oddly enough, like my coffee maker, so is my toaster. And my microwave. I knew I shouldn't, but I opened and quickly closed the fridge to get the milk out so I could at least have cold cereal. The milk was still cold, and I didn't fall ill or die from food poisoning, so I guess the refrigerator did its job through the night.

I fiddled around for a while, doing some things I rarely do, but should, like going through the stacks of mail and assorted papers that seem to multiply when you're not looking. But that was boring so after a few minutes I began running through a list of possible other options, all of which relied on electricity. I didn't even have anything to read as I'd finished my book the night before. I spied a water color paint set my sister sent me for Christmas. I hadn't painted a picture in years, but why not? I sat down and amused myself with paints and a brush for a little while.

I decided to walk into town for coffee and a visit to the library. As soon as I rounded the corner into town I saw the electricity was functioning elsewhere. Along the way I ran into an acquaintance and stopped to chat for a minute, then saw Noreen and Paudie, in town doing errands. Noreen and I went to a nearby café for coffee while Paudie took care of some business.

As we drank our coffee Noreen related a funny tale about a wedding she'd recently attended and a series of mishaps and misunderstandings straight out of a romantic comedy. We chatted a bit, getting caught up on local news and gossip, then she exclaimed 'Now, that's the story!' as she so often does after such exchanges, like news anchorman Walter Cronkite's famous line, the way he ended every newscast, 'And that's the way it is!'

We left the café and Noreen took off in search of Paudie and I continued on to the library. The door was locked. The library is closed on Monday. I knew that, and being the day after the Sunday night trad session, it was indeed Monday.

I went next door to the tiny bookstore, wondering who thought it was a good idea to open a bookstore next to a library. I imagined Monday was surely their busiest day. A short while later after spending twelve euros on a new book, I left. I strolled around town, ran into four more people I knew and realized I'd reached the stage in my residency in Kenmare when I could no longer run out to do an errand without makeup and hair not done, or I just had to get over caring about it. I would always see someone who knew me.

I went to Hallisey's and bought a keychain flashlight so I wouldn't be in the dark again. Next stop was Bella Vita,

Kenmare's Italian restaurant. I took my time sipping a cup of tea while people-watching through the large front window, then ordered a burger for lunch.

It was mid-afternoon when I arrived back home and was pleased to find the electricity had been restored.

I'd been caught blind on a dark street without a flashlight, dined on peanut butter and crackers, and missed my morning wake-up coffee and shower, but with the help of kind strangers from France, candles, a long distance phone call, and friends, I'd managed to turn lemons into lemonade, even though they don't have lemonade in Ireland. Well, they say they do, but it isn't lemonade, it's more like 7-Up.

39

ON THE ROAD WITH NOREEN

September 25, 2014: Summer has returned! Woo-hoo! Just in time for a road trip with Noreen. I'm packed and ready to go!

A few weeks after the horse races summer had returned and I was off on another adventure, this time, a road trip with Noreen. The day before we were due to leave I sent her a text message, WHAT TIME DO YOU WANT TO LEAVE ON THURSDAY? She responded, MAYBE 11 OR IT MIGHT BE LATER. OR MAYBE 12 OR IT MIGHT BE LATER.

Near noon she arrived. I stowed my overnight bag in the trunk, hopped in the car, and away we went. I was responsible for maps and navigation because she hadn't been to the Dingle Peninsula since she was a teenager. We'd talked in advance about which way to head out of town and I suggested it might be a nice change to take the straighter road through the fields and rolling hills, rather than the winding mountain route she normally takes. She agreed. But we headed out toward the mountains.

'Didn't you mean to go the other way?'

'Oh, I think it's nice to go the scenic route,' she said.

'Yes… this is scenic,' I said, confused. 'I think the other route is scenic, too, in a different way.'

'Oh sure 'tis,' she said, and kept driving. Time, direction… it was Ireland, and in keeping with Noreen's carefree spontaneity.

We continued on our Disneyland ride through the mountains at breakneck speeds, whipping around corners, Noreen's rapid-fire talk exceeding the speed of the car. I kept my eyes on the road to avoid getting car sick and in case I had to suddenly yell, 'Watch out!' I just knew some hapless sheep would appear in the road around the next bend. I reminded myself she was Irish and a sheep farmer. Maybe she had a sixth sense.

We stopped for tea or food or to consult the map to determine the route we *wanted* to take – and might even take. Green and gold Kerry flags flew from homes, pubs and shops after Kerry's recent championship win over Donegal. Noreen said they'd be flying for the better part of a year.

Noreen found someone to talk with at each stop. Sometimes strangers, sometimes people who knew someone she knew, a friend, a cousin, a cousin of a cousin, an aunt of a friend. On the road she entertained me with many stories. Their indignant disbelief when she and Paudie were accused of laughing during a town meeting ('We *were not* laughing!'), and the annual special meal she and her classmates enjoyed when she was a schoolgirl, courtesy of an English company who wanted to show the world how well they were 'taking care of the Irish.' We talked of childhood Christmas traditions, how much sheep weigh (on average, about seventy pounds), and the lovely summer weather we were again enjoying so late in the season.

In Camp we stopped in at O'Neill's Railway Tavern where you can sit outside at a picnic table on a wooden deck surrounded by pots of geraniums, and look out across the sea. If cars are more your interest, there are Volkswagen Bugs in various states of repair, the proprietor's hobby. There were three on the day we were there, one emblazoned with large white hand-painted letters across the rusty exterior, '*Let me rust in peace!*'

The pub is low-ceilinged and dark, filled with signs and photos and relics. On that day Kerry flags flew inside and out and a pair of Kerry football socks were draped over the fireplace screen. The owners live upstairs and although the top half of the split front door and the back door both stand open, during the daytime hours the pub is usually empty. Their Jack Russell terrier, Jess, alerts them when they have customers. When we walked in Jess came skittering down the wooden stairs and hopped into the first friendly lap he found, as he always does. On that occasion, it was Noreen's.

The proprietor, Michael O'Neill, a big sixty-something Irishman with wild, longish gray hair and a wild, bushy gray beard to match, came downstairs after a few minutes and took our orders. At first he was gruff, but in short order Noreen drew him out and he relaxed and became more outgoing and friendly. He talked about the pub, established in the 1800's, and the old railway to the sea, which no longer exists. The pub was a gathering place for those traveling or meeting the train to receive family, friends, or parcels. I could imagine the hustle and bustle, the farewells and greetings, the lone traveler sitting in the corner, the families with cases and parcels stacked up around them. I wished for the days when that old railway was still in operation.

Arriving at Inch Beach, we couldn't quite shake the clouds and fog that had returned that afternoon, but at least it wasn't raining. We were shown to our upstairs rooms at the Strand Hotel and I was amazed at my large two room balcony suite, the suite I should have had on my earlier visit instead of the ground floor monkey house. The hotel's owner had graciously offered a free night after that stay and I had accepted. The views were wonderful. Noreen's room didn't have a balcony, but it was spacious, nicely decorated, and also had a sea view.

We had dinner down the hill on the beach at Sammy's. Within minutes of a group being seated at a table next to us, Noreen, in her easy way, had struck up a conversation with one of the gentlemen. There's something about Noreen: people like to talk to her as much as she likes to talk to them. She is far from a gossipy sort; she simply enjoys having a chat. I followed her lead and had a pleasant visit with an English woman in the group.

After dinner Noreen sipped her wine, I drank my Irish coffee, and we both savored decadent desserts. Sammy himself came over to ask if everything was to our liking. His inquiry developed into a fifteen minute chat. He started out standing, then moved to leaning against an empty table, then finally sat down in a chair. They were both Irish; I had neither the wit nor the speed to do much more than nod and smile and listen.

We finished our deserts and went to the bar to pay as is the usual custom in Ireland, paying on your way out rather than getting a bill at your table. I paid and left the dining room to use the ladies' room (no matter how long I lived in Ireland, 'toilet' would never roll off my tongue naturally).

When I returned I scanned the busy bar looking for Noreen. I spotted her by one of the tables occupied by a large group. She was enjoying herself, laughing and talking, her hand resting on the back of the chair of a smiling woman. Not wanting to interrupt, I waved and caught her attention. Moments later we walked out of the restaurant.

'Someone you know?' I asked. No, she didn't know the woman or anyone else in the group, but she had learned she was there for her daughter's wedding. The woman had also offered her name, the names of her daughter and son-in-law to be, the location of the wedding, and where the wedding party and guests were staying. Noreen had bid her farewell as if she was an old friend and I suppose after all of that, she nearly was.

Back in my room that night, a soft breeze and the sound of the sea through the open window lullabied me to sleep earlier than usual and sooner than I wished. I wanted to enjoy that sea air and the music of the waves a little longer.

◫

We left the hotel after breakfast the next morning, the sun shining on the water and the sands of Inch Beach, and headed toward Dingle. Noreen mentioned she wanted to see the local parish priest there, but I don't recall why or how it was she knew him. Maybe she didn't. I knew where the church was as it was the same church where I'd stood in the crowd after the dawn parade on St. Patrick's Day and received the priest's blessing as the dark sky came alive with the day's first light.

When we arrived and parked in the car park by the harbor, I told Noreen the church was a short way up the street, around the first corner, and half-way up the hill. Using blocks to clarify the distance would have been helpful, but I knew they'd have no meaning.

While I was aiming my camera at Dingle Bay, Noreen disappeared without a word. I turned around and she was gone. Sometimes she seems to move quicker than the eye can follow. Then I spied her across the road, standing in a precarious position near the edge of the roadway at a three-way intersection, vehicles whizzing by. She didn't seem to notice the traffic and was undistracted from her conversation with an elderly gentleman which they were both clearly enjoying. When a car came very near them she finally took notice, grabbing the man by the arm and hopping up onto the curb with him where they continued their chat.

When she returned I asked, 'Who was that? Someone you know?' I don't know why I kept asking.

'Oh, no, I don't know him,' she said.

She'd been visiting with the man after getting directions to the home of the priest. I reminded her again that the church itself was just a short way up the street, around the first corner and half-way up the hill, in case she couldn't find the priest's house or he wasn't home.

'Oh, his house is just down the road here!' she said. 'I won't be long!' And she was off.

After taking more photos of the bay and the fishing boats, I sat on a low stone wall near the car park, figuring it would be a good vantage point to wait and watch for Noreen. About fifteen minutes later she appeared and sat down on the wall next to me, closed her eyes and turned her face toward the sun. 'Isn't it lovely?' she said.

I nodded. It was indeed a spectacular blue-sky day.

'You found the house?'

'Oh, no,' she said, 'I went to the church. 'Twas only a short way up the road, around the first corner and half-way up the hill...' She'd either been listening when I gave her the directions, or she'd been thinking about the dozen things she needed to attend to back home and had figured out the directions on her own. Hard to say.

''Tis a lovely church and he's *such* a lovely man. The funeral – there was a funeral this morning – it was over, but there are two

241

weddings later today, and there was a lovely nun there and I knew they must be busy but they asked me to come in for a chat and everyone was *so* nice. 'Twas just lovely. He's really a lovely man. The nun was quite lovely, too.'

She chatted on about the kindness of the priest and nun and about the local man who had passed away and the folks involved in the upcoming weddings. I was again impressed by the amount of information folks so readily offered her in mere minutes. She would never be an outsider anywhere. As she talked, a hearse made its slow way past us. Never missing a beat in her story, she crossed herself.

We got back in the car and continued down the road, leaving Dingle town behind, curving along the peninsula on Slea Head drive. I'd made the trip several times, but it is always impressive, made more so in beautiful weather. The sky was cloudless and the land was showing itself in all its brilliant blue and green glory. Sheep grazed in the velvet green of the sloping fields between the low dry-stone walls running in asymmetrical patterns, walls built long ago with stones cleared from those fields. Looking out across the sea it was almost blinding in some places, the sun dancing on the water, exploding the surface into millions of dazzling diamonds. White frothy waves churned around shiny black rocks and crashed against the cliffs, sending sea spray into the air in giant, fan-shaped, sparkling wedges. Each corner we turned brought with it another phenomenal view.

Noreen exclaimed a few times, 'Oh, 'tis lovely!' but she was happiest when we ran into other folks and she could have a chat. When we pulled over at one viewpoint I'd visited in the past, she sat on a large flat rock near the car and chatted with others who stopped there, too, instead of accompanying me down to the cliff edge for what I assured her were stunning views. Earlier in the day she'd mentioned she doesn't like empty, solitary places – the kind I love. She wondered if it might be because she lives in such a remote location. That makes perfect sense. Surrounded daily by nature, views, and quiet open spaces, the chance for human interaction means more to her than scenic vistas.

We continued our picturesque drive and looped back through Dingle, stopped for tea and cake, then headed toward Kenmare. It was a fun trip. I think Noreen enjoyed it, too, because on the way back, interspersed with talk of her youngest grandchild's upcoming first birthday, how she needed to buy more credit for her mobile phone, and inquiries about my family back in the States and how I was finding life in Ireland, she was full of enthusiasm and ideas about where we might go next. If I can get her nailed down on a date and a time and a general route, another road trip will be in store for us. And no matter the weather, where we go, or how we get there, on the road with Noreen could never be anything less than an interesting, grand adventure.

40

GOD SAVE THE QUEEN!

October 13, 2014: Had a great time in Dublin all weekend with some ladies from Indianapolis I met five years ago on my first trip to Ireland. We've stayed in touch ever since. Now I'm off on another adventure, sitting at the airport waiting to fly to England – first time!

Liz had invited me several times to come to England for a visit and I finally made plans to go. I'd been in Ireland more than a year and hadn't yet made it out of the country. It was time.

I flew out of Dublin and into London, landing at Heathrow Airport. Such a familiar name, it seemed as though I ought to be more familiar with the place, but of course I wasn't. It was a complete unknown to me and I was apprehensive about navigating my way around the airport and London's underground. I'd done a little research before leaving, including looking at an airport map, but I wasn't very confident.

I need not have worried. Armed with a picture of the map in my head and my memory of what I'd read on Tripadvisor and the hotel's website, finding the underground and the right train was surprisingly quick and easy. As soon as I lined up with several others beneath the sign clearly designating the stop for the Piccadilly Line, the train which would take me to Earl's Court, the neighborhood where my hotel was located, the train glided up and the doors swooshed open. I hopped aboard, cursing myself for bringing such a large, unwieldy bag. Rumbling along on that train both above and underground, listening to the recorded announcement with the British accent saying over and over, 'Mind the gap. This is the Piccadilly Line. Next station, ...', made me feel like I was in a 1960's newsreel, the ones shown before the feature film at the movies, those grainy black and white clips showing celebrity Brits of the day, like The Fab Four or Twiggy, frolicking around the streets of London, hopping off and on the underground, the only soundtrack the upper-class British accented voice of the narrator reporting on their comings and goings.

In Earl's Court it took inquiring of several people before I was able to find my hotel, which was 'just around the corner from the underground station.' The problem was – which corner? The map in my head failed me and I was completely disoriented. I cursed my cumbersome bag again as I walked up and down the windy streets, the rain beginning to spit. The sidewalks were jammed with people. I asked many of them for directions, but no one knew where the hotel was, including workers in a café and a shop I passed by, so I didn't feel quite so stupid.

Retracing my steps for the third time, I was again outside the underground station, standing in front of a newsstand which proved to be my salvation. The newsstand guy knew immediately where the hotel was and around which corner and it took me just a few minutes to find it.

The hotel was a pretty white Georgian building with sturdy looking pillars and broad front steps leading up to the entrance, on a quiet side street away from traffic. The man at the front desk checked me in and gave me my room key. I squeezed myself and that blasted bag into the smallest elevator I've ever seen and was relieved it was a quick trip to the third floor. Opening the door of my assigned room I immediately noticed its diminutive size, but the décor was modern and pleasant. I stepped inside and heaved my bag onto the bed as I noticed the location of the window. It was long and narrow, running horizontally almost at ceiling level, high above me. I knew I'd ridden the elevator up three floors but everything about that window said basement. I pondered this as I proceeded to get settled.

I wasn't sure how I'd do in that room. I'm a little – no, a lot – claustrophobic. The room was just big enough to house the bed, a tiny narrow built-in desk where the TV sat, and the attached bathroom. The only place I could find to put my bag was on the floor in front of the door. Small was one thing; I could live with that for a night. Not being able to see out the window was an entirely different matter. I thought of the windows at the Inch Beach hotel, big nearly floor-to-ceiling panes framing the gorgeous beach view, the one I couldn't see because I had to keep the curtains drawn for privacy. The irony of it didn't amuse me.

After a bit I went out to get something to eat, thinking I'd inquire at the front desk about my room, hoping to get another if they were any with normal windows. There were several people at the front desk when I passed by, so I decided to stop on my way back.

On my return to the hotel, the lobby was empty. I approached the front desk. The dark-haired gentleman smiled and said in what was possibly a Pakistani or Indian accent, 'May I help you?' Al Jazeera TV played silently on the flat screen television on the wall behind him, headlines flashing in Arabic symbols across the screen.

'Yes, please.' I smiled. 'I was wondering about my room. It seems to be a basement room but I'm on the third floor... so I don't get it.'

'Ah,' he smiled, white teeth gleaming, recognition lighting up his eyes. 'Room 308!' Another dark haired man with equally white teeth joined him behind the desk and they nodded and smiled at me and each other.

'Excuse me?' I was confused.

'Room 308! You must be in room 308!' he said, apparently delighted.

'Uh, yes, I am.' I was missing something.

He said nothing, just continued to smile. I'd stopped smiling.

'I was wondering, what's the deal with the window? I can't see out of it. It feels like I'm in the basement, but I know I'm on the third floor,' I told him.

'Yes, yes! Room 308! It's the only one like it in the entire property!' He said it with pride, like it was the presidential suite.

I was at a loss. I remembered when I was a kid the way my Mom often became defensive and sometimes snippy with sales clerks in her effort to assert her right to return merchandise. My sister and I would stand silently, cringing and pressing ourselves up against the counter wall, trying to disappear under the overhang of the countertop. I don't recall Mom ever losing the battle.

Now I raised my chin and my eyebrows and with a sniff and something of Mom in my voice I suggested it might have been nice to let me know about the room with the small window, placed so high I couldn't see out of it, *before* I checked in.

'Oh, I'm very sorry,' he said, his smile fading. I felt guilty. Then his enthusiasm picked up again. 'Many people like room 308; it is very quiet! We often get special requests for this room!' His eyes and teeth flashed once again.

I found it more than a little difficult to believe that anyone would request that room, but I didn't want to be rude. I really didn't know what to say, so stayed silent.

'You are wanting a different room?' He seemed somewhat incredulous.

I nodded, relieved. *Finally!* 'Yes, please.' My mother may have had a tendency toward snippiness with sales clerks, but she taught me good manners.

'Oh,' he said, his voice quavering with sincere regret, 'I'm afraid we have no other rooms; we are full tonight.'

Both men looked downcast and shook their heads in unison, sorrowful brown eyes looking at me, then at each other, then back at me.

'We cannot offer you anything else.'

I almost – *almost* – felt sorry for them. I thanked him and turned to leave.

'But tomorrow!' he announced triumphantly. 'Tomorrow we can give you another room!' he was happy and smiling again, enthusiasm restored.

I told him I was only staying the one night.

'Oh…' He gave a small half smile. 'Next time,' he said more softly, 'please be sure to mention you do not want room 308 and we will do our very best to accommodate you!' Both men nodded at me and at each other, smiling again, apparently satisfied that the situation had been well-handled.

I rode the elevator back up to my third floor basement room, reminding myself that I was lucky it was at least clean, the TV worked, and the bed was comfortable.

It took serious concentration and mind over matter to not let myself panic and succumb to a severe attack of claustrophobia during the time I spent in that room. I was glad when morning arrived and I was able to close the door behind me and step outdoors, the space and fresh air offering instant rejuvenation.

After breakfast at The Blackbird Pub where I met Liz and Mary for our day of sightseeing in London, we began our excursion under the London sunshine aboard one of the red double-decker tour buses. We wound our way slowly through the incredibly traffic-snarled streets of London, hundreds of cars and buses all trying to get down the same street at once causing frequent bottlenecks. It was worse chaos than I'd ever seen in Southern California. Horns blared, people hopped on and off buses, hurried down sidewalks and crossed the busy streets; sirens pierced the air and British Bobbies strolled the sidewalks or chatted with shopkeepers on street corners. Red, white and blue British flags and signs were everywhere. It was noisy and crazy, and exactly as I'd imagined London might be.

We toured past lovely tree-filled parks, majestic buildings, and the iconic red telephone booths. We saw the gold-tipped fences surrounding Buckingham Palace, the soldiers standing guard looking like wax museum statues, and saw the flags that flew above the palace indicating whether her majesty, the Queen, is at home or away. Every now and then a rain cloud passed over and sprinkled us with rain, the sun regaining its territory within minutes.

We walked through aptly named Green Park with its big leafy shade-giving trees and wide empty expanses of green lawns dotted with green and white striped canvas lawn chairs with large 'For Rent' signs on them. I had never seen such a thing. They were actually renting lawn chairs to people so they could sit in the park. I wondered whatever happened to park benches.

'What will happen if I sit in one without paying?'

Liz and Mary looked at me with raised eyebrows but didn't say anything. It was clear they didn't think it was the best idea I'd ever had.

I chose a chair and sat down, just to see what would happen. Nothing did. Liz and Mary continued to slowly stroll along the pathway, not looking at me, probably trying to politely distance themselves from the crazy American. I think they were somewhat appalled by my cheekiness, but when I rejoined them, they laughed good-naturedly.

Back on board our big red bus, we rode past Hyde Park and Trafalgar Square, down boulevards lined with statues and fountains and more stately old buildings, and throngs of people walking past the ground floor shop windows housing oodles of red, white and blue souvenirs.

And then, 'We are approaching Piccadilly Circus,' announced our driver. Piccadilly Circus! A place I'd always heard of, but really knew nothing about, other than how it looked in my imagination, a place that was worthy of its name. Surely there would be colorful magical looking structures with peculiar angles and striped awnings, maybe even tents with fortune tellers, food vendors selling popcorn and caramel apples, men in bright yellow high-waisted trousers with red suspenders towering above the sidewalk on stilts, beckoning passersby into exotic side shows, and jugglers and mimes and acrobats on every corner – the kind of place that might be found in a child's storybook. I couldn't wait to see it!

I looked eagerly down from my second level perch on the bus. When the Piccadilly Circus in my mind met the real one, I was sorely disappointed. It's an intersection. Nothing more. There was nothing exceptional, nothing magical about it at all that I could see – and believe me, I was looking – it was just another busy intersection in London. I don't suppose I was the only disappointed tourist who didn't know 'circus' in this context is from the Latin word meaning 'circular' and simply refers to the circular nature of that particular intersection.

Throughout the day we made many stops for tea. Many cups of tea. We were, after all, in England, and I was, after all, with two Irish women. Ireland is one of the top tea-drinking countries in the world, ahead of England! The many cups of tea led to many searches for toilets, most of which were down steep, winding, spiral staircases barely wide enough for one person, and one which didn't exist at all after we followed the sign into the depths of a spooky concrete tunnel complete with piles of rubbish and crumpled blankets and a broken-down man sitting on the ground playing a mournful tune on an old fiddle.

In late afternoon we walked across Westminster Bridge over the River Thames, the late autumn sun low in the sky, a hazy golden glow lighting up the city's skyline, the Big Ben clock tower gleaming and looking even more impressive than it already is. It was beautiful. We boarded a boat for a cruise down the river, sipping wine, floating under the many bridges and past the London Eye shining in the afternoon sun, relaxing and chatting as we watched the city drift by. It was a perfect escape from the traffic and noise and crush of people on the streets, and a lovely way to end our day of London sightseeing.

We bid farewell to Mary who returned to the retreat she was taking part in with her fellow nuns that week, and Liz and I traveled by train south to Bristol. Frank picked us up and took us to their cozy home in the delightfully named village of Chipping Sodbury. From there, days of more sightseeing were book-ended by Liz's delicious breakfasts and dinners, cheerful fires, interesting chats, and laughter.

Liz and Frank were wonderful companions for touring the English countryside. We visited story-book villages and drove past broad green fields and gently rolling hills stretching to the horizon. I saw swans on the lawn on the banks of the River Avon, had a look at Anne Hathaway's cottage and a wander through the surrounding gardens. We walked through ancient marketplace buildings, floors paved with stone, sturdy columns still standing, baskets overflowing with cascading flowers in autumn colors.

The sun continued to shine most of the time and what rain fell only made the old pubs and tea rooms cozier, some dating back to the seventeenth century. In search of the ever-elusive cleverly hidden 'loo,' I was delighted more than once to step outside the back door and discover flower-filled courtyards, the toilet facilities situated in ivy-covered out-buildings made of stone, tucked away in far corners.

It was a wonderful visit. England is a pretty country with a varied, neatly arranged landscape, and more to see and do than my first visit allowed. It seems more civilized, less wild than Ireland, but that does not detract from the beauty of either place, it just makes them different. Ireland hase my heart, but England did capture my interest. Hail, Britannia! God Save the Queen!

41

SECOND TIME AROUND

October 25, 2014: Today smoke came from many chimneys on my street, including my own, turf fires scenting the autumn air. Halloween is coming!

I'd long since stopped lamenting over losing summer and was enjoying my second autumn in Ireland. Fall was in full swing with crisp nights and mornings hinting at frost. The sun's hazy glow dappled the changing landscape as clouds drifted across mostly clear skies. Rusts and browns and orange-golds crept over summer's colors. Pumpkins ripened, apple tarts and soda bread baked in busy ovens, and soups simmered on the hob. Walking along, newly fallen leaves dried and curled, rustling and whispering around my feet like wispy, confused little creatures while the older ones, those fallen weeks before, collected in sodden, sulking clumps.

There was something about it all... It tasted and looked and felt like days gone by and evoked memories of jumping in colorful piles of crunchy leaves, starting a new school year, anticipating Halloween, and the joyous freedom of Saturdays in childhood.

In Kenmare the local oil truck was busy topping off oil tanks for winter heat, firewood was being delivered, and the sweet scent of turf fires drifted on the air by late afternoon. Visitors came in and warmed themselves by the fire and we talked of summer and wondered where it went and planned for winter, knowing we sat precariously near the edge. We remarked on and enjoyed the change in the weather over cups of tea, and marveled yet again over how each year the seasons come and go so much faster than they did before.

Walking up the street to attend the first night of Kenmare's Halloween Howl festivities, I realized with a little thrill that I knew exactly what would happen. It was my second time; I was no longer a newcomer. I again watched the horses carrying their riders, galloping down the street, their hooves marking out a loud staccato on the pavement, the headless horseman at the lead. The torch bearers followed, marching with torches held high, then stopping in a semi-circle to light the bonfire, the crowd pressing inward as the fire crackled and grew, flames leaping into the air, sparks flying bright against the black night sky.

I listened as the music volume increased with the height of the flames, and the little kids, some in costume, began dancing, squealing and laughing with giddy excitement. Others sat on dads' shoulders, wide-eyed and mesmerized by the spectacle; the teens gathered in clumps, playing it cool. I heard again the voice telling the annual ghost story, then 'Thriller' and 'Werewolf of London' pulsing from the loudspeakers.

With the rest of the crowd I watched the skill and grace of the two masked fire dancers in their black and red costumes swinging and twirling flaming balls of fire in unison, just as they'd done the year before.

I enjoyed it all, but I didn't marvel at it like I did the first time, so new was the experience then. Instead, I relaxed into and blended with it, finding comfort in its familiarity, along with a tickle of delight when I realized I truly was part of the community of a rural Irish village. I was a local. Or something very much like it.

◙

On a cold, clear day just after Halloween I returned to Strawberry Field Pancake Cottage for another visit, this time with Noreen, Liz and Janet. Janet is an American and a regular visitor to Kenmare, friends with Noreen and Liz years before I ever met them. We have much in common, being Americans of the same age with a passion for Ireland.

With Noreen at the wheel it was time for another wild ride through the mountains and glens. Irish luck was with us and the sun shone as it so often did for me on such occasions. It didn't go unnoticed; everyone appreciated it mightily after a couple of weeks of gray skies and heavy rains. Recent cooler temperatures left the landscape looking wintry, more barren and less green, yet still dramatic.

Several sheep had strayed from the mountain fields that day, grazing on the long grass on the roadside. The blue and red markings helped make them more visible to drivers, but the paint on their backs was not for that purpose, but to show to whom they belonged. I asked Noreen why it seemed there were so many more sheep on the road than usual that day.

'Oh, I don't know. They're probably thieves,' she said off-handedly.

Thieves? I had no idea what that meant, so asked her to explain. Thieves, she said, were sheep always looking for greener pastures and they're a headache for sheep farmers. It seems they will do anything to get at the grass they want, including jumping fences and walls or even more problematic, getting themselves stuck in fences in the process. In other words, they exhibited very un-sheep-like behavior, not content to follow the rest. It occurred to me if they were people this might be seen as an admirable characteristic. They'd be known as 'go-getters' or 'movers and shakers' instead of thieves.

Arriving at the Pancake Cottage, I was eager to again see the sweeping view. It looked different than the lush green of summer, but was still expansive and striking. The last of the autumn flowers drooped in window boxes near the entrance, but the brilliant yellow gold and deep red of the exterior blazed with color and the huge 'Céad Míle Fáilte' lettering by the front door still welcomed visitors.

Inside, a blazing fire in the stove drew us to the table in front of it and we sat down, surrounded by the rich colors of the walls and the paintings adorning them. Seated by the fire we were warmed by the flames and the ambience, eating and talking and laughing, lingering over tea and coffee, remarking on how we needed to do such things more often. It was hard to pull ourselves away from the warm fire, the easy chat, and the cheerful coziness of the place, but eventually we headed back outdoors into the crisp air of the late afternoon.

I took the ladies into the side garden to show them the abandoned shack I'd discovered on my summer visit, the one I had imagined restoring and living in, and it still held my imagination. The only thing missing was the splash of color from the wild fuchsia bushes.

After a final admiring look across the valley to the hills and mountains beyond, we hopped in the car for the ride back to Kenmare, the sun sinking low in the cloud-streaked sky.

'Oh my God! Look at the sky!' I exclaimed. It was a washed-out winter blue, the sun shining through a translucent cloudbank hovering on the horizon, edging it with gold. More wispy clouds shot vertically into the sky in wide swathes, turned to golden shafts of light by the sun. They looked like pathways to heaven. It was incredible and I couldn't stop looking at it. I got Liz and Janet's attention, but not Noreen's. I insisted twice that she look, but she remained unimpressed, laughed at me, put her foot on the gas and sped off down the road.

I couldn't decide which was the better experience, eating pancakes outside on a summer afternoon listening to birdsong and the wind in the trees, or cozy indoor dining by a roaring fire on a chilly day? I couldn't possibly choose one over the other – and lucky me, I didn't have to.

◻

In keeping with my skewed sense of time ever since summer, with the months and seasons racing by at too great a speed, I had no sooner opened my stubborn arms to autumn than winter began its final approach. Rain, heavy rain, and more rain. When the skies cleared and the sun appeared, it gave miserly light, becoming stingier by the day, and what warmth it brought was more imagined than real. Winter was settling in like a giant billowing parachute floating down from the sky. Fires crackled in the local pubs, folks walked faster, hats adorned heads, and I started my own home fire by midafternoon.

So far the wind had kept its distance, no doubt howling with ferocity far out in the Atlantic somewhere. After the endless raging back-to-back storms the winter before, no one was hoping for an encore.

A cold winter was predicted, with the possibility of snow. While reported by some with lowered voices, perhaps fearful if spoken too loudly it increased the chance of it happening, I was happy to hear it. Snow! But I didn't dwell in a drafty stone cottage on a distant mountainside and had no sheep or cattle to worry over. A nice light snowfall would have been welcome – the kind with the big flakes that easily cover the dark and barren landscape, coating the naked trees and brown shrubs and muddy roads in a frothy icing of white. But alas, this is the Irish lowlands, just above sea level, and so it would more likely be rain falling from the sky, lashing against the window panes, forming deepening puddles in the back garden, dripping off the roof, and running down the street along the curb line in miniature rushing rivers. It was not ice but green moss covering the back patio which made going into the garden slightly treacherous.

I was ready to take on winter; I knew how to dress for the cold and wet and defy it with blazing fires, copious amounts of tea, and the occasional hot whiskey. And I've always loved the feeling of coming indoors to warmth and cheer after being outdoors in the cold, and the tingle and tickle in your face and fingers and toes when they begin to thaw. Unlike my silly wearing-blinders approach to autumn, I was prepared to face winter full-on.

I suppose my upcoming winter break was another factor contributing to my bravado. I'd be away three weeks, far away in the land of sunshine and palm trees where oranges grow in groves by the roadside, movie stars dart into neighborhood grocery stores wearing sunglasses and baseball caps, a backyard barbecue in December isn't unusual, and surfers surf on Christmas Day. Three weeks in southern climes surrounded by family and old friends would be fortifying, like hot chocolate with marshmallows on a cold winter's morning.

I thought of the seasons I'd seen in Ireland and the differences not just in the weather, but in the atmosphere and pace of life. From St. Patrick's Day until mid-autumn, I'd watched visitors flock to Kenmare. The better weather, longer daylight hours, explosion of color, and festive atmosphere are obvious benefits enjoyed by tourists and locals alike. But when I gave up my lamenting over summer's passing, accepted autumn and saw my second winter on the horizon, I appreciated its virtues in a way I couldn't the first time around.

After more than six months of the crowded hustle and bustle of spring and summer, I could see the benefits of the quiet, slower pace and space of the off-season when the town is left to those who live here. It is in winter one can move freely along the uncongested streets and sidewalks, at any pace. And it is in winter when there's no waiting for a table in a restaurant or a drink in a pub, and one can more easily get to know the locals. There is something to be said for all of that.

So Old Man Winter and I, we were friends and he was welcome back – so long as he didn't repeat the storms his nasty mood and destructive ways brought us the year before.

When I returned after Christmas, the days would begin to grow longer, like a snowball rolling down the hill wrapping itself in ever increasing layers, growing in circumference, and by the time it reaches the bottom of the hill and summer solstice, it will have nearly doubled in size. And then we'll sit at tables on the sidewalk sipping cider or Guinness or tea in the sunshine, all thoughts of early fires and short days long forgotten.

42

A CALIFORNIA CHRISTMAS

November 27, 2014: I'll eat turkey today and talk with my family by phone, but otherwise I'm kind of ignoring the holiday this year.

Another second: my second Thanksgiving in my home away from home. Even though I'd told myself I would not let sentimentality gnaw at me again and would simply carry on as though I was Irish instead of American on that day, I couldn't help but remember Thanksgivings past and imagine the celebrations in the homes of family and friends across America.

A holiday dinner is always a long, leisurely affair in my family. There is something about those meals and the after dinner lingering. It is then when the best stories are told, the camaraderie is greatest, the laughter deepest, and the love most felt.

For the second time I'd miss Thanksgiving in America, but I'd give thanks on that day for the blessing of the many Thanksgivings I'd enjoyed in the past, and for my good fortune in being able to return to California for Christmas – to see dearly familiar faces, to eat too much, to talk, to linger, and to laugh – and most especially, to feel the love. My enchantment with Ireland couldn't hold a candle to returning to the fold at certain times of the year.

◲

I stepped into the jet way, stiff and tired after the long flight. After sixteen months of being away it was strange and exciting to be back in California. The Christmas before had been tough, especially the days leading up to it. I'd made the best of it, but still, it wasn't the same.

My pulse quickened when I saw the car pull up in front of the airport and the dear familiar faces of my brother-in-law and my Dad, there to pick me up. After a flurry of hugs and excited chatter on the freeway heading south, we arrived at my sister's welcoming, always fully-decorated Christmas home where I was met with more hugs. Everything sparkled and felt both festive and familiar. All the sights, the scents, the sounds, and the people of Christmas were there. It was the shot of family and old friends I needed. I'd missed them all.

I know my family is no different than most, although they are all very special to me. The holidays weren't without periodic tensions between some of us and small dramas from too many days of togetherness and too many people with too many opinions. We are, if nothing else, a family of individuals with strong personalities. Still, we are saved because we love each other and we like to laugh – and we do so, often.

As materialistic as it sounds (because it is), shopping in America was high on my 'To Do' list and along with my shopaholic sister and mother, and more trips with just my sister, we shopped our way around town. It was something my sister and I did often before I moved, and I'd missed it. I had a list of items I intended to buy, but… Well, anyone who is a shopper knows how that goes. After those many days of shopping I bought more and spent more than I'd planned – far more. I could blame it on my encouraging sister ('Oh, yes, that's very cute!' or 'If you like it, I think you should buy it!'), but I won't. I must take full responsibility. But whatever. We had fun.

In between the shopping trips I met and caught up with some old friends. It seemed just like old times, as though I hadn't been away for so long, and it was so good to again be in their company.

Outside of shopping and seeing friends, I visited with my family. I sat in the kitchen and talked with my sister and my mother while my sister baked cookies, her favorite pastime, and in the family room with my rookie police officer nephew and his wife, listening to tales of life on the mean streets. In the backyard (no more back garden; this was California) I sat in the California sunshine on a purple and lavender wicker bench beneath the bush which blooms in matching purple flowers and visited with my Dad and my brother and my niece.

I talked with my architect brother-in-law when he wasn't working, or surfing, or didn't go to bed early so he could go surfing early the next day, or wasn't taking a nap to recover from going surfing that morning. He is a hard-working, hard-surfing man.

Food is a big part of the holiday scene, of course. I'd only very recently started to shed a few pounds, but all bets were off in California. I savored my sister's chocolate chip cookies and Russian teacakes; real dill pickles (those delicacies more rare in Ireland than uilleann pipers); wonderful breakfast feasts complete with a bounty of fresh fruit and homemade cinnamon rolls; and tacos from Taco Bell at every opportunity, my fast food guilty pleasure.

All of us ate popcorn, and apples, and too many bowls of M&M's as we played board games, always ending in laughter, win or lose. We ate burgers from In & Out and watched 'The World According to Garp' just to see if we still liked it after all these years. We did – the burgers and the movie. My sister and I ate more popcorn while we talked and watched recorded episodes of 'Say Yes to the Dress' and 'Everybody Loves Raymond' reruns on TV. There's never *not* something to talk about when we're together.

On a cool damp night we drank champagne on a gondola cruise down the canals of Naples, Southern California's mini-version of that Italian place, where the multi-million dollar homes are spectacularly decorated for Christmas, ablaze with lights, made even brighter and more magical by their reflections on the surface of the dark, still waterways of the canals, and the occasional song of a gondolier.

We drank more champagne and ate filet mignon and shrimp on New Year's Eve, played more games, ate more M&M's, and went to the movies.

We went out to dinner at a favorite local Mexican food restaurant that had recently added 'new and improved' lighting. The food was as good as I remembered, but the atmosphere was washed away in the harsh blaze of light. I've never had dinner in an operating room or undergone police interrogation under a floodlight, but I felt as though I might have a better understanding of what those experiences would be like. Complimentary visors and/or sunglasses for diners would be a nice touch if they can't find lower wattage light bulbs.

We also dined at an Irish pub where decent pints of Guinness are served and the servers wear T-shirts with 'Póg Mo Thóin' printed on the back. I know how to pronounce that and what it means, but because most people don't unless they ask, it seems quaint and cute instead of impertinent.

We celebrated my sister's birthday with boysenberry pie and party horns, and of course, we had our Christmas dinner feast. It was delicious, good tales were told, and yes – I did feel the love I'd so looked forward to and wished for the Christmas before, when longing to be with family weighed heavy on my heart.

It was a California Christmas, to be sure, covered in sunshine, bordered in palm trees, filled with food and talk, and surrounded by family and old friends. As lucky as I knew I was to be living in Ireland, I knew I was twice as lucky to have those good folks I love, and who love me – despite the subtle, but definite, shamrock green tinge showing though my red, white and blue.

◉

It was hard to say goodbye, but I did look forward to being back in my Irish home. On the day of departure I arrived at the Orange County airport at 6:20 in the morning, two hours before my flight. Perfect! A grand start other than the far too early wakeup time that morning. I checked my bags and paid the excess baggage fee, my punishment for all that shopping. That's where it all began to unravel.

'That flight has been delayed by two hours,' the smiling United agent advised me with what seemed unwarranted enthusiasm.

Just great. My flight wasn't departing until 10:20, but I had only myself to blame. I hadn't checked on the flight before leaving for the airport. I knew better.

The agent wasn't concerned when I mentioned I had a connection in Chicago. She didn't know why, but she couldn't give me an Aer Lingus boarding pass for the Chicago to Dublin part of my flight; the system wouldn't let her. I would need to check in at the Aer Lingus desk in Chicago. And then it hit her. Her eyes lit up and her smile widened.

'So you're going to Dublin?!'

I confirmed I was and told her I was living in Ireland. That was all she needed. She started talking rapidly, wanting to know all about it. In between her questions, she talked of her son who lived in England and how she hoped to make it there someday soon and she would definitely also love to make it to Ireland and 'how cool that you live there! I've always wanted—' ... Another agent interrupted her and reminded her there were others waiting to be helped. Relieved, I stepped away from the counter. It was too early in the morning for such intense cheeriness.

Proceeding through security I checked the monitor to see that the 'estimated' departure time was not 10:20, but 10:45. So it wasn't a two hour delay, but closer to two and a half. And with the addition of the sly 'estimated,' who knew what time it would *really* leave? I managed to kill the next two hours doing a whole lot of nothing.

Just before 9:30 I approached the departure gate and was surprised to see the same agent who had advised of the two hour delay. She had been re-stationed to the gate. The flight status screen still indicated an 'estimated' time of 10:45. I asked if the time was correct or might be changed again.

'Yes!' she exclaimed, '10:45! That's right!' She looked at her watch as though the current time might have something to do with it. She made no mention of her original estimate, but went on to contradict herself again.

'In fact, the plane is on its way and we hope to shave about fifteen minutes off that time! We'll be boarding about 9:45 and should be departing by 10:30!' She seemed excited about it, but I decided it was just her cheerful United agent persona.

I thanked her and walked away, not in the mood for more discussions of Ireland and England. It wasn't even noon yet and it had already been a long day.

Finally, we boarded the plane and ten minutes short of three hours later than the scheduled departure time, the plane took off. I guess there'd been good reason for the 'estimated' status on the flight monitor board.

With the even later departure, my time in Chicago would be down to two hours. Thank goodness I'd originally had five hours between flights. Two hours was cutting it close but I didn't have a choice.

We flew in over snow-covered Chicago and touched down. I was encouraged; we'd made up time so I had just over two hours before the Aer Lingus flight. I was relieved not only over the timing, but over escaping the plane where I'd endured a large fellow falling asleep and tipping over onto my shoulder off and on throughout the flight. He was a nice enough young man, but that wasn't the point.

My relief was short-lived. The plane came to a stop in the middle of the tarmac, nowhere near the terminal.

'Sorry for the delay, folks,' announced the pilot. 'We should be able to get into our gate in about ten minutes. Thanks for your patience.'

Wishful thinking on his part, on both the time estimate and the patience of his passengers. A few more similar announcements and *one hour and ten minutes* later, the plane pulled up to a gate.

I had just over an hour before my next flight. Anyone who's traveled through Chicago's O'Hare airport knows getting from Terminal 1 to Terminal 5 *and* going through security requires time, a commodity in short supply that day. Many passengers had connecting flights but we were on our own. There was no agent at the gate to assist any of us. So much for customer service.

I took off at a fast pace, scanning the signs until I found the one pointing to the underground train. I boarded, got off at the last stop, and headed for the Aer Lingus check-in desk, at the opposite end of the terminal of course, to get my boarding pass. My connecting flight was scheduled to depart in forty minutes, but the agent didn't think I'd have any trouble making it.

'You should be fine. Just ask one of the people in blue to help you when you get to security.' She smiled sweetly.

Boarding pass in hand I raced back to the other end of the terminal, and approached the first blue-uniformed TSA agent, eyeing the long line behind him. He put me in a line with two others marked 'Priority.' Maybe customer service wasn't dead after all.

The first lady in the priority line started toward the large, grim-faced, harsh talking, I-hate-my-job-and-I-hate-people, passport-checking female TSA agent perched on a stool, only to be waved off and told to return to the line. The procedure would be one person from the long line, then one person from the priority line. Four passengers later it was my turn. I again expressed my worry that I wasn't going to make my flight. The TSA woman checked my passport and without looking at me pointed to another agent behind her. 'See him!' she barked, then summoned the next passenger. 'Next!'

I approached the third agent with my dilemma and he nodded, then began looking at the long security lines, multiple lanes crammed with people taking off their shoes, removing belts and watches, placing laptops on the conveyor belt or standing waiting their turn. I stood by helplessly, now sweating from worry over possibly missing my flight, while his large head swung back and forth like a pendulum, scanning the lines. I assumed he was looking for someone else to help, someone with the authority to put me to the front of one of the lines. My anxiety accelerated with every swing of his head. Tick-tock. Tick-tock. Finally, he pointed at one of the lines. Thank goodness!

'This one looks like the shortest one,' he announced, and walked away.

I stood there for a second, nonplussed. I couldn't believe what had just happened, but the need for speed kicked in and I got into the line; there wasn't time to stop and try to figure out why I couldn't have determined the shortest line on my own. With minutes to spare, I made it through security, put my shoes back on, returned my zip-loc bag to my carry-on, threw my scarf around my neck, and took off for the gate, then realized I'd left my new travel pillow on the conveyor belt. Drat! It was a very long way back to Ireland and I wasn't getting on that plane without that pillow. I ran back and grabbed it and set out again, arriving at the gate over-heated, heart pounding, and out of breath. I was the last passenger to board the plane.

The plane took off on schedule. It had been twelve hours since I got out of bed that morning and too many of them had involved stress. Things were beginning to get blurry around the edges. There was nothing memorable about the flight until we came to our final approach to Dublin.

As we slowly descended, I looked down through the misty dawn and saw the lights of the city below us, anticipation building. I was back! Before my little excitement butterflies could even get their wings fluttering, in mid-descent the plane swooped back up into the air and the passengers gave a collective gasp. The loudspeaker crackled.

'Ladies and gentlemen, we're experiencing a delay. The runway must be cleared before we can land. The plane that just landed hit a hare and it made a bit of a mess. Thank you for your patience.'

At first I thought it was a joke, but the lady next to me assured me sometimes that happens and it must be cleaned up so as not to get sucked into the plane's engines. It seemed odd until I learned Irish hares are much larger than little cotton-tailed bunny rabbits. Either way, I didn't like picturing it.

We descended again, then leveled out in the clouds, circling low through the turbulent skies over Dublin for several minutes. The unstable air caused sudden and frequent drops, carnival-ride style. I'm not a fan. I gripped the arm rests and each time we rose and fell I steeled myself, my stomach lurching. I tried to block out the sound of the child two rows back crying and screaming 'I'm going to throw up! I'm going to throw up!' as his mother assured him he was fine. There was no place in this scenario for excitement over being back in Ireland.

And then, finally, we landed. Unlike nearly everything else about that trip, disembarking was quick and smooth and soon I was in line for Customs, then at the window where I offered my passport and Irish ID card to the agent, ready to explain that yes, I am an American but I live in Ireland. But no questions were asked of me. The customs official handed me back my ID and passport with a big smile and a 'Welcome back!' and I was on my way to baggage claim. All the irritations and worries of the trip up to that point melted away and I relaxed. I was back in Ireland.

I located the baggage carousel where most passengers had already collected their bags, except the non-Europeans among us who'd had to go through Customs. I stood watching as the conveyor belt chugged in its endless loop carrying the same half a dozen unclaimed bags around and around. Two more slid down the chute, neither of them mine, and the conveyor belt jerked to a halt. Silence. Would the joys of this trip never end?

I wasn't alone in my predicament. There was a long line at the 'Baggage Enquiries' desk. The agent assured me they would deliver my bags to my residence as soon as they arrived. He was sure they'd be on the next morning's flight. It dawned on me I wouldn't have to transport those two large cases from the airport to my hotel to the train to the bus. A silver lining.

I made my way outside into the cold morning without a jacket, for hadn't I packed mine, along with my umbrella, in one of my checked bags? Of course! I must have been in California mode at the time. The scarf I'd wound around my neck, the only thing I had with me that fell anywhere near the 'outerwear' category, was caught and unraveled by the wild wind the second I set foot outside. I ran up and down in front of the terminal trying to find the taxi rank, holding my scarf with one hand and pulling my carry-on bag with the other, cursing myself for the stupidity of not bringing a jacket. When I found a cab I hopped in, shivering, and was taken to my hotel. I'd been up just short of twenty-four hours.

I tried to keep up my end of the conversation with the friendly Irish cab driver, but didn't do well. It didn't matter much as he was on a roll about foreigners coming in and driving taxis, taking business away from the Irish cabbies. I sympathized with him, but I didn't have enough energy to get too involved. All he really needed were periodic sighs of agreement and an occasional 'Oh, that's terrible!' and I managed both.

We pulled up in front of my hotel on the busy Dublin street just as the rain joined the wind. I dashed into the lobby. Check-in time was still several hours away so my room wouldn't be ready. I'd planned to go for a walk, maybe have something to eat, but going anywhere without a jacket or umbrella was out of the question. Resigned to sitting in the lobby, I forced a patient smile and gave my booking details to the young lady at the front desk. It was then the journey took another turn. I heard her say something, but I wasn't sure I had heard correctly. 'Excuse me?'

'Your room is all ready for you!' She smiled and handed me the key card. 'You're on the second floor, on the Christ Church Cathedral side of the hotel, as requested.'

Almost goofy with exhaustion and relief, I thanked her, took the key, got into the elevator, and found my room with the view of Christ Church across the street. I gazed outside as the rain pelted the windows, an Irish flag flapped furiously, and the wind buffeted the dark gnarled branches of the bare winter trees. I wasn't sure which was more responsible for blurring the view, my tired eyes or the rain streaking the windows.

There were two beds in the room which I swear stood up and waved at me, as though I might not notice them. I dumped my bag, kicked off my shoes and collapsed onto the nearest one, smiling as I realized the luck of the Irish was still with me after all. I'd had a great time in California and it had been wonderful to see family and old friends, but it was good to be home.

43

MIND GAMES

January 30, 2015: I've been back from California for about three weeks. It somehow seems much darker and colder. Maybe it's just because I'm no longer surrounded by family and old friends? Or maybe it's that INIS demon I have to face....

The predicted snow came early to the nearby mountains. It snowed often and I loved the scene it created, the rounded mountain tops looking as if they'd been coated with a heavy dusting of powdered sugar, flanked in front and on either side by the green of lower elevations, a sort of Irish layer cake. It was beautiful, but I wished for snow to come to town. One day shortly after my return from California, it did.

Of course I'd seen snow before. I had lived in Alaska, the Pacific Northwest and the Midwest, all places that get varying amounts of snowfall. But on the first day I saw it falling in my back garden in Ireland, I was transfixed. I walked outside sans coat or gloves and was like a child again, the snow swirling around me. I looked up and let the snowflakes fall into my eyes, a figure in my own snow globe. I held out my hands and watched the fragile, frozen flakes fall and melt on my outstretched palms. When I went back indoors to put on a jacket I was tickled to see a few tiny perfect flakes clinging to my sweater. I held my breath so as not to disturb them, but in an instant they melted and disappeared, leaving behind clear water droplets in their place.

After an hour, the snow flurries diminished. Within minutes the only thing falling was darkness; the snowflakes had ceased.

Despite my hope for deep piles of the stuff, it collected only a little, white patches scattered here and there, but it was snow. After more than twenty-five years in Southern California where seeing snow was never on the agenda, it was an event and something I'd wished for ever since I moved to Ireland. I had such fond memories of snow days from my childhood in Washington; building snowmen and having snowball fights, and night sledding with a bonfire on the hill, noses running, eyes dancing, wet mittens being dried by the open oven, the steam from mugs of hot chocolate and chicken noodle soup warming us.

It was one of those little bits once a part of my dream of a perfect life in Ireland: watching the snow fall upon the green fields as a cozy fire roared in the fireplace. It was an occasion to again be reminded how lucky I was to experience another sweet and magic moment and have one more of my daydreams come to life. I love when 'wishful thinking' becomes reality.

◻

Sometime in late winter I found myself thinking more of my homeland. I wasn't sure exactly why at first, other than missing family and old friends which, to be sure, was no small thing. Maybe it was the childhood memories the snowfall had triggered. I considered the possibility that there wasn't any special reason, maybe it was just time for my adventure to come to an end. I let that thought roll around in my head for a while, but it wasn't fitting very comfortably.

I thought about all the family gatherings and events I'd missed. Two Thanksgivings. One Christmas. The Fourth of July. Birthdays: my father turning eighty-eight… and then eighty-nine. My mother turning eighty-seven and fast approaching eighty-eight. One nephew had graduated from college, another graduated from the police academy. A niece was engaged and would be married as my second year in Ireland drew to a close. These were all events that would never again occur and I often wondered if I was doing the right thing by being so far away and missing so much.

I'd thought about going back once before, during that first rough winter when my immigration status was uncertain for nearly five months. Although I'd ultimately received permission to stay, and the long process had given me extra time since the year doesn't begin until permission is received, nearly a year had passed since I'd obtained that permission. I'd recently sent a renewal letter to INIS to apply for another year and I was in the limbo period of waiting to hear back. I wondered if thoughts of returning to America might partially have been an attempt to prepare myself for another rejection. I was planting my feet in a wide, firm stance, standing solid and tense, ready to be head-butted in the stomach. I didn't want to have to go through that again, but if it happened, I wanted to be more prepared.

I had initially hoped the renewal process would be easier than the original application, but that hope was dashed when I learned that having an income which covered your expenses and a backup fund for emergencies no longer sufficed. Immigration was requiring an annual income of *fifty thousand* euros, an income few people living in rural Ireland would have, and I was in that group.

And that wasn't all. They wanted to see evidence of a lump sum sufficient to purchase property in Ireland. So it had gone far beyond self-sufficiency; Ireland only wanted you if you were wealthy. Lovely. I couldn't meet those requirements, but decided to ignore them and give it a shot anyway. They hadn't thought my income was high enough the first time around, but they'd changed their minds and given me permission to stay. The whole process was so odd and vague with INIS, you just never knew. It was worth a try.

In late January I applied for renewal, submitting evidence of funds to support myself and pointing out what I felt was surely the key fact – I'd been doing so for nearly sixteen months.

I guess it was about then my attitude about staying began to shift slightly, along with my feet, and I took that wider stance to brace myself. Being rejected once by the country I loved had been a tough thing and I wasn't looking forward to a second time. If I made the *choice* to return to America, wouldn't that be better than being rejected a second time? It seemed like it would be; I needed that feeling of being in control, or at least feeling like I was.

Before moving to Ireland I knew I likely wouldn't stay forever – in fact I'd only planned on a year or two. I thought again about the issues I knew would have to be faced at some point. They boiled down to one underlying thing: money. I wasn't allowed to work in Ireland; I could work in America if I wished. I'd soon be paying for Medicare which was no good to me in Ireland, and the Irish medical insurance I was required to have as a condition of my permission to stay didn't cover normal medical expenses like prescriptions, which were costly, and doctor visits. I couldn't afford to pay for coverage in both countries indefinitely.

I had to consider that even if the unexpected happened and I was approved to stay another year, it might be time to return to the USA before that year ended. But the best case scenario was getting approval so I'd have more time if I wanted it and more flexibility in choosing a departure date, as well as greater freedom to more easily return.

I set a date for August, six months away, and hoped I could somehow get at least that much more time. If INIS rejected me maybe I could still get permission for a shorter period, especially if I had a return plane ticket for a specific date. Maybe.

In the coming weeks, I tried on the idea of returning to the USA many times, in a tentative way, like tasting a strange food for the first time, unsure if the unfamiliar flavor is good or bad. Gradually, I began to acquire a taste for it. But there was a sticking point and it was a big one. Yes, I was learning to like persimmons, but I didn't want to give up apples! Obviously, going to the USA meant *leaving Ireland*. Could I bear it? But it was a dumb question. I'd have to at some point.

It is said all good things must come to an end and I suppose, in one way or another, that's true, whether by choice or circumstance. But I reminded myself an end can also mean a beginning and that's where I needed to put my focus.

I knew no matter where I lived, I would probably always and forever miss Ireland and feel, on some level, that longing to return I'd always felt after every visit, before finally making the move. I'd miss walking to the pub 'where everybody knows your name' to catch up on local gossip and listen to lively tunes. I'd miss scenic rides twisting through the countryside past hedgerows and ruins and remarkable sea views; the chime of the church bells ringing the hour, the smiles and greetings on the street, the scents and sights of the open air market... Ah, yes – I would miss Ireland.

But I was surprised when a small glimmer of excitement surfaced and I started thinking about living in the USA not as a banishment from Ireland, but as another adventure, another new chapter in my life. Mind games? Perhaps. I preferred to think of it as an attitude adjustment. If I had to go, I wanted to make the best of it.

The door might be closing on my time in Ireland, but another stood open, and above it I was starting to see something. It was hazy, but I could just make out the slight glow of a red, white, and blue sign, the lettering spelling out, '*WELCOME TO YOUR NEXT ADVENTURE!*' I hoped I would have the time to get ready, to let that sign come into better focus, clearly visible and ablaze with light, so I could more easily walk through that door. And when I did, I'd take and guard the key to the door that was closing behind me, the one that would let me back into Ireland when I wanted to return.

◻

Nearly two months passed without word from INIS, but rather than feeling impatient, I was thankful for the slow processing time. I wasn't optimistic I'd be approved. The slowly turning cogs of the INIS wheel gave me more days to enjoy in Ireland.

It was still very much winter, but early March sunshine, longer daylight hours, and enthusiastic birdsong were so reminiscent of spring. Another spring in Ireland. On a cool damp afternoon with the sun peeking through high clouds I donned my trusty wellies and walked down the nearby cobblestone pedestrian street toward the river as I talked to my sister on the phone, discussing my tentative return to the USA.

I stopped on the old footbridge near one of the town's car parks where there are three large recycling bins for glass, 'bottle bins' the locals call them. Each is clearly labeled, one for green glass, one for clear and one for 'other.' While my sister and I chatted about family and shopping and covered a myriad of other subjects, I absent-mindedly watched as a large truck pulled up and dumped each of the bins, one for green, one for clear, and one for 'other' – all into one pile in the truck, and drove away. I saw nothing unusual about it; the humor of it didn't dawn on me until later. I wondered if that was another sign I was becoming more Irish.

◲

Strangely, after turning myself into a cheerleader for returning to the USA, in the following weeks I felt myself becoming even more enamored with Ireland and wishing I could stay forever. Perhaps it was the curse – otherwise known as the magic – of an Irish spring; even the bare hint of it? I realized I wanted it both ways; I wanted to be able to have a home in both places. Like another of my mother's favorite expressions, I wanted to have my cake and eat it, too. As a child I always wondered what that meant – why not? But in this case, it was true. I didn't have the massive amount of money it would take to buy such an expensive cake. This was not a wish I could make happen, barring a miracle like landing a rich bachelor or winning the lottery. I'd made a dream come true before, a dream that had once upon a time just been a wish, but chances were knife-edge slim to none that I could do that this time.

I had seen all four seasons in Ireland, and some of them twice. I longed to stay through spring and just one more summer. *Just one more summer.* My logic and reasoning for returning to the USA had not changed, but I needed more time.

Somehow, departing two years after arriving – not nineteen-and-a-half months or twenty-two months, but a full twenty-four, seemed better, more complete, more orderly, less painful. It didn't seem right to have to leave mid-cycle, like jumping off a carousel before it stopped, your jet black pony with the golden saddle and jewel encrusted bridle still going up and down, reigns limp, riderless. It changed the dynamics of the experience. I wanted to come full circle, keep riding, be in Ireland through two autumns, two winters, two springs and two summers. I promised myself I would be ready to leave if I could just have that.

With a bit more of that Irish luck – of which I'd probably already had more than my share – INIS would see it my way and tell the carousel operator to let *That American Woman*, the one with the big ideas and crazy dreams, ride on.

44

Money Matters

March 8, 2015: Crazy weather and crazy banks! Had a most unusual banking encounter, but definitely not one to complain about.

Still no word from INIS, but life went on. February took over for January, then graciously made way for March. Winter lingered and I huddled deeper into my jacket while I waited for the ATM machine to produce four-hundred euros so I could pay my rent. Grabbing the cash as it emerged, I shoved it into the envelope already containing twenty-five euros, sealed it, removed my debit card and put the card and the envelope into my pocket.

On the way home, head bent against the cold wind, I stopped and slipped the envelope through Michael's mail slot. Unless I saw him outside and gave it to him in person, I'd adopted that procedure ever since the time he'd laughed at me when I hung the money in the back garden in a plastic bag.

The next day the bank rang me.

A woman's voice said, 'We're so sorry about the trouble you had with the ATM machine yesterday!'

I hadn't known I had any trouble. 'Excuse me? I'm not sure what you mean.'

'You withdraw money from the ATM yesterday about six o'clock, did you not?'

'Yes, I did.'

'And you received the amount you requested?'

'Well, I assumed that I did, yes. Didn't I?'

275

V. J. Fadely

'No, you did not. Could you tell me how much you were shorted now?'

Oh, dear. I thought I'd received the amount I'd requested. 'You know, I feel foolish admitting it, but I didn't even count it!' I explained that I'd requested four hundred euros which I'd put into an envelope and given directly to my landlord for my rent.

'What amount was I given?'

'I don't know. I'm sorry.'

'You don't know the amount I received?' It seemed strange the bank wouldn't know exactly how much the ATM had spit out.

'No, I am very sorry. But we'll check with the head office and let you know. I'll ring you in a couple of days. In the meantime, don't worry, we've credited your account with the full four-hundred.'

I told her I'd check with my landlord to see if I could determine how much I was shorted.

I felt terrible knowing I'd short-paid the rent. How embarrassing! Michael wasn't home, but I rang him on his mobile phone.

'Hi! I'm sorry, but I think I accidentally shorted you on the rent money! The bank just called to tell me there was some problem with the ATM yesterday. I didn't even count the money, just took it and put it in the envelope. I'm so sorry!' I felt like an idiot. 'How much more do I owe you?'

There was a pause and then he laughed. 'I don't know. I took it out of the envelope and put it in my pocket. I didn't count it either – and I've been spending it.'

'Oh no!' I laughed, too. 'Well, I don't know what to do...'

'Just a minute. Let me check.' The phone went silent for a few moments and then he came back on the line.

'Looks like maybe it's short by fifty? That's the best I can tell.'

'Okay – thanks. The bank is supposed to be checking on it and they'll let me know.'

I took fifty more euros out of my account and gave it to Michael.

After two more days and hearing nothing from the bank, I checked my account online and sure enough, it showed four-hundred out and four-hundred back in. I called the bank.

'I spoke with my landlord. He thinks it was short by fifty.' I assumed she'd either confirm this or tell me a different amount.

All she said was, 'Oh, alright.'

'Is that correct? Was I shorted by fifty?'

'I'm afraid we don't know.' It was a bank. A *bank*. Didn't they keep pretty strict financial records? Were they just going to take my word for it, or what? She offered nothing further.

'So…if it was just fifty short and you put the full four-hundred euros back into my account, you'll now be debiting the account three-hundred and fifty?'

'Oh no!' She exclaimed. 'We wouldn't be taking money out of your account without your permission! Now, if you'd like to come in and talk about it…' Her voice trailed off. Silence.

I wasn't sure what else to say. 'Okay, thanks!'

Actually, no, I had no desire to go to the bank and have a further conversation about their malfunctioning ATM machine, but I did go there on other business a few times and was never once asked about it.

At first I wrestled with the whole thing. It was absurd they were so sloppy in their record-keeping, of course. But shouldn't I go in and specifically request they take three-hundred and fifty euros from my account? Maybe. But did I really even know if I'd been shorted by only fifty? Not really; we were only guessing. I guess I'd had enough run-ins with – and heard enough horror stories about – financial institutions that I decided not to worry about it and let it ride, and enjoy that month of the fifty euro rent for my 19th century Irish cottage, where chickens wandered through the garden and my landlord told me stories of days gone by…

45

KIDS!

March 20, 2015: Another mix of weather today, but lots of sunshine between the showers. I made it all the way to the supermarket and back during a dry stretch.

The middle school students in Kenmare are allowed to leave the school grounds at lunch time and many make the short walk into town to buy lunch. I started noticing them whenever I was out during a time that coincided with the school's lunch break. I see them often in their navy blue uniforms crowding into the little market, usually in packs of six or eight, sometimes more. They emerge hungrily devouring sandwiches or little cardboard trays of chicken fingers or chips. Those with bigger appetites, and wallets to match, walk further up the street to the sweet shop where I'd bought the candy canes and peppermints my first Christmas in Kenmare.

One never has to guess whether those kids are Irish. Like the cows and sheep in the fields they are unconcerned with the weather. Some wear uniform sweatshirts or jackets, but even in winter some don't. Very few pull up their hoods or carry umbrellas for the rain. Jackets non-existent or hanging open, they walk along eating, talking and laughing, the wind whipping around them, the rain falling on their bare heads and sandwiches. They don't duck their heads or hurry, they stroll along as though the sun is shining on a warm and pleasant day. They made me think of Noreen and it was always amusing to watch them.

When I got caught one day on the narrow sidewalk leading from the school into town the rose-colored glasses through which I'd been viewing these children lost some of their tint. I was coming from the supermarket near the school, heading back into town carrying two full shopping bags. The students were coming toward me, returning from town after lunch.

There were hordes of them. More than I'd imagined the school could hold. The sidewalk is wide enough for two people to walk next to each other or pass one another, but only just. When the first group of a dozen or so students approached me, managing to walk three abreast, forming a tight human blockade, I smiled like I normally would when passing someone on the street. Sure they were teenagers, but they were Irish! When none of them made eye contact or any move to give me the right of way, I squeezed myself and my shopping bags up against the stone wall. They breezed past me, animatedly talking to one another and laughing, as though I wasn't even there. This pattern repeated itself with wave after wave of blue-uniformed laughing and chattering teenagers flooding past me until I decided to see what would happen if I held my ground and kept walking. I wasn't really annoyed, just curious to see what would happen. Surely they'd move and make way for me, an adult, and a senior citizen at that?

After I was run into and nearly knocked down a few times without ever hearing 'excuse me' or 'I'm sorry,' I abandoned that theory, changed tactics, and again squeezed myself thin (no small feat) against the wall and let them pass. As the last few passed by, two young lads, I started to step aside but they beat me to it, politely moving out of the way. There are, of course, exceptions to every stereotype.

Were the others being thoughtless? Rude? I didn't see it that way, although some might. I would venture to say they were simply acting like normal self-involved teenagers. Away from parental or other adult guidance and moving as part of a pack, they were like most teens everywhere. Lost in their own world. Oblivious.

My bet is most of those kids will grow up to be solid Irish citizens, polite, friendly, and full of humor, just like their parents.

In the interim, I'll be more conscious of my timing and my route when I go out to do errands, but will still always enjoy watching those kids from afar as their jackets flap in the breeze and they talk and laugh and eat their soggy sandwiches in the rain.

46

THE WAITING GAME

March 31, 2015: Unbelievable how cold it still is! And it isn't just me; everyone has been remarking on it. Sunshine has been frequent but still waiting to feel that soft spring air.

Technically it was spring, but winter was reluctant to move on. The chill in the air and the snow in the mountains made it clear winter intended to outstay its welcome. Immigration was still dragging its slow feet, too, but that only meant more time in Ireland for me. Waiting to hear was starting to wear on me, but I kept reminding myself every day I didn't hear was another day I got to stay.

All around Kenmare daffodils bobbed their sunny heads and other early spring flowers appeared. Buds formed on bushes and trees, ready for a few days of warm weather to burst forth in full color. The sky looked different, the clouds lighter, wispier. People and traffic increased and other accents mixed with the Irish accents along the sidewalks of Kenmare. When the sun was out, so, too were the sidewalk tables in front of the pubs. Every now and then it was even warm enough to enjoy sitting at one of those tables without your jacket. Shop doors stood open with goods hanging outside, colorful bits and pieces flapping in the breeze. Shop fronts and pubs were given fresh coats of paint and window boxes waited to be filled with flowers. All of this promised winter's demise. It was looking like spring and it was only a matter of time before it would feel like spring, too.

Near the end of March I went to town to do errands. A storm had raged all night, wind and rain pounding Kenmare. The brunt of it passed through by morning, leaving behind sunshine and gusty winds. No tables sat out that day. In the post office the wind ruffled papers on the counter and threatened to blow post cards off the rack every time the door was opened. On the street, people walked quickly through the chill of the swirling gusts.

Inside a small gift shop I found the tiny sheep figurines I wanted for a friend in America. I remarked on the weather. The proprietor agreed it was unusually cold and we exchanged further comments lamenting the lateness of spring and wondering when it would really arrive. Then, as if catching himself and realizing this was not the customary positive attitude one should have about Irish weather, he remarked, 'Ah, but we'll pull through!'

He handed me the little sheep inside a small paper bag. 'Wednesday is Fool's Day. We could well have a change in the weather and 'twill be nice for the weekend, in time for Easter.'

'We can certainly hope so!' I said. But he was now convinced.

'Oh, i'twill, i'twill,' he remarked. I smiled at him, amused by his Irish optimism, and left the shop.

Mid-afternoon Noreen stopped by. I told her I'd like to get some flowers planted in my back garden. I was feeling like spring even if the weather wasn't.

'Oh, we must go to John Ore's!' she declared, as she had mentioned several other times. It was apparently a Home Depot kind of place, on a smaller scale.

'Do you have time today?'

'Of course!' she replied. Yes, she had time – in between the shift she'd just finished at the gift shop and the cleaning of her holiday cottage which she'd not yet started, not to mention the sheep, dogs and husband waiting for her at home. But she's that kind of person. She made the time.

'Let's do it, then!' I said.

And so we did. It was cold, but at least the sun was shining. We wandered through the racks and tables of plants outside the store, looking for nasturtiums, then went inside to enlist the help of one of the men working there to find them. He walked back outside with us just as a stiff breeze blew up, causing me to shiver, clutch my jacket and hold it tightly around me. The man and I looked at each other with raised eyebrows over the unexpected wind gust and unseasonable cold. I saw Noreen up ahead perusing the plants, jacket flapping open, unbothered by the unspring-like weather. A sharp March wind blowing through tables of plants was nothing to someone accustomed to roaming the mountainside in all weather hunting for stray sheep or newborn lambs.

'Oo-oo, it's...' I caught myself and revised the sentence before it left my mouth. '- not warm, is it?' I remarked to the employee, huddling deeper into my jacket.

He laughed. 'Ah, you're avoiding the 'C' word!'

I laughed. I was, of course.

''Tis fresh, so!' he said.

We laughed together. 'Yes! That it is!'

Noreen and I paid for our purchases and were directed to drive around to the side of the store to pick up the large bags of soil we'd both bought. Noreen pulled the car around and while it would have seemed logical for me to get out and find someone to help us while she remained in the car with the engine running, I had neither choice nor chance. In her lightning speed way, she managed to put the car in park, open her door and get one foot on the ground before the thought even had time to form in my head.

Sitting there waiting for her, I noticed a large sign on the side of the building 'John R. McCarthy.' Strange. I had thought we were at John Ore's. When she got back in the car, I asked her about it.

'Are there two shops here?'

'No,' she said, looking puzzled.

'But I thought we were going to John Ore's?'

'Yes!' she said, backing out of the parking lot.

I was confused. 'But the sign says 'John R. McCarthy.'

'John Ore McCarthy's – that's where we are!'

It finally dawned on me. Translated, 'ore' is how 'R' is pronounced in County Kerry, and 'John R.'s' is what the locals call John R. McCarthy's. It was another one of those nickname things born of too many McCarthy's running around. For the rest of my time in Ireland, I called it John Ore's, too.

That afternoon I planted the primroses I'd bought instead of the nasturtiums which weren't yet in stock, dependable hardy violets, and the geraniums and sweet peas I'd grown from seeds, planted indoors until the danger of such things as rogue hail storms and overnight frosts passed. Within an hour my fingers were nearly frozen and I was forced back indoors. But I didn't mind. I knew winter had already had more than its fair share of time and spring would soon politely, but firmly, send it on its way.

The next day the weather persisted, this time the sunshine and wind joined by intermittent rain. During a sunny period I walked up the street and ducked into the market for bread. The wind that had chased me from home followed me through the door. The cashier looked up with raised eyebrows and remarked on the cold. 'Yes!' I agreed. 'I'm enjoying the sunshine, but the wind is icy!' I hoped that might be the proper mix and not seen as too negative. It was. She shook her head in sympathy, rolling her eyes. 'Oh, you wouldn't stand it for long!' she said.

I set the bread on the counter and she rang it up. The door flew open as another customer came in, stomping her wet feet. It was raining again. I paid the cashier, grabbed the bread, put my hood up and said goodbye.

'Walk between the drops!' she called cheerily as I stepped out the door.

I headed down the back street to Hallisey's, no path between the drops showing itself to me, thankful I'd worn my wellies. Inside the shop I chatted with the same cashier who'd worn the Kerry jersey and been so earnest in his support of the team in the All Ireland Football Final.

'It feels nice in here!' I said, enjoying the heat. 'It's so cold out there today!' I said it without thinking and anyway, it had gone on too long to ignore.

''Tis, so - yes, 'tis!' he said, shaking his head.

'And last night! I couldn't believe how cold it was last night!' I exclaimed.

He looked up from the cash register. 'Oh, you should have been on the mountain last night. I was on the tractor looking for stray sheep. I found one with her newborn twins. 'Twas fierce cold and windy on the mountain. Had I not found them they'd have frozen, so.'

I didn't know of which mountain he spoke; it could have been any of those surrounding Kenmare, but I could imagine the feel and the sight of being on a mountainside in the frigid rains and winds and coming upon a sheep and her tiny babies, their wooly outlines pale shadows in the darkness.

I remembered last spring and the sudden warming. The man in the gift shop was right; it could happen overnight. Until then, I walked with more care, making my way through the knots of tourists on Kenmare's sidewalks, kept a sharp eye out for reckless rental cars unfamiliar with the custom of jaywalking, enjoyed the new color in my back garden, and stayed warm by my fire in the evenings.

I knew spring was gathering strength, ready to meet us 'round one of the next corners. As the shopkeeper had said, the next day was Fool's Day and it sounded exactly the sort of day when one might turn the very corner we all hoped to find. And spring meant new life, renewal. Maybe that meant I would find a letter from immigration around the same corner, one that said, 'Céad Míle Fáilte! Please make yourself at home and stay awhile!' More of my wishful thinking, but surely it couldn't hurt.

47

GOOD FRIDAY

April 5, 2015: An Easter morning walk today was not the spring like affair I enjoyed last Easter! But at least the sun was shining so the children had a good day for the egg hunt in the park.

On Good Friday I received a delivery of firewood. It was the second time I'd had to replenish my wood supply in the face of winter's stubborn grip. The delivery was made by a friendly courier who remarked before I could on the chill that was still in the air. I dutifully chatted with him for a moment about the weather, appreciating the sunshine and remembering how warm it was *last* spring. I was getting pretty good at the weather thing. I could prattle on about it as much as anyone, and enjoy doing so. As I did, a light rain began to fall from a single defiant cloud, the sun still shining. The courier and I looked at each other, smiled, and shook our heads.

Courier services were on the job that day, but the postal service was not, I discovered, after walking to the post office to mail those sheep I'd purchased. The door was locked, a sign announcing CLOSED 'TIL TUESDAY FOR EASTER WEEKEND. Hm-m-m… I hadn't realized it was a long holiday weekend. I had a vague recollection of Good Friday being more of a recognized holiday in the States when I was a child, a three-day weekend with many businesses closed, but I didn't think that had been the case for years.

That evening I went out for the Friday night trad session. I tried to get myself out at least one night a week so I didn't become too much of a hermit as was my tendency when I was in writing mode. The pub for the early Friday or Sunday night trad session was often my destination. This time I planned to stop in at a couple of other pubs on the way to say hello to some friends. When I stepped out the front door I was happy to see the cold winds had finally ceased and swept the sky clear of clouds.

At my first stop, several tables were occupied by diners, but the bar was empty. Even my friend Kieran wasn't there. I'd hoped I might run into him as I hadn't seen him in a while. There's never a time I don't enjoy a chat with him so I was disappointed he didn't seem to be around.

I looked around the pub, wondering why it was so empty. Surprising for a Friday night, and a holiday weekend no less, but it was early.

I asked if Kieran had been in.

'He was here, but he went across the street,' said the bartender.

'Really?'

He nodded. That seemed strange, since this was one of Kieran's preferred pubs. He practically had a reserved stool. I hadn't known him to frequent the place across the street. Oh well, that was my next stop so maybe I'd catch him there.

I talked a little longer with the bartender and barmaid Mandy, the young lady from Scotland who'd introduced me to walking man Mick, then told them I was going to go see Dierdre and Chloe who worked at the pub across the street. Just before I stepped out the door, I told Mandy I'd come back later for a drink.

'You have to buy a meal to drink!' she called out. Always the jokester.

I laughed and said, 'Yeah, right! See you later!' and left.

I walked into the pub across the street and sat down at the bar. It was quiet there, too, but there were a few other folks sitting at the bar. I greeted Dierdre and Chloe and ordered a glass of Guinness.

'Have you seen Kieran?' I asked.

'He was here, but he just left. He has to work in the morning.'

Okay, it was looking pretty likely that a chat with Kieran wasn't in the cards that evening. I was still curious why he'd been there instead of at his usual pub, but it seemed it might sound rude to wonder aloud, so I didn't.

Chloe left to wait on a table of diners and I told Dierdre I'd just come from across the street and remarked on how empty the usually crowded pub was.

'It's Good Friday,' she said as she finished filling the glass of Guinness.

'Yes, I know,' I said. 'That's why I'm surprised how quiet it is – it isn't just Friday night, it's a holiday weekend!'

'It's Good Friday,' she said again and looked at me pointedly. I didn't know what she was getting at.

'Everyone's at mass,' she said.

'Oh!' I hadn't thought of that, but guessed I should have.

'No alcohol on Good Friday,' she continued.

'What? What do you mean?' I was perplexed. Had I not just ordered a glass of Guinness and had she not just poured it for me?

'No one can serve alcohol.' She gave me the glass of Guinness and took my money.

'But...?' I looked at the people at the bar with glasses of what looked like beer or wine in front of them and at the glass she'd just set in front of me.

She put the money in the cash register, turned back around, and said, 'It's all non-alcoholic.'

For a couple of seconds she had me. I'd actually wondered why I'd never heard of non-alcoholic Guinness.

She said the only way pubs could serve alcohol was with a meal. Otherwise, it was against the law. I laughed, knowing she was still kidding. She insisted she was not joking and then it clicked. Now she was serious! Yes the Guinness was real, but technically I should have ordered food, too. So Mandy wasn't kidding about having to buy a meal! She must have thought I was stupid with my laughing response. She was right. I definitely had not known about the Good Friday law.

But something still wasn't right. How were they able to serve alcohol to me and the others sitting at the bar? None of us were eating. I wondered aloud to Dierdre.

She shrugged. 'Oh, Gerry has some sort of arrangement…' she trailed off without finishing her sentence. 'They don't bother him.'

And then the rest of it registered: that's why Kieran had not been on his usual stool across the street. He'd had to come to Gerry's for a drink.

We discussed why it was a law since it was a religious thing, separation of church and state and all that, but she said it was just one of those things that had been around forever.

'So… what about on Easter Sunday?' I asked. In the USA, that was the day most celebrated, the day when everything would be closed. 'I suppose everything's closed, right?'

'Oh, no – it's a regular day. All the pubs will be open.'

'Really? But it's Easter!'

She shrugged again.

'And Saturday? Does it have some kind of religious significance for Catholics?'

'No, Saturday is nothing. It's just a regular day, too.'

Okay; now I knew the score for Easter weekend in Kenmare, and later learned it was the same situation in the whole of Ireland.

After chatting a while longer, catching up on the news and gossip, I walked back home. The streets and sidewalks had emptied; it was as quiet as a winter day – and not much warmer. The only thing that hinted at spring was a banner over the street advertising Kenmare's spring music festival, another advertising a bike race taking place in May, and the lights of the open ice cream shop, hoping to lure in a customer or two. The rest of the shops were dark. Pub doors were closed and locked, I noticed, except for those with a restaurant, and even a few of those establishments were closed.

I encountered only three other people on the street on my way home. A couple was using the ATM machine outside the bank, talking in soft voices in a language I didn't understand. A skinny young man in bike shorts, shirt, and helmet stood astraddle his bicycle in the middle of the empty street taking photographs with his mobile phone. A rook called from one of the tall evergreens in the park, the harsh cry too loud in the peaceful quiet of the evening. It clearly was Good Friday in Ireland, a different sort of holiday than most, when the streets are crowded with people. Oh, they were there, alright, you could be sure of that, but they wouldn't be out and about until the next day.

Back at home, I went into the garden to check on the laundry I'd hung on the line earlier in the day, for the first time since August. Despite the wintry temperatures I'd decided to give it a try and do what I could to show my faith in 2015's timid spring. The clothes weren't much drier than when I'd put them out so I had to switch to the *Plan B* method.

It was eight-thirty and I marveled at how the daylight lingered. I lingered, too, after taking the laundry off the line, watching as the sun sank behind the hillside, accompanied by the birds singing their twilight song. I was certain they were doing their part to welcome spring, and surely spring would get the message and be encouraged.

48

RIDING THE WAVE

April 11, 2015: Time for another trad fest in Kenmare so guess everyone knows where I'll be this weekend!

It was easy to find me the weekend of Kenmare's annual traditional music festival. Wherever there was music, I was there, surfing the festival waves through the pubs and streets. I was thrilled to have the chance to enjoy it again. The festival came at a good time; it was a lovely boost up and away from too much thinking about my immigration status. Even the less than warm weather didn't matter; it all took a back seat to the music.

During the course of the weekend I was mistaken for a woman on a nearby roadway whose car was on fire, was in the right place at the right time to hear a soulful tune about the loss of some Kerry boys in a battle with the British, and watched with sadness as an old man was helped out of a pub after a long last day of drinking. I spoke with musicians like piper Mick O'Brien, bodhrán player Colm Murphy whose recordings I'd been listening to for years, and a flute player, Harry Bradley, who was a dead ringer for Colin Farrell.

Finding Mr. Bradley standing next to me at the bar waiting for a drink during a break in the music, I couldn't help but say something to him, so intrigued was I by his resemblance to Colin Farrell. Knowing he would be tired of hearing about it, I tried to avoid saying the name. 'So how often do you get told you look like someone?'

'What do you mean?' he said, feigning innocence.

Forced into it, I had to say it. 'Colin Farrell, of course!'

'Oh, Jayzus, the poor man hasn't aged well, has he?' He smiled, flashing his deep dimples, picked up his pint and returned to his chair to resume playing.

I couldn't wait to hear the uilleann piper, Mick O'Brien, and arrived at the pub hours ahead of the scheduled start time to make sure I had a seat with a good vantage point. It was wonderful to hear him play although due to the late start time of the session, it was noisy because of the number of tourists and young folks more interested in drinking than in listening to the music. I was glad there would be another opportunity to hear him the next day.

Saturday afternoon's session started in my own front room on a cool damp day, sitting before a warm fire with a glass of wine, eating sausage rolls, bread and cheese, and apples. The music was not that of pipes or fiddles but of the soft patter of rain, the crackle of the fire and the chat and laughter of the friends I'd invited over, Molly and Eric, and Noreen and Paudie. We moved on to a little pub up the street, the site of Mick O'Brien's second appearance, where we were among the first few in the door. The music started and soon the dark old pub was packed.

An hour into the music an older local gentleman sang an emotional folk song, a true story, a lament over the loss of lives of some Kerry boys during the rebellion against the British in 1921, in a battle not far from Kenmare. As the man sang, Mick the piper leaned forward, listening intently, the emotion written all over his face. The pub was packed with people, completely silent but for the singing. Midway through the song, Mick and the singer clasped hands. They remained in a tight grip for the rest of the tune. Irish or not, anyone who wasn't moved to tears at least fought a lump in their throat – or they weren't paying attention.

In between pub sessions I was entertained at a concert in the local theater. Seamus Begley, vocalist and accordion player, appeared with a guitar virtuoso, an award-winning musician from England, Tim Edey, who had recently returned from a USA tour with The Chieftans. Tim wowed the audience with his astounding guitar skills. I'd seen Seamus in concert with my mother and my sister in the USA and we'd all enjoyed him, but in his homeland Seamus did less singing and playing and more joke telling.

'The Mother Superior gathered the young nuns together. 'I have an announcement, girls!' she said, 'and 'tis very serious! We have a case of gonorrhea in the convent!' 'Oh, thanks be to God!' said young Sister Mary. 'I was getting quite sick of the Chardonnay!''

Noticing a child sitting in the front row after he'd told a string of definitely not child-friendly jokes, Seamus struggled to come up with a clean one. 'What did the mother turkey say to the misbehaving little turkey? 'If your father could see you now, he'd be turning in his gravy!''

More jokes and more music and then the concert was over. It was time to move on. There was more music to be heard.

On Sunday I met up with Kieran just before one of the early evening sessions. Noticing all the texting and phone conversations going on around us we got into a passionate discussion about the rampant abuse of mobile phones, the viral epidemic of 'smart phone-itis.' We speculated what the world might be like twenty years hence and wondered if there would be any face-to-face social interaction or if we'd be the only two left still talking directly to each other in an otherwise silent world of people glued to their mobile phones. Like mine, his phone isn't a smart phone. It simply makes and receives calls. Strange as it probably seems to most people, we both thought that's what phones were meant to do. We agreed we'll hang on to those phones as long as we can and go down fighting when technology advances to the point where we can no longer use them.

The music started, we hopped down from our soap boxes, and most of those attached to their phones put them away. There were a dozen musicians, among them three talented members of Kieran's family: his sister on bodhrán, her husband on guitar, and their daughter on harp, the three of them sitting elbow to elbow. During a break in the music one of the fiddle players stood up and walked over to me, smiling as though she knew me.

'Excuse me?' she said. I looked at her. 'Weren't you on the Killarney road today?'

'No, I wasn't.'

'Oh, I could have sworn it was you! The woman looked just like you!'

'No, it wasn't me – sorry!' I smiled.

I wondered what this mystery woman was doing on the Killarney road, so inquired.

'Her car was on fire! Big billowing clouds of black smoke!'

'Oh my goodness! Was it the engine?'

"Twas the whole car! And I swear, she looked just like you! She was even wearing a scarf like the one you're wearing! Are you sure it wasn't you? Where were you?'

'I'm sure. It wasn't me!' I was a bit thrown by the fact that she didn't seem to believe me. Kieran was trying to contain his laughter, quietly snickering into his pint of cider.

'When did this happen?'

'Today! Just a few hours ago!' she exclaimed. 'She looked exactly like you. I can hardly believe it *wasn't* you!'

At this point I was actually starting to wonder about it myself. Had I been on the Killarney road and forgotten??

'Well, no, it wasn't me – I promise you!' I said. I was getting a little exasperated.

'Okay!' She laughed, then sat down and picked up her fiddle, and the tunes began again. Kieran by now was laughing without restraint. My exasperation evaporated and I started laughing, too.

After the session I took off to hear more of Colm Murphy, the bodhrán player, and Harry Bradley, the flute playing 'Colin Farrell.' They were playing in a pub not often frequented by locals, more of a tourist hang-out, and I wasn't sure what it would be like to hear them there. But hear them I would, sitting at a table I secured directly in front of them, not ten feet away. It wasn't crowded and for the first hour I had to share them only with other music lovers.

Rumors traveled around the pub about a nine year-old concertina player and were confirmed when a young boy walked in, his concertina in one hand and his mother's hand in the other. Colm and Harry saw him and waved him over. He played two songs of his choice with them. It was fun watching him and amusing and sweet to see the older, more experienced musicians treat him with such delighted respect.

When the music ended I left the pub. It was late, but I hoped to catch a couple more tunes at a nearby pub where I'd told Kieran I'd meet up with him. The bartender was standing in the doorway as I walked out.

'You're leaving now?'

'I am,' I said. 'I'm hoping to catch the last few at the Tin Whistle!'

'But we're just getting started!' he said as he switched off the outdoor lights and unlatched the hook that was keeping the door open.

'Aren't you closing up?'

'Well, yes, we are, but that's when the fun begins! They'll be headed this way from the Whistle!'

I wasn't sure I believed him, but smiled and told him maybe I'd be back.

At the Tin Whistle a full session with at least a dozen musicians was just winding down and it was standing room only. It was almost 11:45, just minutes from closing time. I asked around and sure enough, the next stop was the pub I'd just left. I was tired by this point; it had been a long weekend. But how could I miss the chance for an after-hours session? I couldn't.

Back at the shall-remain-nameless pub, not a light shone. The street was dark, everything was closed up. The pub looked locked up tight. If someone hadn't told you, you wouldn't have known anything was happening behind that door. I gave it a tentative push and it swung open. The party was just getting started.

Harry and Colm were at the bar ordering drinks and Harry was wishing for a prawn cocktail, receiving the news of 'burgers only' with a brooding look from his dark Colin Farrell eyes beneath his dark Colin Farrell brows. I'd have been happy to just sit and stare at the man all night, and if I'd had any prawns in my fridge I'd have surely made a fool of myself by running home to get them.

A few other people stood at the bar and a dozen others sat around in groups talking and laughing. Behind me several musicians drifted in the door, instrument cases in hand, and over the next ten minutes the noise level increased as more people filtered in.

A local man started pestering one of the headliner fiddlers, to 'say something about Dan Murphy!' The fiddler protested, said he wasn't prepared, but the man persisted. Eventually he gave in, stood up, and began to speak of the late Dan Murphy, a man who had passed away the week before. He spoke of his life, about his importance in the traditional music scene, of his step dancer wife and his musician sons, and he told of attending the funeral service that very day. He and some other musicians were asked to play a tune at the service and from the altar, they played a hymn.

The fiddler followed this speech by playing the same hymn, a beautiful slow air, on his fiddle. Thundering applause, raise your glass to Dan Murphy, and the party was on.

Fiddles and accordions, bodhráns and whistles, guitars and banjos were taken from cases and the music resumed. A young Frenchman played his guitar and sang an American-sounding folk tune. A thin young woman with a nice smile sang a love song in Irish in a clear and sweet voice, and well-known sixty-nine year old accordionist Jackie Daly played a solo.

Despite the 'Sh-h-h's' and the clinking of glasses a group of young people near the bar continued to talk and laugh during Jackie's solo. He never stopped playing, but slowly stood up and made his way over to the group. There he stood directly in front of them, inches away, straight-faced, staring at them and never missing a note. They took the hint, and he returned to his chair.

Afterwards he passed by me and I told him I had enjoyed the tune. He grabbed one of my hands in both of his and thanked me. I said I was sorry for the disrespect of the young folks. He said 'I was so mad I wanted to hit someone!' The man has been a professional musician for forty-five years. I imagine things have changed a bit over time and the respect that was once deep and automatic is lacking in that arena just as in so many other aspects of life these days.

I sympathized with him, and we exchanged remarks about 'the good old days,' and I told him again how much I'd enjoyed his playing. He repeated a heartfelt thanks with another firm shake of my hand. I said 'No, thank YOU!' His playing had made me smile and as he walked away, I was pleased to see my remarks had affected him the same way.

That after-party was as close as I'd get to being in the inner circle, a member of that group of musicians and their friends and families, people who'd played and laughed and hung out together for decades. I didn't have to wish to be a fly on the wall; I was. And on that night hanging out on the wall was a cool place to be, a very cool place, and another Irish experience I was glad I had not missed.

Sometime in the wee hours of Monday morning, the last note from the last tune faded away. Two hours after closing time, fiddles were stowed in their cases, the last joke was told, the last glass raised, the last story shared, and farewells made amid handshakes, hugs and bursts of laughter. At two and a half hours into tomorrow I went to bed, the swirl of the pipes, the beat of the bodhrán and the lilt of the fiddles and whistles echoing in my head. I slept with the light of dawn too near, while the Irish voices, laughter, and music played on, weaving in and out of my dreams.

49

SEANCHAÍ

April 19, 2015: Michael was just here to pick up the rubbish and had another good story to tell, but it's always hard to remember all the details later.

I thought of my landlord Michael as my personal seanchaí. I always enjoyed the varied, numerous, and detailed stories he shared with me. Seanchaí is the modern accepted spelling of the old Irish word meaning 'bearer of old lore' or 'traditional storyteller.' While not as entertaining to read his stories as to hear them in Michael's voice, the authentic experience can only be had in Ireland, unless one has the good fortune of running into him somewhere else – maybe Las Vegas? No matter where one might find him, he's sure to have the time to share a story.

Recalling the rich details of one particular long story after Michael told it would prove to be impossible, but I would always remember the main storyline.

Long ago, before Michael was born, there was a woman in England who had grown up in an orphanage, and remained living there as an adult. Someone in Kenmare knew her, or knew of her, and thought she would make a good wife for a lonely Kenmare bachelor. She was brought to Ireland to meet him.

The first introduction was to be in the bog where the men were cutting turf. Looking across the bog, the woman laid eyes on Michael's father, Daniel, already married, mistaking him for the man she was to meet. She was quite taken with Daniel and remarked on what a handsome man he was. She was set straight on his eligibility, but it was believed she always had a crush on him. In later years, Michael reported with a laugh, his father always remembered her as 'the woman with the big, flat feet.' Coincidentally and ironically, she had seen Daniel barefoot one day all those years ago and said, 'Oh, you have lovely toes!' Michael spoke the words in a funny falsetto voice, laughing, and I laughed along with him.

He continued the story. After the bachelor of Kenmare and the English woman were introduced, they stepped out together a few times. The man was kind and behaved like a gentleman. They went to the local pub, where the young woman had an orange squash, and to her surprise, so did he. This happened each time they went out together; orange squash was the closest either of them came to imbibing any alcoholic beverages. When the woman returned to England she reported to everyone he was not a drinking man. This news did not go without notice and raised the man's value as a prospective husband in everyone's eyes.

After the woman received a series of romantic and beautifully written love letters from him, the bachelor of Kenmare won her heart. She agreed to marry him and moved to Kenmare where they were wed.

Alas, it did not turn out to be a happy marriage. The man was not an abstainer from drink; in fact, quite the opposite: he was a drunk, and a mean one. He beat the woman, and drank up all their money. They ended up poor and homeless.

In order to get free housing from the government, it was necessary to submit a written application. Busy with the children who had been born into the now loveless marriage, the woman gave the application to her ne'er-do-well husband to complete, but he could not. The man had to confess that he could neither read nor write.

The woman was confused; she couldn't understand how that could be. What about those love letters she'd received before their marriage, when her future had looked so bright and filled with romance? As if the orange squash ruse and shabby life she'd been living was not enough for the poor woman to bear, the rest of the old fantasy was crushed when she learned the whole sorry truth.

When she'd been in England dreaming of him, she'd had no way of knowing how he'd encouraged some of his friends to meet him at the pub every week. She didn't know of the willingness and delight those more literate men had taken in cleverly crafting the words of love he himself could not. The tender and amorous letters which had stolen her heart had been written by the man's friends for the price of a pint, courtesy of the crafty bachelor of Kenmare.

That will always be my favorite of Michael's stories.

Many of Michael's stories chronicle his adventures as a flight engineer, including time working for a Saudi Arabian sheik, stories from around the world. One tale had to do with being in a small plane somewhere like Somalia, or some such place – somewhere I wouldn't want to be, especially in a small plane – and being under fire from the ground. I didn't get the details of that particular drama as it was sandwiched in between several other stories that day. I regret that I didn't ask.

There've been many stories about the sheik and his wife. She isn't happy, and lets it be known, when the sheik wants to go to Las Vegas without her. She knows full well what her husband will be doing there. The man has lots of money and he loves to gamble. It takes little imagination to guess what other things might amuse him in a place like Las Vegas, without his wife, sometimes for several weeks at a time.

One story dates back to the time just after smoking was banned on commercial airlines. Michael and a buddy were on a flight to Belgium, traveling there for work. His friend was a smoker and once the plane was in the air, he lit a cigarette. Michael immediately warned him to get rid of it. A 'blue-haired lady' passenger a few rows in front of them bellowed 'I smell smoke!' She turned around and pointed at them. Michael grabbed the cigarette from his clueless friend and tried to figure out what to do with it, how to put it out. There were still ashtrays in the armrests, but they were no good, they were bolted shut. The woman continued to yell and there was Michael, as the flight attendant bore down on them, stuck holding the cigarette, his friend looking out the window, the picture of innocence...

One afternoon Michael noticed a poster on my kitchen wall entitled 'First Cup,' a picture of a young man sitting at the counter in an old-fashioned diner drinking a cup of coffee. He was reminded of his first time in New York City, also his first time in America.

Michael was young, in his early twenties. On this occasion he was employed on a plane carrying a load of horses to New York. He recalled before he left folks at home warned him about America in general and most especially New York City, telling him he should be very careful there. It was imperative he not run anywhere if police were around or he might get shot. He should be extra cautious if anyone knocked on his hotel room door; you never knew if it might be a criminal with intent to harm on the other side.

He was told caution needed to be paired with common sense, and a horror story concerning a hotel guest was cited. The guest had answered his door after a knock and the announcement 'Room Service!' Not expecting room service and knowing what might wait for him on the other side of the door, the man wasn't just suspicious, he was terrified. Loaded pistol drawn and aimed at the door, he flung it open and pulled the trigger, shooting the man dead. He had, indeed, been a hotel employee, but he'd made the fatal mistake of knocking on the wrong door. Chances are good this was a tall tale, but it likely served its intended purpose and put young Michael on high alert before his trip to wild America.

With these admonishments and stories fresh in his mind he arrived in New York City. After checking into his hotel he looked out the window and was met with a view of Central Park, an unexpected site in the middle of the bustling concrete jungle. But he didn't have time to look at the view; he was tired after the long flight, and very hungry. He decided to chance going back out onto the street to find something to eat. He must have been very brave, or hunger was overriding the warnings about America and the big bad city.

He found a diner, went inside, and sat at the counter. As he described the woman behind the counter I could picture her, a stereotypical loud-mouthed, overbearing New Yorker, an old-school gum-chewing waitress of the kind you see portrayed in the movies. She accosted him as soon as he walked in, order pad in hand, the pencil she'd removed from behind her ear poised and ready to write, demanding to know what he wanted. He was young; he was tired; he was hungry; he was an Irishman in America, a stranger in a strange land. He didn't want to make decisions, he wanted it to be like walking into his mother's kitchen where you sit down and eat what's put before you. He just wanted food to fill his belly.

In response to his soft query, 'What do you have?' the waitress started in with a rapid-fire list of options including a multitude of bread choices and the various ways he could have his eggs cooked. She was not sympathetic to the young Irish lad. Overwhelmed, tired, and weak with hunger, he spied the large wall menu showing different numbers for different meals and pointed to one. He just wanted food! That did the trick. He sighed with relief as the waitress hollered to the cook, 'Another number six, Fred!' He watched silently as she stuck her pencil back behind her ear, slipped her order pad into her apron pocket, snapped her gum, and walked away in her starched pink uniform, her white rubber-soled shoes squeaking on the vinyl floor.

Michael has led an adventurous life, to be sure, and his adventures continue. The stories here are but a few of those he's told me. In the retelling, I've undoubtedly confused, forgotten, and embellished details, but I've done the best I could without benefit of notes or recordings on which to rely for accuracy. I know he'll forgive my clumsiness and failings.

Michael often asks me 'How's the writing going?' I tell him it's going fine but once remarked I thought with all his stories it was he who should write a book – perhaps two. He said he isn't a good writer. I suggested the idea of a ghost writer. I later got to thinking that might be a good idea. Maybe someday I would write a book after all, but it would be *his* stories, not mine.

50

THE GIFT

April 24, 2015: Still writing, but I long ago switched gears from the all-encompassing memoir Kiwi Ned had once suggested back to his original idea, life in Ireland, a more manageable subject.

One morning I was deeply absorbed in writing. Somewhere on the edge of my consciousness I heard the *click-squeak-ka-thunk* of the mail coming through the mail slot in my door and dropping onto the floor. I wondered, as I had wondered for many weeks, whether this time I'd find the letter from INIS, but it was just a fleeting thought and I kept writing, knowing it wasn't likely.

A few hours later I took a break and scooped up the small pile of mail from the floor. A red and yellow flyer advertising sale items at the market, a white envelope with my sister's return address, and a thin brown envelope that glared at me like it was lit with some kind of phosphorescence. Oh, my. It was a letter from INIS, the only indication the telltale brown of the envelope with its single black imprint of a tiny harp. But it was probably just a request for more documents or information. That was the usual procedure. That's what I told myself as I opened it, the pace of my heartbeat belying my nonchalance.

Unfolding the single sheet, I held my breath. I saw the words *Seirbhís Eadóirseachta agus Inimirce Na Héireann* followed by the English, *Irish Naturalisation and Immigration Service (INIS)* in bold letters across the top. Gripping it with both hands, I skimmed the letter.

Dear Ms. Fadely... Trying to remain calm, telling myself I already knew what it was going to say, *it's not a big deal, just read it,*

I continued. After the first paragraph I read it again, more carefully, eyes wider. I was absolutely astonished. Ireland had not pulled the welcome mat; I was approved to stay for another twelve months. The held breath whooshed out of me. *Approved??* Approved! Well, well, well. This put a new spin on things. I didn't know what to make of it. I felt tingly and tearful and confused.

I read the next paragraph. A single sentence stated there would be *no further renewal.* So this was it, the last hurrah. Twelve more months than I expected, but only twelve more months.

I didn't care for that last bit, but still, another year! Where I'd once felt like a jilted lover I felt this time as though a love affair had ended, but I'd been let down gently, been told, 'I think the world of you and hope we'll always be friends.' It wasn't a happily ever after, but it wasn't as bad as it might have been.

I just had to think about it in the right way. It was, after all, unexpected and barely dared hoped for. It gave me another year of freedom. It was a gift, really, and that's how I needed to see it. More time in Ireland if I chose, and time to plan and accept the final chapter of my Irish adventure and the opening chapter of my *Return to America.*

I was surprised it took only a day to scrap the plan to return in August. Just like that, I decided to stay on. The carefully thought out logic of why it was time for me to go disappeared like a snowflake melting in my palm. I was excited thinking about a second summer in Ireland, the one I'd so wished for, actually happening. And the more I thought about it, the more I liked the thought of a third autumn, a third winter, and most of a third spring... Of course the reasons to leave were all still valid, but I decided it was worth the financial hardship to take the time I was given.

Would staying longer make it easier to leave? Probably not. I knew I'd always have mixed emotions and it would never be easy to leave. But it was with great appreciation I accepted that lovely gift of time. The work I'd done to convince myself that August was the right time to go had not been easy, but it had been a good practice run. I felt I'd be more prepared now, better able to go when the time came. It would never be easy, but maybe it would be *easier*.

I promised myself to renew my efforts to take more notice of every day of my remaining time in Ireland. Like a beachcomber finding treasures on the beach, I would keep collecting as many more moments of delight and amusement as my sand bucket could carry so that when the time came and I was back in America, I could take them out and enjoy them all over again, my small beautiful nuggets of Irish treasure. I'd touch them and hold them up to the light for closer inspection, then carefully put them back in the bucket for safekeeping. On particularly humdrum days or when extra luck might be needed, I'd slip one or two into my pocket. And during really tough times, I'd just take the whole dang bucket along.

51

GATHERINGS & WANDERINGS

May 27, 2015: Just back from Galway and Dingle, another fun trip but nice to be home.

The greens were greener and the flowers were blooming. Spring was definitely trying, but temperatures stayed unseasonably cool. It was more like March than May.

On the heels of a trip to Gougane Barra with a glorious walk through the forest and another perfect overnight stay, I took off by bus and train on a four-day jaunt to Galway and Dingle.

After two sunny days in Gougane Barra the weather reverted to its Irish self for the Galway-Dingle trip. In keeping with the sort of spring we'd been having, the cool temperatures returned with alternate periods of rain, clearing, wind, and repeat – many times. Still, the beautiful scenery along my journey was worthy of spring, complete with a multitude of baby animals. I was amused by one little calf who took advantage of a break in the rain and charged a flock of birds who had the audacity to land in his field, scattering them into the air. Little lambs frolicked everywhere, staying close to their mothers in the rain, and bouncing through the green grass as though their tiny feet had springs on them during periods of sunshine.

In sharp contrast to the new life, Radio Kerry played on the bus speakers, the announcer's voice naming the dead and associated funeral details for all those who'd recently passed away in County Kerry, one of the four times daily death notices are broadcast. I never grew accustomed to that.

In Galway at Tig Cóilí, my go-to pub for music, I tried desperately to make the pot-bellied, partially balding old guy behind the bar be my young, curly-haired, handsome singing bartender Luke, but failed. No Luke in sight. Perhaps he'd lived my fantasy with another woman and accompanied her home where he sits by her fire and sings love songs to her? I felt jealous.

It was the day in spring in Galway when the locks are opened and a small footbridge is moved to allow the boats who've wintered in the protected harbor, a small area next to the River Corrib, out into Galway Bay. The procedure is repeated in reverse in autumn, before winter sets in.

I stood on the shore and watched and chatted with another spectator, an English transplant who'd lived in Ireland for twenty years. If you didn't move your boat today, he told me, you're there for the summer. Anyone who wants in or out had better know the schedule and be prepared to move.

Yellow-vested, hard-hatted men pulled open the chain wrapped locks with the assistance of a crane. After several minutes of tinkering around with the bridge, removing bolts and screws, they wrapped the same chains around the bridge so the crane could hoist it up, completely removing it and setting it to the side, onto the grassy bank. My fellow spectator and I discussed the idea of a simple draw-bridge and wondered why they didn't build one so they didn't have to move the entire bridge, but decided it was just one of those peculiar Irish mysteries. I thought about the day I'd seen a van slowly driving down the road, a metal gate sticking out the back end, supported by a man jogging along behind the van as fast as his wellie-clad feet would carry him. Surely there was an easier way??

When the bridge was removed and the way was clear, sailors trudged along the bank, towing their crafts by pulling the heavy ropes they'd attached to them, guiding them down the narrow channel. I was reminded of little boys playing with toy boats.

Throughout, the sun shone, the wind blew cold, massive billowy white clouds skipped across the sky and elegant white swans sailed on the glassy surface of the inlet leading to Galway bay. It was invigorating and in the truest sense of the word, indeed a *fresh* day. I wished for a bit less fresh and a touch more warmth, if only enough to allow me to remove my hood and keep my fingers from freezing while taking photos.

After one strong gust of wind the man I'd been talking with remarked, 'Mild winter, we're having!' We both smiled at his clever description of the cold spring. He may have been English, but twenty years in Ireland had given him a talent for the art of weather talk.

After the big event of the day I was standing and enjoying the scene – the blue and white sky, the sun dancing on the surface of the water, swans serenely floating by, gulls soaring and sailing on the wind – when a flurry of activity across the road caught my attention. There in front of a church, a hearse had pulled up, gleaming in the sunshine. A crowd of people began slowly spilling through the tall open doors of the old church and congregating on the broad steps. At the side of the church I could see a long line of giggling children, the little boys in white shirts and dark slacks, the girls in white dresses and veils, many wearing jackets or sweatshirts against the chill breeze. They pushed and shoved and skipped around as a few adults roamed up and down the line trying to contain their youthful energy.

As I watched, a casket was carried out the front doors of the church, the crowd stepping quietly to either side to allow its passage, the end of a life marked with dignified, somber ceremony. As the casket reached the hearse, the mourners proceeded down the steps and the bouncing line of boisterous children began moving toward the back door of the church, their excitement visible even from a distance. The funeral was over; First Communion was about to begin.

◉

Back in the Southwest of Ireland, Dingle was as always, bright and happy. Weather continued with its mixed bag format, but temperatures were warmer than in Galway. Sitting in the Dingle Bay Hotel pub waiting for the music to begin, a man stepped up and stood uncomfortably close to me. I wondered, who was this fellow crowding my space? I looked up and it was Brendan, the tour guide I'd first explored Ireland with in 2009 and several times thereafter, being his usual funny self. I ran into him from time to time when he overnighted in Kenmare, but hadn't seen him for a while. He was in Dingle guiding a group of Americans and he invited me to have dinner with them. I accepted the invitation.

I enjoyed catching up with Brendan, talking 'Breaking Bad' episodes which I'd been watching every night on a British television channel, and learning that his van is no longer the Mercedes van I rode in so many times, but has been reincarnated as a Volkswagen. 'Two seasons ago, Jane,' he said, looking at me like I wasn't very bright. Well, I'm not, when it comes to things like vehicles. Mercedes or Volkswagen, it was still a van with the same bright green and gold lettering and logo emblazoned on its sides, with the same guy at the wheel.

The folks in the tour group were all welcoming and friendly, but I chatted mostly with the woman sitting next to me, and the young college student and the man across from me, all of whom seemed to be a family. The man was around my age, the woman seemed younger. They were all friendly, especially the husband. He reached across the table and took my hand. *Oh no! Here we go again!* I couldn't help but remember the man in Glenbeigh, and a few other similar encounters.

'I really admire you for making such a move!' he said with great enthusiasm. He raised his pint of Guinness and we toasted. I responded to his many questions, but knowing he was someone's husband tried to avoid the situation becoming awkward by talking more with the wife and son. He was nothing at all like the Glenbeigh fellow, not pushy or over-flattering, but still. He was attached!

Brendan invited me to join the group on their tour of the Dingle Peninsula the following day. The friendly man encouraged me to go, and expressed his disappointment when he found out I decided against it in favor of a day in town. 'We have room for you! There's an extra seat!' he said.

I thought he probably was just a friendly kind of guy, and would have been someone interesting to talk with, but he was not unattached and I didn't want to risk getting myself into an awkward situation, so I felt I'd made the right decision.

I spent the day in town, shopping and walking and trying to capture the green of the hills, the sun on the bay and the gleam of the fishing boats in photographs. In a small gift shop a little ceramic Irish angel caught my eye and I gently plucked her from the shelf. The tiny gray-haired Irish lady behind the counter was in the mood for a chat (imagine that), not only with me, but with the customers ahead of me as I stood in line and waited... and waited. But then it was my turn and together we admired the sun that was shining and commented on the cold spring, before she launched into a lengthy, but cheerful, dissertation on appreciation of every moment of the weather, good or bad, every moment of life, good or bad, and 'sure now, the young folks don't realize it yet, do they? It's a learning curve... Have a lovely day! Slán go fóill[2]!' She turned her attention and her smile to the next customer.

回

After returning home, I exchanged e-mails with Brendan and learned I'd paired the friendly man in his tour group with the wrong woman. He wasn't her husband, nor her significant other. And he wasn't the college lad's father. He was, in fact, not attached. He was single. A bachelor, for heaven's sake.

I was more than a little miffed that Brendan hadn't informed me of that rather vital information at the time. His excuse was 'I think he's committed to living the single life.' I told him I was, too, but that didn't mean I wouldn't welcome having a nice, interesting, unattached man in my life.

I'm Facebook friends now with the man who isn't anyone's husband, but somehow that isn't the same as a day out on the Dingle Peninsula. And we won't even think about the fact that the next night the group was in Kenmare and I purposely stayed home to avoid being the cause of any awkward or unpleasant moments between the man and the woman I thought was his wife.

---

[2] Goodbye for now (*slawn-guh-foal*)

回

Before my Galway-Dingle trip I'd planned a gathering for a couple of days after my return, brashly issuing the invitation *seven* whole days in advance. That was really pushing the outer limits of planning in Ireland. It is one of my many deeply ingrained ways which hasn't changed – like the habit of saying 'dollars' instead of 'euros,' and trying to get in on the wrong side of the car. My Irish friends laugh at me, but I don't mind.

All ten guests showed up at '7-ish' as planned and we ate and drank and chatted before proceeding up the street to the Atlantic Bar where there's dancing on Sunday nights. I'd long been hearing about Noreen's set dancing prowess and had only a glimpse of it one night at a pub when she and a few other ladies were inspired to get up and step to a tune.

Set dancing is similar to square dancing without a caller. The name of the set is called out, for example, the 'Kerry Set' and they go to it. Noreen was much in demand as a partner and it was great fun watching her dance the 1-2-3 quickstep, twirling and skipping and sashaying around the dance floor, weaving in and out and around with the others. She can add dancing to her many other talents.

回

As May drew to a close, Clare was in town from Dublin for a few days ahead of Colin who would join her on the weekend. She invited the ladies of the group for an afternoon at their holiday home, a spectacular multi-level structure in an idyllic setting. As lovely as their home is, it wouldn't have mattered where we were, it was the hostess and the guests who made the day. Liz was in town for a few weeks, too, and that made it an extra special gathering. Our impressive surroundings only enhanced the experience of one of those 'wine in one hand, tea in the other' occasions.

The reluctant spring gave us just enough warmth to sit outdoors on the wide deck looking out over the green of the lawn, woods and forest, glimpses of the river below peeking through the trees. In the adjoining field sheep grazed and lambs bleated and scampered about under bushy hawthorns heavy with white blossoms. Almost-to-bloom foxglove lined the fence, the buds still closed, but giving you the impression they might burst open at any moment. The day was mostly cloudy and breezy, but it didn't rain and the sun smiled on us from time to time. A grand day by Irish standards.

We relaxed into the afternoon, drinking and eating, talking and laughing. We wandered around through the woods and along the edge of the lawn to look at, try to identify, and remark on all the beautiful flowers and trees. Cooling temperatures and increasing wind soon took us indoors, wine in one hand, tea in the other, and there was no break in the chat or laughter. I knew in the future, no matter where I lived, I would do my best to recreate that sort of lovely, storybook, Irish afternoon.

�«▣»

Spring finally gave way to something like summer in late June – about as close as we were going to get to summer, we would eventually discover – bringing warmer weather and occasional bursts of sunshine. I watched as the sun stayed high in the sky and the days stretched until well past ten o'clock at night. The extra daylight and increased buzz around town left no doubt that another summer in Ireland was unfurling.

On the Fourth of July, I celebrated the holiday with barbecued burgers in a country pub, a modest little place on a narrow tree-lined road surrounded by green and mountains, across from the shores of a picturesque lake. The red, white and blue banners, the taste of the grilled burger and the scent of the barbecue lingering in the air were strong reminders of the USA. The only thing missing was the fireworks. I was glad I'd come instead of opting to do nothing more than put an American flag in my window as I'd done the year before. I hadn't known one could find a place in Ireland where Independence Day was celebrated.

The pub looks as though it's been there for many years and has none of the kitschy 'Irish' décor, it's just a small, plain pub in beautiful surroundings.There were entire families inside and outside, people of all ages, most Irish and most local to the area.

As the place filled up, Will, the proprietor, had his work cut out for him, in constant motion pulling many pints of Guinness, topping off those that had sat for the required resting period, opening bottles of wine, grabbing cans of Coke and Orange Squash from the shelf, taking money and returning change, all with a smile and an occasional comment.

I sat at the bar with Noreen and Paudie and we were later joined by Eric and Molly. From time to time I helped young kids barely tall enough to see over the bar get Will's attention so they could give him their order for – usually – 'a Coca Cola, please.'

After everyone had eaten, Will's wife circulated through the crowd carrying a platter of leftover sausages from the grill and offered them to those patrons whose appetites had not yet been satisfied. On an announcement by Will, folks began making their way outdoors. I followed the crowd, not knowing why, a fleeting thought of fireworks entering my head but no, it was still far too light that summer evening.

I gathered with everyone else in the cool breeze by the side of the pub, the late sun still hovering above the horizon, causing everyone to shade their eyes from the glare. Puffy white cotton candy clouds punctuated an otherwise finally blue sky after a stormy afternoon.

We were there, I soon learned, for the launch and dedication of the pub's new defibrillator unit. Even one of the local senators was present, the very man who'd helped me with my permission to stay in Ireland. He was looking dapper dressed in a suit, as he always is, no matter the time of day or day of the week. Speeches, photographs and applause ensued, along with a hope and a plea that every household would send at least one family member to be trained in the use of the unit. At first I was amused by the idea of such a ceremony but then realized this was a big deal. We were far from medical facilities. People had worked hard to raise the money to purchase the unit and it could very well save lives. Fireworks would have been nice, but this was certainly more worthwhile.

I'd become separated from Noreen and the others outdoors. I returned to my seat at the bar and soon met a group of men from

Dublin. I later learned they'd been friends since childhood. I'd noticed them earlier; not noticing the group of five jovial, singing, Guinness-drinking men would have been impossible. I was nursing my second glass of wine when I met them. It was the last one I purchased for the rest of the evening, the drinks magically reappearing at regular intervals as they took turns buying rounds. There seemed to be some sort of unspoken understanding that I was one of the group.

I spied Noreen and the others at a nearby table but decided to stay put and enjoy being surrounded by attentive, jovial men who made me laugh. It seemed a more attractive option; a nice alternative to being the fifth wheel with the two couples.

The featured entertainment in the pub that evening was a guitar-playing singer. He sang all the favorites, the old Irish folk songs as well as several American standards. The little pub filled with the sound of singing as the patrons joined in. *If you're Irish, come into the parlor, there's a welcome there for you...*, *Country roads, take me home, to the place I belong...*, and to my surprise, *Que sera, sera, whatever will be, will be...*, that old song my mother used to sing to me as a child, the one I'd thought of that time I'd watched the hens in the gathering storm. Everyone was there in celebration of the 4th of July in Ireland. The best of both worlds!

During a break in the music my new friends provided the entertainment, their strong voices raised in both solos and harmonies. One impressed me with a brilliant rendition of 'God Bless America,' missing not a single word of the lyrics. It being the Independence Day of my homeland, I added my voice to his as not doing so would have felt unpatriotic.

At one point, two of the men prepared to go outdoors to go for a row on the lake. They wondered, would I like to go, too? I declined, thinking that although it would have been a wonderful and unique experience on that peaceful summer evening, I wasn't quite willing to risk being out in the middle of a lake with two strangers who'd probably had more than their fair share of Guinness.

There was more joking and back slapping and laughter as we talked and sang our way through the evening that too soon ended, and the late summer twilight which fell so softly through the pub windows was gently swallowed by darkness.

It was a lovely summer evening with old friends and new, celebrating American Independence Day in a country pub in County Kerry, across the road from a beautiful lake where green hills met blue sky. God Bless America – and 'if yer' Irish, come into the parlor…'

It was yet another of those times that seemed to keep coming, like putting a quarter in a gumball machine expecting to get a single gumball, but they just keep rolling out. You cup your hands together and watch in delighted amazement as they pile up. I'd never take those precious gumballs for granted.

◻

Knowing how fast time gets away I made plans for the coming months. In late July I'd spend too much money for a weekend stay in Killarney at an over-priced hotel to attend a three day music festival. In August I had a date with some horses who like to race on the beach. I booked a B&B a short walk from where the festival celebrations and all-night shenanigans would take place, having learned my lesson the year before. Directly in the village square was a great place to sit at a picnic table and hear music after mass on Sunday morning, but not where someone like myself wanted to book a room for the night. Experience had made me wiser.

There would be more visitors, more events, more gatherings and wanderings, more encores and firsts; good times were in store. There wasn't going to be much searching needed to find more Irish treasures for my sand bucket; they were everywhere. It occurred to me I might very well need to get a larger bucket.

As another summer in Ireland bloomed I planned to sit in the golden saddle of that jet black carousel pony with my eyes wide open, a gentle hand on the reins, letting its handsome jewel-adorned head take me where it may, sometimes wandering slowly, other times galloping swiftly just for the thrill – and savor every minute of it.

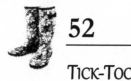

52

TICK-TOCK

October 26, 2015: My third autumn in Kenmare and I'm still on the carousel! I've come full circle, through two autumns, two winters, two springs and two summers, just as I'd hoped to do. But I'm still not ready to go. I don't know that I ever will be.

As the extra months I'd been given passed by, time trickled away too quickly. After the cool spring melted into Ireland's 2015 tongue-in-cheek version of summer, the days slipped by on soft swift feet. The date of my second anniversary in Ireland passed and summer was slowly being eclipsed by autumn.

◻

Six days after they arrived, they departed Kenmare for the airport in their rental car at four in the morning. My sister, Gail, and her husband, Dave, had finally made the long trip from California to visit me in Ireland, two years after I made the move.

After a flurry of hugs and thanks on the dark street outside my front door, Gail got in the car. We continued chatting through the open window while her husband Dave finished putting their luggage in the trunk, then went around to the opposite side of the car and got in. His first clue that he was on the wrong side of the car was the absence of a steering wheel. I've lived here over two years and I still try to get in on the wrong side. And in fairness, it may have had something to do with the fact that Gail was sitting in the driver's seat. Neither of us had given it a thought. It felt perfectly normal, like she was on the passenger side of the car.

Seats switched, the engine roared to life and I waved until they disappeared down the street into the quiet and dark of the pre-dawn October morning.

Their visit had started with a gathering in my home where they met some of my new friends. The fire blazed, wine was poured, stories were told. I did little more than offer refills of wine and plates of food as chat and laughter filled the room. It felt like if I talked too much, more fully participated in the socializing, I might miss something. I needed to stay just a little apart that first evening, to better listen and watch, to fully enjoy the surreal pleasure of having family in my Irish home and among my Irish friends. I had wished for it for so long, and they were finally here.

We hit as many pubs, restaurants, country roads, viewpoints and ruins during their visit as time allowed. We drank wine and tea and Guinness; ate fresh salmon, crab, and oysters and delicious brown bread, and enjoyed decadent desserts using large spoons, the European desert weapon of choice over forks.

Despite the russets, browns and golds of autumn, much of the Irish green and the flowers of summer remained. The cool temperatures and later start of summer made the flowers bloom later and last further into autumn than they usually would. Streets, shop fronts and stone bridges were still graced with hanging baskets cascading over with blooms, and bright red wild fuchsia, yellow gorse and a few patches of purple heather brightened the roadways and hillsides.

The sheep were down from their summer grazing in the hills and mountains and plentiful in the fields, on the roads, and also in Kenmare for two days as it was the time of year when several of the farmers bring their sheep to town to sell instead of taking them to the mart. There were more than I'd ever seen and the smell was strong, overpowering the sweet scent of turf fires which drifted from Kenmare's chimneys.

Weather was fairly cooperative; a day of sunshine, a day of rain, and the rest fairly gray, but dry and not too cold. On the Irish scale of October weather, it scored quite high. That didn't keep me from wishing for more of those clear blue sky days when the sun lights up the landscape and shows the true colors of Ireland in all their glory.

By the end of the first day of driving Dave would have been happy to return the rental car and never get behind the wheel again. Irish roads can be very trying to those not accustomed to left-side driving on roadways wide enough for one-way traffic, perfectly fine except for the fact that they are not one-way. Admiring the view isn't an option for the driver if he uses any amount of caution and common sense. 'Keep left!' became the regular refrain as he careened down the narrow lanes and roadways, periodically slamming on the brakes for sheep, oncoming cars or something he wanted to see, and Gail began counting (and announcing) the number of times he ground the gears and killed the engine.

In that fashion, we toured as much of Southwest Ireland as time permitted and, back in town, went out every night.

And then there was the early night. We planned to have a pub dinner and catch the seven o'clock trad session. By my calculations, we'd be back home by shortly after nine o'clock. After dinner my friend Kieran joined us and the chat commenced in earnest, along with a second round of music following the trad session, a vocalist, harp, guitar and sax producing a rich set of jazzy, bluesy tunes. We were still firmly there when the lights were switched on in the pub.

We followed the crowd outdoors and down the street which took us by Kenmare's disco, that place of pulsing lights and ear-splitting music where I'd gone during the summer of excess with Kiwi Ned. I decided we should at least poke our heads in so they could say they'd been to an Irish disco.

The lights were flashing and the music was blaring and within seconds Dave had whisked me out onto the dance floor as I passed my purse off to Gail to hold. Moments later, she flew by in the arms of a man I'd never seen, the purse dangling. Like plucking a floating leaf from a rushing river I reached out and grabbed it from her before she was swept away, the man raucously dancing her diminutive barely-over-one-hundred-pound frame around the floor like she was a Raggedy Ann doll.

About the same time I mentioned to Dave he ought to rescue her, he was on his way in that direction. The man apparently spoke no English and didn't want to give up his partner, oh no, he did not! He was well pleased with her. But then he figured out if he handed her off to Dave, I'd be free, so he let her go and grabbed me and it was my turn to be twirled and jumped and slammed around the floor.

The man had zero rhythm and grace but enormous energy and enthusiasm. After my face smashed into his I disentangled myself and we made our exit. Outside, Kieran and several others stood chatting and we paused to talk for a bit before making our way back home.

At 2:00 a.m. our early night ended. The early in our evening wasn't supposed to relate to the wee hours of the following day, but that's the way it goes sometimes, especially in Ireland, in County Kerry, on an autumn night without rain.

On their last night here, we had dinner by candlelight at a small intimate restaurant where we dined on scallops, crab claws and prawn-stuffed sole. After dinner we strolled home and ended the evening where their stay began six nights before, sitting by my fireside. As we shared a parting chat the fire's warmth dispelled the chill which had hitched a ride on our backs and accompanied us into the house, as though reminding us winter was waiting. I didn't let myself think about the fact that it was their last evening. I really wasn't ready for them to go.

It was a visit I'd long hoped for and the feeling of having them here almost defies description. It took only a day before it felt normal, as though they'd always been here, and so it was a shock when they were gone. There were so many more places I wanted to show them, more people to meet, more ruins to explore, more subjects to discuss, more laughs to share. But even with double the time it still would not have been enough. I tried to see the full half of the glass instead of the part remaining to be filled.

I'll never forget the time my sister and brother-in-law made the long journey from California to see me in my Irish home, chatted with my friends, raised a glass in my favorite pubs, smelled turf smoke in the air, listened to my music, walked past the same stone walls, gardens, and shops I've so often passed, and saw with their own eyes the mountains, fields, valleys, villages, and sea views I've so often admired. Those five days and six nights added another dimension to my Irish world.

◎

It seemed as if autumn was holding its breath, just waiting for my sister and brother-in-law to leave before drawing to a close. Leaves started to wither and fall with more seriousness, no longer just teasing. The green rampage of grass and ivy and shrubbery thinned, and the brilliant greens and vibrant hues gave way to autumn's colors.

The town square would soon fill with folks of all ages on a damp October night. Torch bearing marchers would set the bonfire ablaze to the tune of spooky music, and I'd put a jack-o'-lantern in my window.

Winter would follow, my third in Ireland, bringing Christmas lights and Santas in shop windows, blazing fires and festive garlands in pubs, and mothers and children wearing warm wooly hats and smiles, humming Christmas songs as they walk along the sparkly streets of Kenmare.

I'd watch winter's approach with varied emotions, delighting in another Christmas season in Ireland, but feeling the pang of missing family. And the significance of that particular winter was not lost on me. It would be the winter before the spring of 2016, the season that contains the month of May, the month that contains the date decreed by INIS that I must take my leave from what has become my second homeland.

I'd hoped to be gracious about the extra time I unexpectedly received, not be too greedy, but that was easier said than done. There were so many things to do, so many places to go – and never enough time. The longer I stayed, the longer I wanted to stay.

53

Winter

December 12, 2015: Dusk comes very early now, but soon we'll reach winter solstice and begin gathering daylight once again.

Winter arrived, as it has a way of doing each year. Winter. A time of regrouping. Thinking. Rethinking. Reconnecting. Planning. Hibernating.

A time for warm fires, hot whiskey, camaraderie in the local pubs, and empty village streets. Rain. Wind. Frost. Sleet pinging against the windows and sliding down in lazy, icy rivulets. *Closed For The Season* signs. Heavier jackets, scarves and knit hats. The chores of cleaning out the wood stove or fireplace and keeping the indoor wood basket filled becomes part of the daily routine and moves to a position of higher priority.

It is a time when you stop for a chat when you run into someone you know on the street – or someone you don't – because everyone has more time now, but you don't linger as long. The wind whistling in your ears, the cold seeping into your bones and the rain dripping off the shop awnings urge you to keep moving.

The earth tones of valleys and hillsides emerge from behind their cover of tall grasses and wildflowers, ferns have turned dark brown and curled in on themselves, and gorse still shows its gold, but it is a ragged shadow of its former self. The colors of the buildings emerge, naked without flowers and outdoor tables and sun umbrellas to camouflage them, their bright facades bringing welcome color to winter's duller palette.

The darkness crept up on me so early one afternoon it took me by surprise. The clock said 4:30. I tapped it and listened, just to make sure it was working. As I filled my arms with logs from the wood pile to get the fire started two rooks looked down from their perch atop a telephone line and scolded me with their harsh cawing.

The instant I stepped back inside the house the heavy skies let loose, dropping their load of rainfall. Complaining, the rooks swooped away. The wind raced and gusted, rattling the trees' nearly bare branches together. In their final shuddering, the trees stopped resisting and shook off the last of their autumn leaves like a dog shaking water off after a swim. On the hillside red holly berries stood out like Christmas lights against the muted landscape, blazing against the dark trees, black rocks and gray skies.

Winter was here and I looked at it with eyes different than those around me, for it was likely the last winter I would be calling Ireland my home. Everything I saw had become more precious.

I awoke sometimes in the middle of the night and counted the months, the weeks, the days and wondered how I would react when the time comes. How would it be? How would I do? And then I'd admonish myself, knowing that sort of thinking is pointless and does nothing but detract from the remaining time. I could not afford to let worry and melancholia overtake me. But it wasn't easy when I was so often reminded of how easy it is to live in this place.

🔳

Returning from errands on a windy and rainy afternoon I found a notice of an attempted delivery of a package. A signature was required. The notice directed me to bring the form and photo identification to the post office and pick up the package.

The next morning I called the post office hoping to avoid a trip out into what was shaping up to be yet another fierce day. Despite the delivery notice's clear command about picking it up, maybe I could get the postman to make another delivery attempt.

Calling the post office here is not the same experience as it generally is in the USA where you listen to a series of recorded messages and push numbers hoping to finally reach an actual person and then, if you're lucky enough to have that happen, try to explain your issue while you tensely grip the phone, fearful of being disconnected and having to go through the entire exercise again. Only four people work at the post office in Kenmare, and that includes the postman.

On the second ring, the phone was answered by a young woman.

'Good morning. An Post Kenmare.'

'Good morning. This is Jane Fadely on Stone Street. I received a notice that I have a package?'

'Stone Street, is it?'

'Yes.'

'Just a moment now and I'll check for you.'

'Thank you.'

Conversation overheard in background: 'Fadely. Stone Street. Do we have a parcel?'

(Unintelligible male voices) I knew they were likely rummaging around in the bin behind the windows where packages are kept for pick up.

'Yes, we've found it. It's here for collection.'

'So I need to come in and pick it up?'

'Yes, you'll need to collect it.'

'Okay. Is it large? I'm only asking because I'll be on foot.'

'Yes, it is large, but not too large, I'd say. Will we have someone bring it to you?'

'Oh, well, if that's possible that would be great!'

'Just a moment.' Conversation in background: 'Will you be going to Stone Street this morning?' (Unintelligible male voices.) I presumed they were checking the mail to see if there were any deliveries for my street that day.

She returned to the phone. 'Hello?'

'Yes, I'm here.'

'It will be re-delivered to you. I'll sign for it?'

I started to question her about that – how could she sign for it if the package was for me and required my signature? – then realized where I was and stopped myself.

'Sure, that would be terrific,' I said nonchalantly. 'Thanks very much.'

'No bother.'

'Goodbye.'

'Goodbye. Bye. Bye-Bye.'

Thirty minutes later the package was delivered.

◩

A few days later I received another delivery, my grocery order, but not all of the wine I'd ordered for an upcoming gathering. Seems it was out of stock. I was annoyed they hadn't substituted with another brand, which they would normally do, so sent an e-mail complaint. Within twenty-four hours I received a phone call from the supermarket headquarters.

The gentleman was very apologetic and could not explain why no substitution had been offered. I had received two of the four bottles I ordered, was that correct? Yes, I assured him, that was correct.

'We'd like to refund your money for the two bottles you received. Would that help make up for the error?' Indeed, it certainly would – more than. He apologized again and thanked me for my business.

◩

At the little stationery shop inside the post office I took the four greeting cards I'd selected to the counter.

'That will be €10.30,' said the man who periodically ran back and forth from the stationery counter to one of the post office windows, depending on need.

I pulled out a ten euro note. 'Let me see if I have some change,' I said, and began digging in my pocket.

'Oh, no bother. We'll round down,' he said.

'Are you sure?'

He smiled, handed me the cards and said "Discount."

On Christmas Eve I made my way to the pub to meet Kieran and a host of other locals for a drink, customary for many in Kenmare and, I suppose, across Ireland. My suspicions about the free drink on Christmas Eve from my first Christmas were confirmed; it is indeed a tradition. If you are a known customer, your first drink is free.

'Have you had your Christmas drink?' was the oft-heard query that evening from the bartenders, Liam among them, all wearing bright red or green or blue Christmas shirts, some with Santas, others with snowmen or Christmas trees. You couldn't help but smile.

The pub was as crowded as a Saturday night in the high season. A string of lights glowed in the steamed over front window and trad music played in the corner, barely audible above the voices of the celebrating patrons talking, laughing, and calling Christmas greetings to one another. The place was buzzing with hugs, exuberant back patting, warmth and good cheer.

What a nice tradition, I thought, gathering in the pub to greet friends and neighbors on Christmas Eve, especially for those of us without family or, like me, too far away to be with them at Christmastime. I'd enjoyed the novelty of that experience the first year in Ireland, but this year it held more meaning, knowing it might be the last time I experienced Christmas as a resident of the Emerald Isle.

I chatted awhile, had my Christmas drink and purchased one more, then walked back home along damp streets through the hushed evening, under the glow of the Christmas lights and a beautiful full moon peeking out between the clouds. *Silent night, holy night; all is calm, all is bright.*

54

FOOTPRINTS & MEMORIES

January 1, 2016: Happy New Year!

As the new year begins, the days grow longer and my time grows shorter in Ireland – barring a miraculous change of heart by immigration.

On days when the wind and the rain are quite convincing reasons to shy away from outdoor pursuits if you have a choice, midwinter's a fine time for such things as sitting by the fire doing nothing but staring into the flames and thinking. Lately, I've found myself pondering my Irish experience. Rather than panic or fall into despair over having to leave, I've tried to get into the right frame of mind for returning to the USA. I've thought about what living here has brought to me, reminded myself to be thankful for the time I've had here, and encouraged myself to dream of new possibilities elsewhere.

Living in Ireland has been a grand adventure – the grandest! – but have I learned anything other than the certainty my fascination with the place is not likely to diminish? What will I be taking away with me when I leave, other than the return portion of a round-trip plane ticket? What, if anything, will I leave behind?

I've made many new friends. I've picked up or improved on certain skills like understanding the accents and the lingo, the art of drying laundry, fire building, and the use of hot water boilers and mini fridges. I've discovered and reawakened old joys and interests, cooking and baking, gardening, theater, and splashing through puddles in rain boots. But there's more than that.

Living far away from America has given me a greater appreciation for my family, for old friends, and for my country, too. At the same time, it has led to a better understanding of a different culture, and the realization of how much life can be enhanced at any age by meeting new friends.

Living in Ireland has confirmed that I am happiest living somewhere with four seasons and can survive, and appreciate, dark cold winters for the pure pleasure of seeing spring's arrival.

I have a different take on time; I know better how to appreciate it. I will always enjoy revisiting the past through memories or immersing myself in big dreams of the future, but I've become better at living in the moment.

I've learned not everyone in Ireland is cheerful and kind – although enough of them are that it seems a fair enough generalization to make. My father has always been a big proponent of having 'the right attitude' and it was preached to me regularly when I was growing up, no matter how obstinate I sometimes was about it. I've long been aware approaching people with good cheer and friendliness helps to guarantee reciprocal treatment. I've become much better at putting that into practice in Ireland. It hasn't been difficult given the cordial nature of most folks, but it is that very fact which has convinced me, along with my father's teaching, that no matter where I live it is simply a better way to go through life. Is it any wonder why everyone loves the Irish? Dad knew what he was talking about, of course.

I've felt privileged to live here and that's made me more aware of how fortunate I have been in my life. We all have our trials and heartaches, our burdens to bear. I know I'm not special in that way, but perhaps I am in the amount of good there's been in my life. One can bemoan misfortune, dissolve into grief or ball up in anger, but what's the point? It only bogs you down, insulates you and distracts you from the good stuff.

I don't want to miss things like rainbows splashed across the sky, the first shy flower buds of spring, the hypnotizing ebb and flow of the sea, and the thrill of hearing a tune that makes my heart sing. I don't want to miss the opportunity to meet more of the good people in this world, to laugh with someone, to hug, or be hugged. To see and feel snowflakes fall and melt in my hands, breathe in the scent of pine forests and freshly brewed coffee. To pick wildflowers damp with rain, be mesmerized and warmed by a crackling fire, and see the smile on someone's face when they're happy to see me. I refuse to be distracted, to let any of it be lessened or tainted by the pain of unfortunate circumstances or people who've done me wrong.

Since moving to Ireland I've developed a habit that keeps that idea foremost in my mind. Every night I give a prayer of thanks for the good that has come my way that day, no matter how seemingly small or insignificant. Finding the right words for that sentence I've been struggling with. A cheerful card received in the mail. Seeing a pretty sunset. Having an interesting chat with a complete stranger, someone who might even become a friend. Sunshine after days of rain. The hundreds of small pleasures which gracefully weave together to make life better, but only if you take the time to notice.

When I depart and move back to the USA, will I leave anything behind other than new friends, the footprints from my wellies, and a piece of my heart? That isn't a question for me to answer. It must be asked of others.

I hope there might be a few who will say I brought them some happiness; that I was good for a chat and a few laughs; that they found me an interesting and caring and sincere person. I hope some might hear faint echoes of my laughter or see shadows of my smile. And maybe there'll be one or two who think Kenmare won't be quite the same without *That American Woman* – remember her? Now, what was her name? Oh, right – Jane Parker – or was it Jane Kenmare? Well, anyway, yes, whatever her name was, I remember her. She seemed a nice lady, so.

▣

Life in Ireland hasn't been perfect, it's not the utopia one might be convinced it could be after short visits living the holiday life, but it has been overall so satisfying and uplifting, and just plain fun. Time has brimmed over with wonderful characters and friendships, exciting adventures, interesting discoveries, and joyous laughter. I've made, and continue to make, soul-deep memories of the kind I'll always treasure.

When I go, I'll miss nearly everyone and almost everything about living in Ireland. My heart will long to see chickens in the garden and sheep in the fields, to listen to Michael in his overalls telling stories on a Sunday afternoon, to splash through rain-drenched streets in my wellies and spend a morning in Morgan's Salon while the buzz of cheerful voices and laughter mixes with the hum of hairdryers. I'll wish for a chat with Liz over the garden wall, and the simple enjoyment of walking up the street to meet a friend for a pint and some tunes. For the pure pleasure of realizing, and saying, 'I live in Ireland!' That never lost its thrill.

Sure, I'll remember the too long, too dark, too wet days; the gross slugs and snails in the garden and the gigantic spiders and occasional mouse in the house, the summertime humidity that causes bread to mold within two days if you forget to put it in the freezer, and the idiocy and red tape of Ireland's immigration bureaucracy. The thoughtless rich neighbors who drive their ridiculous over-sized SUV far too fast down the otherwise quiet little street, the annoyance of not having a full-size well-functioning washer and dryer, and the desperate ache of missing family at certain times of the year. But those things will dull and nearly disappear from memory, leaving behind the beautiful, the funny, the warm and happy memories.

I'll have only to close my eyes to imagine the changing colors of twilight and dawn, the enchanting, star-studded night skies, and the way the moonlight looks shining through the trees. The sweet scent of turf smoke drifting from chimneys, and the incredible feeling of touching an ancient standing stone or the walls of a crumbling castle.

I take comfort in knowing I can take some of it with me, not only in memory, but in practice. I can continue the custom of greeting folks I pass on the street, drink tea in the afternoons, wear my wellies to walk in the rain, and watch the night sky.

As hard as leaving Ireland will be, I *am* looking forward to being an American in America again. To having no need to ask for permission to remain or prove to anyone I can support myself.

It's exciting to think of again being part of family gatherings and seeing old friends and having the freedom to earn a few extra dollars if the mood strikes or the need arises.

I can't wait to go shopping with my sister, to buy new clothes and shoes in sizes I recognize, at bargain prices. I like the idea of being able to talk to American friends and family on the phone and not have to consider an eight hour time difference. I look forward to celebrating uniquely American holidays like Thanksgiving and the Fourth of July in America with my fellow Americans, and buying genuine dill pickles that don't come bubble-wrapped inside a cardboard box, and without the need to take out a loan to pay for them. All of those things will be grand; no doubt about it.

I won't find ancient ruins, laughing Irishmen, and sheep being sold in the town square, but I might find a place with friendly folks, four lovely seasons, and air that is fresh and clear. With luck I'll have a fireplace or a wood stove and still be able to enjoy the warmth and ambience only a fire can bring. And certainly if I look, I'll find colorful flower-filled gardens, someone looking to chat, and the occasional rainbow after the rain. It may at first take some attitude tweaking and periodic reminders to myself that just because I'm not seeing and experiencing those things in Ireland doesn't make them any less special, but I'm confident I can convince myself to a reasonable degree.

In my return-to-America research I found a small town near the Pacific Ocean, on the banks of a mighty river, where I'm told you can watch the ships go by, ride a trolley car along the river front, and go to the second largest open air market in the state. Its Victorian buildings, hilly streets, and foggy weather are reminiscent of San Francisco, minus the big city and the cost of living. The sight of the green hills across the water could easily fool you into thinking you were seeing the coast of Ireland, and its small size and sense of community remind me there are other places besides Kenmare where I might happily live, where new discoveries and adventures await me.

I'll always have a strong connection to Ireland and will suffer periods of intense longing, but with time the yearning will become easier to handle. At least that's what I'm telling myself. I'll find a way to damper it, like turning down the regulator on my wood stove to slow the flames. Like the coals in the stove, memories will be a warm glow. And when I can, I'll add to them by returning to this green place, sand bucket in hand, to wander past old ivy-covered stone walls blooming with flowers, down village streets and country lanes, and stop to drink pints of stout or cups of tea while sharing stories and laughter with old friends who once were new.

Wherever I end up, I'll still be the retired American lady, but I'll be the retired American lady who once upon a time lived and laughed in Ireland, who walked through rain puddles in her wellies past spring's first flowers, autumn's leaves, winter's frost, and summer's lush color. And always, everywhere, saw the smiles and heard the voices of dear neighbors and friends. Wasn't she lucky?! And who knows? Sure now, someday she may even see chickens in her garden again.

Without convincing myself I will someday be able to return, it is certain I couldn't bear the pain of leaving. I feel very blessed for the time I've had in such a magical, peaceful, delightful place and I will forever humbly consider myself a wee bit more Irish. Now, please excuse me – my sand bucket and my wellies are waiting. There is still time – and I don't want to waste it.

When I was an old woman, but not too old, I lived in Ireland. I went for morning walks, sipped tea with the locals in the afternoons, and sat before a cheerful fire on cool evenings... I wasn't just an American in Ireland, I was Irish, and I felt like I was home.

Ch. 3: *I felt like I was in a place I'd been before, a place I'd missed.*
(White Park Beach, Antrim)

Ch. 5: *I opened the door and stepped out into the cool quiet of the morning.*

Ch. 7: *The antiquities…never became commonplace to me.*
(Kilcatherine Church, Beara Peninsula)

Ch. 9:…*I wandered in and out of pubs, never able to get my fill of the music.*

Ch. 12: …'It's relaxing to watch them,' he said.

Ch. 15: …Like a warm fire, tea had a way of improving things, too.

Ch. 18: …there is no shortage of torrential downpours.

Ch. 19: …Christmas Eve began with a stormy sea at dawn…and ended by my familiar fire and the twinkle of my own Christmas tree.

Ch. 21: ... *Galway...never disappoints me.*

Ch. 21: ... *A girl can dream at any age.*

Ch. 23: *It had been the simplest of days, but somehow perfect.*

Ch. 25: *'Now it's directions you're needin', is it?'*

Ch. 27: *Green was on a rampage, decimating the brown of winter...*
(Dingle Peninsula)

Ch. 27: *Soaking up the sunshine and spring beauty, I thought again of how lucky I was to live in such a place.*
(Glenmore Lake, Beara Peninsula)

Ch. 30: *Ah, Gougane Barra!*

Ch. 30: *Ireland showed its best face to my visitors...*

Ch. 33: *...we stopped wherever we wished, at beaches and viewpoints, pubs and markets.* (Ballydonegan Beach)

Ch. 36: '...and it's SANDY COVE! IT'S SANDY COVE IN FIRST PLACE!!'

Ch. 37: *I would have liked to say goodbye to sweet summer.*
(Cloonee Lake, Beara)

Ch. 39: *...the land was showing itself in all its brilliant blue and green glory.*
(Slea Head Drive, Dingle Peninsula)

Ch. 40: *…Had a great time…in Dublin…*

Ch. 42: *'Look at the sky!'*

Ch. 42: *...the abandoned shack...still held my imagination.*
(Strawberry Field Pancake Cottage)

Ch. 48: *I took off to hear more of Colm Murphy, the bodhrán player, and Harry Bradley, the flute playing 'Colin Farrell.'*

Ch. 51: *I was reminded of little boys playing with toy boats.* (Galway)

Ch. 51: *All ten guests showed up at '7-ish' as planned...*

Ch. 52: *It took only a day before it felt normal, as though they'd always been here...*

Ch. 52: *The sheep were ...in Kenmare for two days...*

Ch. 53: *Winter was here...*

Ch. 53: *Have you had your Christmas drink?....*

Ch. 54: *I don't want to miss things like...rainbows splashed across the sky...the incredible feeling of touching an ancient standing stone... the opportunity to... be mesmerized and warmed by a crackling fire...*

Ardgroom Stone Circle, Beara

Cariganass Castle, West Cork

Ch. 54: *...who once upon a time lived and laughed in Ireland... Wasn't she lucky?*

ACKNOWLEDGMENTS

Chickens in the Garden owes its existence to many. Thanks must first go to my dear parents and sister, the three people who have always been the most supportive of my writing, along with every other aspect of my life.

To those who agreed to read all or part of various drafts of this book, among them Pat Bearden, Janet Beimfohr, Gail Chartier, Mel Chartier, Maggie Daly, Diane McDougal and Melinda Rusaw, I am grateful for their time, encouragement, and suggestions.

I thank my author friends Cathie Borrie (*The Long Hello*) who kindly read an early draft and provided helpful feedback, and 'Kiwi Ned' who once upon a time convinced me I could write this book.

To those who donated toward the cost of editing I am deeply grateful for their kind generosity and confidence in me: Neal & Su Amsden, Chuck & Pat Bearden, Rob & Terri Bearden, Theresa Burkhardt & Lori Johnson, David & Gail Chartier, Susan Gaughan, Guy & Cindy Hinderberger, Susan McClain, Maureen Ozolins, and Deborah Stephens.

I never thought I would thank my brother-in-law Dave for his comments over the years regarding my penchant for using too many words in my writing, but I do thank him. I took that criticism to heart and employed it, although perhaps not to the extent he might have wanted, but I didn't think five or six pages would be quite long enough to be called a book.

Certainly I must thank my brother Tracy who, with just one thought-provoking question on a summer's evening made me begin to believe I could turn a dream into reality. Many more thanks are due to the friends and family who encouraged and supported me in my quest to make the move to Ireland and live that dream, because had I not accomplished that bit, this book would not exist.

A special thank you is offered to the many who have expressed interest and encouragement during the long writing, editing, and design process, and those who patiently responded to my many queries seeking feedback.

And then there are those who have been part of my world in Ireland, especially the good folks of Kenmare, without whom both the book and my life would have been far less interesting. I am very thankful to have met them.

My sister once sent me a greeting card imprinted with, '*We are all here to be angels for each other.*' Thanks to everyone for being my angels during this endeavor. Cheers and blessings to all of you.

May joy and peace surround you
Contentment latch your door
And happiness be with you now
And bless you ever more.

Kilmalkedar Churchyard, Dingle Peninsula

'*... in quiet places where silence sings...*'

Born and raised in the Pacific Northwest, V. J. Fadely is an American with Irish ancestry. She retired from her career as a legal secretary in 2013, a job she always found too structured and monotonous for her active imagination and creative nature. She enjoys travel and new adventures and looks back with fondness on an earlier time when she worked unconfined by office walls in the Alaska wilderness, employed as a laborer on the Trans-Alaska Pipeline, more an adventure than a job. She has lived in several different states, most recently California, and traveled through nearly every one of them.

Writing since she was old enough to put pencil to paper, her current favorite topic is Ireland. Her latest adventure, living in County Kerry, Ireland, was still in progress at the time this book was published. She loves sharing her passion for the country with others.

Ms. Fadely has authored a small booklet, *Irish Bits & Pieces* (©2015), a compilation of tips and information for visitors to Ireland and 'bits and pieces to bring back memories after the journey.' She has written for Untours, an American travel company specializing in European holidays, IrishCentral.com, and IrishCultureandCustoms.com.

Find her on facebook.com/VJFadely.

23926708R00221

Made in the USA
Lexington, KY
18 December 2018